INDIANS OF THE SOUTHWEST

BY

M. JOURDAN ATKINSON

Illustrated by

RALPH J. PEREIDA

and

DONALD M. YENA

THE NAYLOR COMPANY
Publishers of the Southwest
San Antonio, Texas

E
78
57
A8
1963

TO

MY FATHER

JOHN BACHMAN JOURDAN

Son of a slaveholder, son of a pioneer, contemporary
of the Texas Indians, who paved the way for any
further anthropological or ethnological knowledge on
my part by first teaching me that

"All Men Have Their Rights"

Foreword

On its 28th anniversary, the writer of this book again greets its readers. Naylor tells me that people now write in for "Atkinson's Indians" — a pleasing sort of familiarity with the text.

So often a request for an index has come that thanks to the indefatigable effort of Britomarte Somers Gibson from Vermont (that other state which was once an incipient nation), an index has been added to this fourth edition. There are also further notes and some new-old illustrations to enhance the eye-witness atmosphere that has been the purpose of a continual survey of Texana and Americana. That my daughter (and now her children) bears an Indian strain through her father's Cherokee Jamison-Swafford grandmother has lent a poignancy to the task.

A quote from Biagi's preface to THE LITTLE FLOWERS OF SAINT FRANCIS applies exactly to the use of language by early recorders of the continent:

> The use of traditional forms and conceptions was not a practice to be condemned by writers of the Middle Ages; it was on the contrary an absolute necessity for imposing with the stamp of truth what was to be represented to the mind of the reader.

Purpose of the old Spanish and Anglo chroniclers was not to dissect out and sterilize "facts" — that is to insulate against play of the imagination. Their purpose was to invoke the imagination to portrayal of the "new world" they had explored; a world that immediately faded out of existence from sheer contact with its explorers.

Whether or not these men knew grammar or could spell, they were determined to preserve what they had seen, which would never be seen again in the form in which they saw it. It has been the task of the writer to attempt to pass on their vision to the reader; and, while reassembling their word-painting to fit the science of ethnology, still to keep faith with them by retaining its essential flavor.

An ethnologist (cultural anthropologist) sees the sum

total of civilization — past and present — as a continually shifting mosaic, which, nevertheless, is made up of distinctively patterned cultures. Each fades into another, as to time, and feathers out into others geographically.

Every culture rests on three patternings that give it the uniqueness of entity: its religious pattern, its politico-legal pattern or "government," and its economic pattern.

Ethnologists are inclined to divide social patternings (cultures) into benevolent patternings and malignant patternings. Born on one of the world's great cultural crossroads — the Old Spanish Trail which is comparable in the Occident to the Burma Road in the Orient — the writer offers twenty years of research in the vestigial cultures evident on the Trail.

INDIANS OF THE SOUTHWEST is one result of this research. Since its initial publication in 1935 as THE TEXAS INDIANS, it has been read and criticised by teachers, scientists and the Indians themselves. The highest tribute it can receive is from the Indians. "It is as our fathers told us."

The scope of the book was never confined to present-day Texas boundaries. Aboriginal tribes and nations had no notion of the carving up of the world west of the Mississippi River into modern political entities. Among their interleagued nations, and even out onto the Buffalo Range, the salutation between allies was *TEJAS*: (tay-has) corresponding to Friend or *Amigo!* — a greeting that accompanied the Pipe of Peace.

Old Spanish spelling used an "x" for this word where modern Spanish spelling uses a "j" but both are pronounced like the English "h." Anglos kept the antique Spanish spelling but corrupted the pronunciation to the English "x" — as "Tex-as." Even so, the title TEXAS INDIANS meant actually "Indian Friends." To avoid further confusion with political Texas, the book's name is now changed to

INDIANS OF THE SOUTHWEST

Contents

Acculturation of the Southwest

Thus far "historic time" in North America begins in 1492, with the importation of the Julian calendar by Columbus. Archaeological time begins — *we know not when*. Sites opened in the southwest set the date of man's occupancy of this region at not less than twenty thousand years preceding the arrival of the Spanish. Documents older than the Spanish archives indicate Euro-asiafrican contacts far preceding the Spanish occupancy. We can only hint at ancient truth until more data come to hand.

We do know that one folk movement was in progress from east to west when the Spanish came; and that, as a result of their coming, a counter movement rocked the Indian universe. The movement of the Old Indians — the *Caddo* and the *Asinai* — in other words, the border nations of the eastern timberlands who were the Mound Builders of the Mississippi Basin area, was out onto the Buffalo Range. The *Jumanas,* or *Pintadas,* seemingly offshoots of the *Asinai,* were fringe peoples in transition from mound building corn planters to buffalo hunters. The *Sioux* are classified as a *Caddo* people who followed the buffalo so far and so long up the northwestern rivers that they became primarily nomadic. By the same token, the Pueblo peoples on the farside of the Buffalo Range are held to be eastern gardeners who crossed over the Buffalo Range into the Great American Desert where they found a new sanctuary in the western canyons and on the mesas. There they remained as agricultural oases in the desert; and there they became the foremost craftsmen in the preparation of buffalo robes — their leading item in that flow of Indian commerce that was to set the pattern for "the Santa Fé trade" of Euro-American history.

The buffalo, it is said in early Spanish documents, "never crossed west of the Pecos" and was unknown to the peoples of New Spain, which we now call Mexico.

THE HOUSE OF STRAW

I
Passing in Review

Indian to Father Hennepin:

"Fie, thou knowest not what thou sayest; thou mayest know what has passed in thine own country, for thy ancestors hast told thee of it, but thou canst not know what has passed in ours before the Spirits (Palefaces) came hither."

BEGINNING OF HISTORY

In 1492, on the eve of the arrival of Columbus in the "new" world, the Southwest was occupied by a startling and picturesque array of peoples, maintaining, among themselves, an amazing panorama of the serial stages of civilization as it was unfolded, fanwise, from the Mexican and Peruvian empires, eastward across the Americas.

CADDO AND ASINAI

In and out of the Piney Woods, over the bright Red Lands, spread carefully tilled gardens surrounding innumerable straw villages — the houses, domed like monstrous beehives, sheltering the confederated Mound Builder Nations.

KARANKAWA AND ATTAKAPA

Over the brackish lagoons, along the Gulf edge, slid pairs

of hollowed logs, always two, one behind the other, poled by tall, grease-and-mud-bedaubed fishers with the longbow, whose only shelter was a careless skin flung over a willow wythe — eaters of putrid flesh! Cannibals!

TONKAWA AND COAHUILTECA

Scattered through the cedar brakes of the central and southwestern Hill Country were the community camps of seminomadic hunters, where women planted an occasional bean vine while men eternally stalked the deer — homes of well-fed, near-naked, semitropic children of plenty, whose mode of life was intermediate between the civilized truck-gardening nations in the eastern Timber Lands and the wild, buffalo hunting Tribes on the western Plains.

Now and then, through the impenetrable Brush Country to the far south, following the *javelina* trails, struggled a starveling from the Mexican wastes to join the hill tribes.

THE PUEBLOS

On the Rio Grande and the Pecos Rivers, and in canyons to the westward, cliffsides were honeycombed with terraced apartment houses. Women, singing on the terraces pestled corn to meal in time with the song, or stoked fires built of the buffalo chips, which, they said, gave their pottery its special glaze. The terraces overlooked the fields where they walked with their hair loose to give the corn fertility. Some said, in their secret hearts: "Nine months after I let down my squash blossom headdress my son will be born!" Below, in the estufas, their men painted with colored sands. With their pictures they consulted the Sun through the Holy Fire, and Smoke, its messenger, to learn the future of the buffalo crop and the crop of precious corn.

APACHE AND COMANCHE

Down the forward slopes of the Davis Mountains scouted fierce wanderers from the northwest, *Apache* explorers, picking up a precarious livelihood among the rabbits and the prickly pear. As for that tremendous, barbaric nomad, the *Comanche*, he did not exist in Texas, when Columbus landed in the Antilles, except as a footsore and often hungry savage following in the wake of the buffalo on the Panhandle grazing grounds, drifting southwest, toward the approaching and equally footsore *Apache*, and toward their common objective, the traditional location of the fabulous "buffalo holes."

A Foot Parade

Thus passes on foot, there being nothing in the Americas to ride, the amazing parade of Texas peoples as they were the day Columbus planted the Spanish flag before the astounded eyes of the distant San Salvadorians, and, by that act, loosed the hordes of Europe upon an unsuspecting world!

THE MOUND BUILDERS

The Mound Builders west of the Mississippi ceased as national entities before Texas was opened to Anglo-American emigration, in 1820, by the Mexican government. According to Anglo historians, the *Asinai* were completely annihilated by intrusive Indians — the *Cherokee*, the *Choctaw*, the *Kickapoo* and other Mound Builder Nations — forced backward from older southern states by encroaching European settlements; though remnants of the *Caddo* remained in Texas until the opening of the reservations. Spanish authorities give the western boundary of the agricultural peoples as the Trinity River, which is also the boundary of the eastern timber area where it verges on the prairie. According to them the *Asinai* and the christianized *Caddo* were so intermingled with the *Adeaseños* (the Creoles settled on Adaes Creek) that they were retired to San Antonio or farther on into Coahuila by government order when the Spanish abandoned the East Texas missions. Gil y Barba returned a portion of these people to Nacogdoches and the Angelina country where they were living when the Spanish province of Texas became first a Mexican state and then an independent republic.

A LEAGUE GALLEY

II

The League of Nations

"The province of the *Asinai* (Tejas) contains many divisions. It extends for more than one hundred leagues (264 miles) in each of the principal directions. To the northward it reaches as far as the banks of the Missouri River."

Espinosa.

THE GRAND FLEET

On the broad bosom of the Mississippi River once floated the Grand Fleet of an Indian League of Nations, the Mound Builders, whose allied confederacies covered the Earth from the Trinity River in Texas to the Atlantic seaboard, from the Gulf of Mexico to the Great Lakes.

Out of the southern empires — Peru, Columbia, Yucatan, Mexico — who can say which or when, their forefathers came bringing tobacco and corn, seeking new lands. Up the rivers they spread from the Gulf, felling the forests with Flame, setting the Earth with tropic garden truck, building their holy mounds with basket brigades, worshiping the Perpetual Fires and the New Fires — worshiping the Sun.

THE SPANISH GOLD RUSH

Ages after, scouring the "new" world in the wake of Columbus, Hernandez de Soto, mad with the Spanish gold lust, fresh from pillaging the ancient southern empires across the Blue Gulf, came up the mighty Father of Waters, seeking gold that was not there — only to meet the plumed flotillas of the Mound Builders, manned by the cohorts of the Sun.

Over the garden lands word of his coming preceded him, passed by swift, unseen runners, racing from village to village, from ally to ally — onward the news flashed by Smoke telegraph, beyond the Trinity, across the prairies, till word of war rang to the edge of the Buffalo Range.

DRESS PARADE

Then, if we may believe the Gentleman of Elvas, star reporter of De Soto's expedition, over the linked lagoons, along the sluggish bayous, out of the river mouths, came quota after quota of war canoes. Loosed from their moorings below the villages were the local fleets — later to be described by the French missionary, Father Membres, as dugout canoes, forty or fifty feet long — sometimes a hundred and fifty to a town. Into the Mississippi they poured, until down that broad waterway swept a vast train of *pirogues;* burned and scraped from the lengths of towering trees; graceful and vivid as tropic water fowl; their prows, for the sake of magic, built into masks of bird and beast.

Squatted along the craft, on outriggers of bundled bamboo, perhaps, were the oarsmen, twenty to a side. Down the centers of the canoes stood double files of warriors, each with a feather-bordered shield to protect the oarsman at his elbow. All were naked save for moccasins, breechclouts, and chaplets of plumes. At the rear of the boats, seated chieftains and their aides, occupying pavilions shaded by tilts — canopies of painted skins raised on spears — directed the activities of the fleet.

Such was the Indian Navy of the south.

TO THE SUN, THE VICTORY

To the legions of the Sun went the victory in that first

7

wild round of war, the armored Spaniards falling back into the Gulf before the stone-edged weapons of the naked champions of the "new" world. De Soto's men, sails spread in retreat, caught the victory song rising from the decks of the *pirogues* halted in the face of the pounding surf— paean after paean shouted to the Sun.

THE MARK OF COLD IRON

Never again was that song to resound across the sea, gladdening the hearts of the allies housed in villages of straw; for De Soto's columns, tramping the country to the sterile edges of the Staked Plains, stamped the symbol of Spain deep into the soil of the ancient garden lands — the imprint of an iron heel.

III

The House of Straw

"The particular traits we have observed in this people (the *Tejas*) are their loyalty to their lands and the skill with which they construct their houses."

Ramón, 1716.

UP IN THE WORLD

Nothing in East Texas seems to have amazed the exploring French and Spanish more than the houses of the gardeners, which, we are told by one witness, "were made of whole trees set up with the boughs interlaced, sometimes towering a hundred feet in the air." Coming down a bit, Father Douay, who was with La Salle, says: "Their houses are fine, forty or fifty feet high, of the shape of beehives. Trees are planted in the ground, and united above by branches, which are covered with grass."

"They live in round dwellings that look like cupolas and are very warm, for they are thatched from the roof to the ground; and they have their beds resting upon poles and sleep between tanned bison skins" — so runs another ancient report on the homes of the *Tejas*.[1]

WINTER AND SUMMER HOUSES

All old chronicles of the southern Indians describe

winter houses" as something of particular note. In Roemer's TEXAS, which was translated from German, appears this description of a Caddo household: "The home of every family consisted of several huts of diverse form. There is always a large conical shaped hut present, about fifteen feet high, which is enclosed on all sides except for a small opening at the bottom. It is thatched with long grass and therefore at a distance resembles a haystack of medium size. This hut is used in cold and wet weather (the winter house). Near it are several other huts, open on the sides, which really are only grass-covered sheds, resting on four uprights under which at a distance of about two feet from the ground, a horizontal lattice-work platform woven from strong twigs is fastened. On this wicker platform men and women squat during the hot hours of the day. The roof shelters them from the hot sun's rays and at the same time the air can circulate freely on all sides, even from the bottom. Finally, there was a third kind of hut used for storing provisions which was nothing but an oven-like container also covered with grass, resting on four high posts."

From other sources we learn that the cooking place, with the gardening Indians, was always removed from the main domicile.

The whole arrangement here set forth compares most interestingly with the old Texas homesteads where every household included a "smokehouse" and a "milkhouse," comparable to the Indian storehouses, and where the kitchen was ordinarily set away from the actual residence. Moreover, the Indian's love of his grass-covered shed, or porch, well compares with the Texan's long hours of repose on his "gallery" or veranda, without which no ranch or plantation house is complete.

THE BUILDING BEE

Espinosa and Du Pratz, Spanish and French missionaries, respectively, give detailed accounts of the "building bees"

10

that took place in Texas and Louisiana whenever a new structure was required, Du Pratz describing the putting up of rectangular houses, and Espinosa discoursing on the erection of round dwellings.

On the list of regular officials among the Louisiana *Natchez* is a "building inspector," or "inspector of public works." Espinosa's report indicates the existence of a similar official among the *Tejas.*

Whenever a family was ready to set up a new or a separate residence, says the latter chronicler, the first act was to declare the matter to the Council. That governing body, discussed under THE LAW OF THE LAND, officially sanctioned the proceeding and public heralds announced the day on which the work would be done. At the same time they informed each citizen as to what part of the building he or she would be expected to prepare in anticipation of the event, which was always a community enterprise.

On the eve of the assigned day, the deputies, or village police, slept at the building site in order to be on hand early for the superintendence of labor. With the Dawn, every citizen assigned the preparation of a lath or a pole appeared, bearing it on his shoulder.

The first step in the construction of a circular house was to set up a heavy knobbed center post — such a post, wherever used, was called an "Indian ladder," says Bartram — to which a cross-piece was attached. The laths were then set upright and tamped down in holes dug on the preceding day. Next, two men climbed the center pole, perched on the crossarm, and lassoed the ends of the laths, drawing them together and fastening them at the top. This part of the work complete, the "ladder" was cut off at the bottom and removed.

In the construction of houses with four corners, no center-pole was used; instead, two climbers ascended opposite laths, taking the end pairs first, bent them over by agile human weight, and tied them to form a ridge — the basis for a peaked instead of domed roof.

After the "ribs" of the house were all firmly placed and braided together with bark or grapevine thongs by the men, the women thatched the wall surface from bottom to top with bundles of grass, cornstalks or wattle, brought from home. When the thatching was complete, says Du Pratz, the house was chinked inside with Spanish moss and clay, and wound outside with grapevines, the result being a structure so serviceable "it would stand for twenty years without repair, no matter how strong the Wind."

"The difference they make in the construction of houses," says Espinosa, "is in the number of poles or laths used, more being required for public edifices and the houses of officials than for the dwellings of ordinary citizens."

Bartram, an early traveler in the Gulf region, gives a detailed account of the method of attaching and bracing tiers of laths so as to form the inner structure of the great Council Houses, which, according to him, were made to accommodate seated gatherings of several hundred persons.

It is said that the houses of the *Tejas* invariably faced the East, that they often had skin doors swung on poles set in sockets, that most of them had lofts, and none, windows.

According to Espinosa, a bundle of grass or straw, worked into a fanciful image, was set atop each finished edifice.

He also says those who came late to the labor were lashed by the police-overseers, the men across the breasts and the women over their shoulders; however the blows were not heavy — being, perhaps, symbolic rather than punitive — and were received with laughing good nature — as a great jest, in fact.

Of the jollification following the completion of the task, he tells us: "During all the time the people are working, the new householders are busy preparing food for everybody, having previously made ready quantities of venison and many pots of ground corn they call *atole*.

"No one, not even the ruling chieftain, is excused from feeding all those who assemble — in fact the feast given by

12

men of prominence is more abundant than that prepared by ordinary citizens.

"They served the crowd according to its rank. From the highest official to the smallest child, all are served in order, abundantly and carefully, in earthen vessels, some large and some small. The feast over, the crowd scatters and each one goes home well pleased."

INTERIORS

"In the house is the Fire," says one narrator in the discussion of interiors, "a Fire which is never extinguished by day or by night. Over the door is a little superstructure, or mound of stones, very prettily arranged. Round one half of . . . (a house we saw) set against the wall, were ten couches made of reed mats suspended from four forked sticks forming the bedstead, or frame. Over the reed mats, or rugs, buffalo hides were placed. At the head and the foot of the couch, two other rugs attached to the ends of the suspended rug formed a sort of arch, which, lined with a brilliantly colored strip of matting, made a very pretty alcove."

Du Pratz tells us these beds had mattresses, with ticks of softly tanned skins stuffed with Spanish moss or shredded corn husks, and that the mat coverings were customarily striped black, red, and "natural," or maize-yellow.

James Adair, a British trader maintaining a business among the southern agricultural Indians for forty years, beginning in 1735, states that by the custom of the country in Louisiana, little boys were bedded on panther or buffalo skins, in order that they might grow into men of spirit, while little girls were couched on fawn skins in order to acquire the submissive temperaments thought becoming to Indian femininity.

Painted skin chests under the beds contained dried meat, clothing, and plumes. Plumes were also kept in bamboo tubes. Being delicate and precious, feathers and articles made of feathers were always carefully handled and given special protection.

13

The smooth earth floors of the houses, say early travelers, were covered with closely woven matting or rugs, "beautifully painted on both sides with vivid figures of birds, beasts, and flowers"; and Casañas, another Spanish missionary sent among the *Tejas*, describes these cane carpets as so well-made "they might have been used to cover European drawing rooms." The matting was, perforce, cut or woven to accommodate the circular Fire pit which served as family altar, cookstove, and hearth.

Among some *Caddo* Nations, particularly the *Pawnee*, to the northwest, "chimneys" or screens were set up about the Fire — circles of poles hung with painted skins resembling, in their illuminated position, richly figured tapestries.

Adair says the better-class houses were calcimined inside with white clay; and other observers comment on the brilliant effect of clothing, weapons, and shields hanging against this stark white background, "like unpolished silver" — an ever shifting kaleidoscope of color and shadow in the playing Firelight.

The Spanish explorers of East Texas tell us a dwelling was ordinarily occupied by two families; each having its allotted semicircle for living quarters. In some houses, the beds went all the way around the wall. Where the residents were not so numerous that the entire wall space was taken up by beds, shelves were placed against the wall, each shelf raised five or six feet from the floor.

On these shelves were large, round, close-woven baskets containing shelled corn, nuts, acorns, and beans and large earthen jars filled with ground cornmeal or bear oil. Though all trace of the baskets is gone, many of these great jars may be seen in the Indian pottery collection at the University of Texas and at the several museums in Oklahoma.

In order to keep the foodstuffs in the baskets free of weevils, the Indians covered the contents of each basket with several layers of ashes; then bound skins tightly over the tops to keep out the rats.

Where there was no room for shelves on the main floor,

Joutel, who explored East Texas with La Salle, says the storehouses were in the lofts.

We are told, concerning the *Tejas,* as of other southern village Indians, "They have all the earthen-ware that is necessary for their purposes, and curious seats of wood for those who come to their houses." Adair says of the seats that they were low stools with four stubby legs, the whole made from one block of wood.

The wooden mortars, carefully hollowed log-ends or log troughs, in which these Indians ground corn to meal for their daily bread, stood always by the door — set there, like other articles, to absorb the beneficent Medicine of the morning Sun.

EARLY AMERICAN APARTMENT HOUSES
THE RANCHO AND THE RANCHERIA

The prime distinction between *Asinai* and *Caddo,* as to the layout of their living quarters, was in the size of the communities. The *Asinai* gathered in small rancherias of half-a-dozen to a dozen houses, each group a few miles apart. The *Caddo* gathered in large villages of two hundred or more houses, and the villages were many miles apart. But in either case a single house usually accommodated not more than two closely related families. This private ownership of homesteads is a major difference between the eastern timber Indians and the *Pueblo* dwellers to the westward — a difference the terrain and climate would force into being as the gardeners moved westward into open desert territory.

"Ranch," like "tank" (from *tanque,* earthen reservoir) is a word the Spanish adopted and gave customary descriptive endings: *rancho* for a big settlement and *rancheria* for a small one. Thus the *Caddo* and the *Puebloistas* lived in *ranchos* and the *Asinai* in *rancherias.*

SACREDNESS OF THE SEED CORN

Among the many picturesque features of East Texas

15

homes was the seed corn, of which Espinosa declares: "They make a string of the best ears of grain, leaving the shucks on, and put it on a forked stick at a point in the house where the Smoke will reach it. For this purpose they select the quantity they will need for two years' planting, so that if the first year is dry, they will not lack for seed the second year."

Seed corn was sacred and not to be touched, even though the family was starving.

The ordinary harvest, before it was shelled, was dried on outside racks over the door, where it, also, received the beneficial rays of the Rising Sun.

Such was the home of the gardener — a dwelling with a pleasant interior and a substantial exterior, of which it is said in Lawson's HISTORY OF SOUTH CAROLINA: These Indians "are often troubled with a multitude of fleas, especially near the places where they dress their deer skins, because that hair harbors them; yet I never felt any unsavory smell in their cabins, whereas, should we live in our houses as they do, we should be poisoned with our own nastiness, which confirms these Indians to be, as they really are, some of the sweetest people in the world."

FOOTNOTE

[1] *Texas* or *Tejas* is not the name of any Indian Tribe or Nation, yet the *Tejas* Indians were well known from the time the Spanish entered Texas. See p. viii for explanation.

IV

The Social Whirl

"The whole Nation (the *Asinai)* is pleasant and joyous."
Espinosa.

THE VILLAGE OF THE ASH

"This village, that of the *Coenis (Asinai),* is one of the largest and most populous I have ever seen in America," says Father Douay, who was with La Salle. "It is at least twenty leagues (fifty miles) long; not that it is constantly inhabited, but in hamlets of ten or twelve cabins, forming cantons, each with a different name."[1]

THE LAW OF HOSPITALITY

The law of hospitality was fully as strong with the Indians as it later came to be with the pioneer. Every visitor who arrived among the *Asinai,* or in any other Indian domain, had to be fed, and at once — no matter if he had already dined within the hour.

Sometimes there were abuses of this fine sense of hospitality, for an entire tribe or nation, desiring to impose on and, impoverish another, might arrive when the public larder was slim — and private larders slimmer still. Nevertheless, no Indian, the old historians assure us, would have demeaned himself by refusing to entertain visitors, even though he knew full well they came with false hearts, intending, literally, to "eat him out of house and home." Nor would any Council have refused them a welcome in the Council House.

Public visits, in fact, amounted almost to a public tax, for the higher a man was in the social scale of the community, the stronger was the convention that bound him to share his last mouthful with a stranger guest. THE PEACE PIPE, THE NEW FIRES, THE GARDEN PATCH, and THE WINTER SOLSTICE all contain evidences of the strength of Indian hospitality.

THE CASTE SYSTEM

A distinct recognition of social differences existed among all the Mound Builder peoples and is particularly commented on among the *Tejas* by the French soldiers and Spanish missionaries, and among the *Natchez*, in Louisiana, by Du Pratz.

As generally set forth, society consisted of four strata: the royalty, or immediate members of the reigning family; the nobility, including Medicine Men, or priests, councilors, and distinguished warriors; the commonalty or "respected class," and the "stinkards," or low class people.

The reigning, or hereditary, or civil chieftain was known, among the *Natchez*, as the Great Sun, and his mother, the person next in importance in the social regime, as the "female" Sun — meaning the Moon or Night Sun — supreme female in the Indian Pantheon. The descent of the feathered sceptre of the Sun, emblem of imperial position, was not from the male side of the house, but from the female side — the hereditary chieftain being succeeded by his sister's child instead of his own — hence the importance of the Woman Sun.

To these dignitaries, looked on as human counterparts of the heavenly Orbs, tribute was paid similar to that paid

18

the great luminary bodies. For instance they were bowed to by the populace, and greeted with shouts of acclaim like those the Great Sun, in his turn, addressed, each morning, to the Sun God.

The *Natchez* claim to have once had as many as two hundred Suns presiding over different provinces, and the reader must keep in mind the fact that the Sabine River was not an Indian boundary dividing different peoples. It is an historical boundary but not an anthropological boundary. Therefore some of these Suns may have presided in what is now "Texas."[2]

We are assured by the very earliest explorers of the southern agricultural region that there were some women chief executives; mention being made, among the *Tejas*, of the *Sanate Adiva*, who commanded the highest regard, had five husbands, and a house of many rooms.

The Gentleman of Elvas makes note of another such sovereign lady in Louisiana, and describes the chivalrous treatment accorded her by De Soto. Having been regally entertained by her, the Spanish commander, setting forth again upon his expedition, seized her person, ordinarily transported in a palanquin on the shoulders of loyal courtiers, stripped her of her jewels, described as quantities of magnificent pearls, and set her afoot at the head of his armored column — it being his custom to retain the chief authority as hostage from one province into the next.

The ancient chronicler gives as an instance of the stealthiness of Indian nature that she was able to make good her escape from the gentle clutches of the Spaniards, and, incidentally, to secure and carry away with her the main bulk of the pearls.

Among the *Tejas*, mention is made of a child, or boy chieftain, who, while all due respect was paid to his person, was allowed to "play about" while the Council proceeded with affairs of state.

The word "reigning," rather than "ruling," is preferable concerning these hereditary chieftains, since their position

19

seems to have held much more of social than of political import.

In order to keep the imperial family — the Family of the Wind, headed by the Sun and the Lady Moon — from becoming a powerful caste in itself, a system of social "demotion" was in order, by which the sons of royalty were not royalty, but merely nobility; and the sons of nobility dropped to the ranks of the commonalty, until such time as they were able to distinguish themselves by notable acts for the public good.[3] Those married to royalty did not partake of the rank of their mates, but were merely consorts. For example, the husbands of royal women were subject to ceremonial execution on the death of the ladies, just as wives, ordinarily, were subject to execution at the death of their husbands, as shown in ORIGIN AND IMMORTALITY.

Ranking next to royalty among the *Tejas*, say the Spanish — that is, ranking above the warriors — were the Medicine Men, or priests. In fact considerable confusion exists in some accounts as to whether the leading Medicine Man did not actually take precedence over all civil chieftains in honor and authority. Certainly it was his distinguished privilege, according to all accounts, to occupy one of the two *tapestles* in the Council House, or in the public square, whenever the other was occupied by the civil chieftain.

The next chapter gives a description of the use and position of these Red and White Seas, which apparently were a feature of all official gathering places. As each *tapestle*, or dais, was long and flat, with a bench below for a footrest, their arrangement, except for the absence of back and arms, must have been not unlike that of a modern boot blacking stand.

According to H. B. Cushman, who was reared among the *Choctaw* by missionary parents, the priestcraft was vested in the Panther Clan.

Next to high rank in the priestcraft or in the military, among the gardners, social prestige seems to have been based on proficiency in the ball play, a sport to be described a little further on in this chapter. Since all men not destined to occupy the regal *tapestles,* were obliged to raise themselves in public esteem by their own efforts, there was great striving for official honors among ambitious young men, and the awarding of these honors formed a very considerable part of village pageantry and social life.

The "stinkards," or low class people, included enslaved captives and male "wives," sometimes politely spoken of as "hermaphrodites" in the old writings. Men of this despised group, Adair says, were always placed at the tail end of ceremonial processions. Their kind, however, seems to have existed throughout Indian society, for there is mention of male consorts accompanying *Comanches* on the war path.

THE PUBLIC SQUARE

The public square was the hub of the village. It was floored with hard-packed clay and such areas, still existing in East Texas, have long been termed "Indian dancing floors" by the local inhabitants. Surrounding the square were public edifices, including the Temple and Council House — the latter where men's gatherings were held and visitors of distinction entertained — and the residences of high officials, including the civil chief and the war chief. Adjacent to this "official circle" were the homes of councillors, warriors, and other men of prominence. From there on the village spread out, either round or semicircular, in honor of the Sun or the Moon.

In some squares, early travelers mentioned the presence of tall Scalp Poles, evidence that here the Tortures were held.

During the day these enclosed courts, with their high Red and White Seats, wore a serious aspect, since they served as the center of local government, but towards evening they took on a festive air, becoming, at night, the theatres of village gaiety.

The Light Fantastic

The principal complaint lodged against the Indians by the Christian fathers who followed the *Conquistadores* into the "new" world was of the fondness they exhibited for the *mitotes,* their ancient aboriginal dances, to indulge in which converts regularly eluded the anxious supervision of the monks and slipped from the missions into the wilderness to "foot it featly" under the New Moon.

Of the Indian dances, Du Pratz tells us "they were all alike; to have seen one was to have seen all." Judging from this statement, the steps and musical measures must have been extremely similar, though the meaning, it is certain, was infinitely varied among the numerous performances. It has to be kept in mind that Du Pratz, like Espinosa, was a missionary monk whose mind was not predisposed to a critical evaluation of heathen festivities.

Assuming that the step was always the same, we have a description of it in THE GREEN CORN DANCE, a description given by John Howard Payne, the poet — who was much more appreciative of the grace and art of the Indians than were the earnest churchmen seeking to win them from their ancient rituals for their souls' sake.

The Circle Dance

Du Pratz describes for us a dance witnessed among the *Natchez* at the Green Corn Festival: "At night they surround the place of festivities with torches made of bound shocks of dry bamboo, which, more than two hundred of them blazing at once, give a great light.

"By this light the Indians dance till Dawn.

"A man seats himself on the ground with a pot which has in it a little water and over it a deerskin drawn tight. He holds the pot with one hand and with the other hand beats a measure.

"Around him the women form an oval, each having her hands in a 'round' of feathers so strongly made that it can

22

be twirled from side to side; that is, from right to left.

"The men surround the women with another circle, the performers staying about six feet apart. Each man has a *chichicoi*, a rattle made of a gourd 'threaded' by a stick, both ends extending from the calabash, the longer one serving for a handle. With this instrument the men accompany the movement of the dance.

"In the measure the women move from left to right and the men from right to left.

"The circles shrink or enlarge according to the measure, and the dancers drop out at will, to have their places taken by others — thus the dance can be kept up all night long without fatigue."

The School Room

The actual dancing masters among the southern Nations were the aged, or "beloved old ones," who taught the infants of the race the holy rituals by the time the babes were able to move their feet to the measures of the *mitote* and twist their tiny tongues to the chant. Once their charges were properly started on the "old and holy" path, the mentors continuously watched over them with the jealous espial of the aged to see that no changes were made in convention and sacred rite. The nursery was always under the supervision of the family patriarch, who acted as schoolmaster to the oncoming generations, and was the repository of all knowledge, there being no libraries save the memories of "those of many winters."

Indian Orchestras

According to a set of clipped notes gathered by Herman Lehmann and published by Jonathan H. Jones, no Indian celebration was complete without music, and the music was clamorous and clanging because of the belief that such sounds appeased angry gods and evil spirits. Among the instruments of native orchestras are listed drums, wood winds, plumes, the shield, and "fiddles" — also, "the stone."

"The sound of the stones," say the notes, "to the ears of the Indian is the most beautiful tone in the world, less tart and rasping than the sound of metal, more bright than the sound of wood, more brilliant and sweet than either.

"They use the sonorous stone singly or in chimes of twelve or twenty-four, and esteem them so highly as to select specimens for their use with great care and regard for color. The majority are used plain; that is, simply cut and polished; but occasionally specimens are carved in the most fantastic shapes. They represent various deities, as birds, fish and animals, and are otherwise decorated with red feathers, gaudy colors and hair tassels.

"The stone chime is one of the most ancient and highly prized of instruments found among the Indians. They are religiously guarded and kept concealed. They are cut out of jade or a kind of calcareous stone which is only to be found in certain localities. The common shape of these stones is the carpenter's square. The twelve stones are arranged in two rows, six above and six below.

"The Indians have fifty varieties of drums, ranging from the hollow tree split open and covered with rawhide, to the rattan hoop covered with a coon skin. The drum which gives the sweetest and most mellow tone has a handful of rattlesnake rattles inside it which softens the tone wonderfully.

"Four square pieces of wood with a neck extended, tightly covered with rawhide and whitleather strings, made the Indian fiddle."

Some of the "instruments," such as the plumes, had only a spiritual quality, though their presence was necessary to complete the symbolism of the orchestration.

THE MAY FETE

Among the *Tejas,* "track meets" appear to have furnished the prime sport, taking precedence even over the ball

24

play. Espinosa describes for us the May-time races of the East Texas Indians, sometimes likened to old English May Fetes.

"At the beginning of May these Indians have a feast and a contest. They secure a very tall, straight, slender pine tree. After cutting off the branches, leaving only the plumed top, they set up the tree in a level space. They make two very wide clear paths that come to a circle round the tree.

"Innumerable Indians gather at the rising of the Sun and begin to run along these paths, one after the other. The one who runs around the tree the greatest number of times without pausing receives the most applause."

THE BALL PLAY

The *Choctaw*, from all accounts, held the palm in ball play. All nations, however, appear to have gloried in the sport. A spirited description of this amusement has been set down by W. B. Parker who witnessed a "try out" while on his way to Texas to join Marcy's expedition. Says he: "Upon entering upon the prairie, we observed in the distance a crowd of natives in gay clothing, the brilliant colours blending with the verdure, and making at sunset a truly picturesque scene. . . . It was a ball-play. Described, as this sport has been, by the able pencil of Catlin, description falls far short of reality.

"About six hundred men, women and children were assembled, all dressed in holiday costume, and all as intent upon the game as it is possible to be where both pleasure and interest combine.

"In this instance the contestants were all *Choctaws*, practising for their annual game with the *Creeks*, and I was struck with the interest taken by all the lookers-on, in the proficiency of each of the players.

"About sixty on each side were engaged in this exciting play, than which no exercise can be more violent nor better calculated to develop muscle and harden the frame.

25

"Each player provides himself with what are called ball-sticks. They are in shape like a large spoon, made of a piece of hickory about three feet long, shaved thin for about nine inches at the end forming the spoon, then bent round until brought into shape, the end securely fastened to the handle by buckskin thongs, the under side or bottom of the spoon covered with a coarse network of the same material . . . (the player) has one in each hand, and the ball — about the size of a large marble — is held between the spoons and thrown with an over-hand rotary motion, separating the spoons when the top of the circle is reached.

"The game is this: two poles are set up, each about seventeen feet high and a foot apart at the bottom, widening to three feet at the top. At the distance of two hundred yards, two similar poles are set up facing these. To strike the poles or to throw the ball between them counts one, and twelve is game. An umpire and starter takes the ball, advances to a mark equidistant from each end of the course, and throws it vertically into the air; it is caught, or, falling upon the ground, is eagerly struggled for and thrown toward the desired point. We saw some throw the ball the whole distance.

"At each brace of poles judges are stationed, who, armed with pistols, keep close watch, and whenever a count is made fire their pistols. The ball is then taken and started anew.

"Among the players, are the runners, the throwers, and those who throw themselves in the way and baffle the player who succeeds in getting the ball.

"The runners are light active men, the throwers heavier, and then the fat men, who can neither throw nor run, stand ready to seize a thrower or upset a runner.

"When a runner gets the ball, he starts at full speed towards the poles; if intercepted, he throws the ball to a friend, a thrower, perhaps. He is knocked down, then begins the struggle for the ball: a scene of pushing, jostling, and striking with the ball sticks, or a wrestle or two, all attended with hard knocks and harder falls. Whilst (we were) looking on, one man was pitched upon his head and had his collar bone broken; another had part of his scalp knocked off; but it was all taken in good humour, and what, among white men, would inevitably lead to black eyes and bloody noses, here ended with the passage of possession of the ball — a good lesson in forbearance and amiability, worthy of imitation.

"The combatants are stripped entirely naked except a breech cloth and moccasins, and gaudily painted; they fasten at the centre and small of the back, a horse's tail, gaily painted and arrayed like a tail that has been knicked by a jockey; some wore bouquets of flowers instead of the tail, but these were evidently the exquisites of the party, which the rings worn in the ears, nose and under lips, and manner of arranging the hair — one having it cut to a point and drawn down over his right eye, whilst his left eye was painted green — clearly proved.[4]

"The grotesque appearance of the players, the excitement, yells and shouts of the crowd, old and young, and the gaudy finery displayed, all combined to make an indelible impression upon our memories. The aged men of the tribe were the most noisy and excited. One old fellow, blind of an eye and quite seventy years old, was wild with excitement; shaking his red handkerchief, he continued to shout, *hoo, ka, li — hoo, ka, li —* catch, when the ball was thrown, and *chi, ca, ma —* good, when a count was made until quite hoarse.

"Doubtless, like the old war horse at the sound of the bugle, he felt all the fire of his youth, as he entered into the full spirit of this Indian sport."

WITH THIS OFFERING, I THEE WED!

The "Building Bee;" the spring planting, which was a festival enterprise; the harvest ceremonies; and the community hunts — all parts of the "social whirl" — have been described in other chapters. Here Du Pratz outlines for us the celebration of the marriage ceremony among the *Natchez*.

"If two people want to be married it is neither their parents nor grandparents who make the arrangements for this affair. They are made by the patriarchal heads of the family — usually the great grandparents, or their parents. These two old people have an interview in which, after the gentleman concerned has requested the lady, they ask if there is any relationship between the two parties who wish to marry, and to what degree; for within the third degree inclusive they could not marry. This interview of the family heads is based upon the supposition that the alliance is satisfactory; and that, besides, the match has been approved by all the important members of the families; for if anyone disapproves, the marriage cannot be consummated. Among these tribes which we term 'savages,' the laws do not authorize sons and daughters to bring into the families of their fathers mates who are not suitable for them, and to give to their posterity something which would be displeasing from the moment of birth.

"With wondrous agreement and dignity, which might well be imitated, they marry only where they love, and those who love are married only when it is approved by their families.

"It is rare that young people are married before attaining the age of twenty-five years. Until this time they are regarded as very weak both in spirit and in experience.

"When the old people have made an agreement concerning the marriage and have set the day, the necessary preparations are made to celebrate it. The men of the bride's family go to the hunt, the women prepare corn, and relatives of the groom prepare according to their circumstances.

"The set day being come, the head of the girl's family leaves his home and conducts the girl to the home of the groom; all the family follow in order, silently, and those who laugh do so moderately.

"Outside the groom's home are all the members of his

28

family who receive him (the official representative of the bride) with the usual crys of joy which were several *Hou! Hou!* He enters, and the head of the groom's household says: 'There you are!' to which the other replies 'yes!' The first repeats the word and shows with pride the beds which serve as sofas, saying 'be seated.'

"After a short rest the family representatives get up and lead the young people toward each other; they ask if they are satisfied with each other and if they love one another. They remind them that they should not marry if there is lacking a sincere desire to live together; that no one forces them to marry; and that they take each other by their own choice; that they shall leave their families and live in peace. After this admonition, the boy's true father brings the gift that he is making to his son and places it in his hands. The bride's father comes forward and takes his place by his daughter's side. Then the groom says to his betrothed, 'Dost thou wish me for thy husband?' She replies 'I do, indeed, and I am happy; love thou me as I love thee, for I shall love only thee.' At these words the groom covers the head of the girl with the gift which he has just received of his father, and says to her, 'I love thee; that is why I asked thee to wife; here is that I give thy parents to purchase thee.' Then he gives the present to the bride's father.

"The husband wears an aigrette on the top of his braid, hanging over his left ear, to which is attached a cord of oak leaves; in his left hand is a bow and arrows. The aigrette bears witness that he is to be married; the oak leaves that he has no fear of the woods, or of camping after the hunt. The bow and arrows show that he will not be overcome by the enemy, and that he will always defend his wife and children.

"The bride holds in her left hand a small laurel (magnolia) branch and in the right hand a stalk of corn which her mother gave her at the time when she received with her father the gift of the groom. The laurel, which is evergreen, indicates the bride's willingness to keep always in good standing, and the stalk of corn, that she will care for the household, and prepare the food for her husband.

"The couple having said what I have just related, the girl lays down the stalk which she held in her left hand and gives her hand to her husband, who takes it in his left hand saying: 'I am thy husband.' She replies, 'And I, thy wife.' Then the husband goes to take the hands of all her family; then he leads his bride to his own family, so that she may offer a like courtesy. Last he leads her to his bed, saying: 'Here is our bed. Keep it clean.' This indicates that she is to guard their nuptial couch against any defamation."

Boiled down, the marriage ceremony among all agricultural Nations consisted of the groom's gaining consent from the bride's parents; the exchange of symbolic tokens between principals — an ear of corn offered by the bride in earnest of the fact that she would cultivate the garden and cook the food, and a haunch of venison submitted by the groom as evidence of his determination to be a provident Nimrod — and the formal announcement to the Council legalizing the affair.

According to Bartram, the young couple, after the celebration, repaired to a specially constructed green bower with two magnolia shrubs at the entrance, there to remain undisturbed for a night and a day.[5]

ETIQUETTE AND SOCIAL CUSTOMS

The following summary of etiquette and social customs prevailing in the southern agricultural area has been prepared from consultation of the authorities listed in the bibliography at the end of this book:

The Indian never bowed socially; bowing was an act of reverence paid only to divinity.

The great chieftains received the same homage that was paid to the Sun — being looked on as akin to the Sun.

Only chieftains, Medicine Men, and distinguished visitors were offered stools. Other persons sat on their heels, or on the beds.

In the Temple, in the Council House, and in all community assemblies, the better places were given to the most honored members of the group, usually the elders and the warriors.

No Indian ever interrupted the speech of another.

It was customary to offer the maidens of the community as consorts when masculine guests arrived unaccompanied by their wives. No stigma attached to resultant births, all children in the Tribe or Nation being identified with the mother's family.

A visitor was offered food the moment he appeared in an Indian home and it was construed as an insult for him to refuse to eat.

All Indians ate when they felt hungry and no regular meal hours were observed.

People of the better class used platters of braided reed to hold their food. Low-class people placed their food on the ground — or on their feet.

It will be noted in descriptions of Indian cooking, as well as by visits to Mexican Indian houses today, that most food is wrapped in corn shucks or folded in *tortillas* so as to be handled without tableware.

Widows had set terms of mourning which they must observe or be classed as wanton.

Babies surviving their mothers might be nursed by women of near kin. If there were none such to nurse them, they were put to death since it was felt that only sustenance from one of near relationship would suffice their needs.

Small children were placed in charge of the most elderly man in the family, who served as tutor-guardian, aided in the physical care of the youngsters by unmarried girls.

Children were allowed to go about naked till several years old, except on fiesta days.

Children were never given corporal punishment.

Quarreling was absolutely intolerable to Indian society, either in the agricultural area or on the Plains. It was punishable in children by isolation from the family, and in adults by banishment from the community.

Any misfortune, such as the burning of a man's house and personal properties, resulted in immediate community aid from the neighbors.

It was customary to offer gifts for the use of the dead at funerals.

BANNERS OF OPPOSING FAITHS

We are told that when some of the early missionary monks crossed the Plains to the gardening area preceded by two banners, one bearing a golden cross and the other the mystic intaglio of the Virgin of Guadalupe, they found, blocking their path, banners made of smooth-tanned buffalo hides, set up on stakes, emblazoned with the rays of the sacred Sun, glimmering to the distraction of Christian eyes in the light of that brilliantly beaming Orb.

It is no great wonder that the Indian, reared from infancy to revere the Sun and the Moon, taught from the cradle to dance in their sacred illumination, accustomed from his earliest breath to participate in the multifold activities of his ancient social and ritualistic regime, found little to exalt his soul inside the grey mission walls. Try as hard as they might, the earnest missionaries whose minds were occupied mainly with discipline found it difficult to keep their converts and to defeat with baptismal water the ancient Holy Fire. They found it still harder to substitute baptismal water for the showering of holy corn meal that is still a part of Indian ritual in New Mexico and Arizona.

FOOTNOTES

[1] In using *Coenis,* the French are using the Spanish word for "ash" — *cenizas* — a name given to these Indians because of their deep veneration for Fire, and their care of the

THE SOCIAL WHIRL

Temple ashes which were disposed of in a heap sufficient to form a landmark.

² With many Nations the great civil chieftain was of the Family of the Wind, insomuch as the Winds were next to the Sun, the Moon and the Stars in the Indian Pantheon. For it was the Winds that were the Go-Betweens of this world and that of the Spirits. In other words, they partook both of the human and the divine, and were the supernal spirits of the Here World.

³ See THE WARRIORS AWARD, Chapter XV.

⁴ The narrator obviously had no understanding of Indian heraldry as signified by painted symbolism, or of the tribal significance of the hair-do. (See Chapters IV and XV.)

⁵ It is interesting to try to analyse Du Pratz's description of the wedding ceremony, attempting to determine how much Christian interpretation he may have given the symbolism. The acorn was a world-wide emblem of conjugal union, among nature worshipers, because of the interplay of acorn and cup; hence its magical import with respect to fertility and its constant appearance in the dress of women.

NOTE: The modern game, *Lacrosse,* is a variant of Indian ball play.

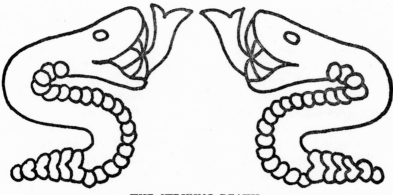

THE STRIKING DEATH

V

The Sacred Fires

"The *Asinai* and *Naichas* Tribes had Fire from their fore-fathers. When asked why they did not go out on the Plains to hunt during buffalo time, like the neighboring Tribes, one of their priests replied that they could not because the wood would fail and the Fires be extinguished."

Espinosa.

"They have houses of worship and a Perpetual Fire which they never let die out."

Hidalgo, *speaking of the Tejas.*

THE PERPETUAL FIRES

The devout agricultural Indians of the south looked on their Perpetual Temple Fires, together with the ever ascending crests of mystic, curling Smoke plumes, as direct descendants of the Sun, eternally compelled to the service of the Great Orb by inviolable, hereditary bonds. The Perpetual Fire, like its Progenitor, the Sun, was a thing alive and sentient, an "all-seeing eye"; and the Indian feared as well as revered its holy Flame. As for the Smokes, they were continuously active messengers, divine and vigilant tattle-tales, whose specific function was to make intimate reports from the Fires to the spirits, to the gods, and to the Sun, on the doings of the Indians in the Middle World.

THE SACRED FIRES

Three sound, seasoned walnut logs, set tripodally, about an earthen cone, perhaps, and burning at the apex — this, according to the Chevalier Tonti, contemporary of La Salle, and according to Lafitau, missionary priest in Louisiana, was the form of the Perpetual Fires. The inception of these Fires remains among the Mysteries. The Indians, when asked, said only: "Our Fathers had them from the Sun; we do not know how they were brought to Earth."

The possibility is that they were kindled from the Sun, as were those of the Peruvians, who brought down New Fire each year with disks of gold — and that the secret was lost in the absence of recorded history.

THE NEW FIRES

The reader must not confuse the Perpetual Fires with the New Fires which were created afresh each year by the priests at the Green Corn Festival. The Perpetual Fires, being direct from the Sun, were, in Indian eyes, supremely holy and subject only to the Sun; whereas the New Fires, though sentient beings akin to the Sun, and therefore influential with the Sun, were thought, without disrespect, to be subject to man, having been produced by man. They were sanctified and used as oracles, but not deified like the Perpetual Fires.

The Perpetual Fires were palladiums, no less, for Du Pratz informs us that should they ever burn to cold grey ash, their cooling would be the signal for the millenium; and that not so much as a coal might be removed to light a priestly Pipe without the entire Nation's incurring the penalty for blasphemy. The New Fires, on the other hand, were maintained from year to year, in Temples of their own, for the express purpose of furnishing brands to rekindle household hearths — that none among the godly might be compelled to eat food prepared over a contaminated or an infidel Flame.

Four sound, seasoned walnut logs, laid in the form of a

35

Maltese cross on a truncated pyramid of Earth, burning at the center of the cross — this seems to have been the shape of the New Fires. Though continuously alight, they were never allowed to burst into blaze save when sacrificial drops of bear oil or pinches of tobacco were tossed to sputter on their glowing hearts — sacrifices cajoling the Holy Essence for the sake of auguries. Down the logs, to their outer ends, the rich odors ran, taking flight with the Smoke, through the four World Quarters, to rise at last and tickle the nostrils of the Sun.

According to old accounts, the Temples for the Perpetual Fires were rectangular, with pitched roofs, while the Temples for the New Fires seem to have been round and domed like the dwelling houses. All were ribbed and thatched.

NUMERICAL SYMBOLISM

It will be noted throughout this book that seven, four, and three appear again and again in southern ritual. Ordinarily, wherever the *trinity* occurs in religious symbolism, it represents the age-old idea of the family — father, mother, and child —whether human or divine. In the case of these Indians it, in all probability, represents the Sun and the Earth, together with man — the offspring of their spiritual union.

Among the gardeners, women's ritual seems most concerned with the number three, and men's ritual with the number four. There were seven worlds in the Indian's conception of the universe. The number seven does not appear in Texas artifacts except in group combinations of three and four, but the Maltese cross, presumably representing the World Quarters, or the four cardinal directions, or the Homes of the Winds, appears over and over — in the shape of the Temple Fires, as described by the Spaniards, and in decorative effects on gorgets and jars taken from East Texas burials. The *triqueter* appears less frequently, but no less distinctly, in the shape, and the decoration of a few beautifully made bottles and bowls — all, apparently, of Temple origin. Its most outstanding appearance is in French descriptions of Perpetual Fire among the *Natchez*.

By general reasoning, we arrive at the hypothesis that the symbolism of three and four, and of the circle and the square, representing Sun and Earth, were interlocking. Thus the cone on which New Fire was kindled, and the round shape of the New Fire Temple, were symbolic of the Perpetual Fire, or the Sun and the Moon; while the pyramidal shape of the Perpetual Fire Temple was symbolic of the four-cornered pyramidal altars on which the New Fire burned, symbolic, also, of the Earth, or World Quarters — this interlocking symbolism of the two phases of Fire worship intensifying the importance of the number seven.

INSIDE THE TEMPLES

Using Adair's detailed descriptions made in Louisiana, which tally in essential details with the recorded observations of Spanish priests and French soldiers in East Texas, as well as with the impressions of English colonials in other southern areas, we find that the principal furnishings of both kinds of Temples were as follows: the blunt-topped Earth mound (rectangular pyramid or cone) on which the Fire burned; two *tapestles*, or tall, table-like seats, one painted white and the other red, with accompanying footrests; the altar, which seems to have been similar in shape to the *tapestles*, but hollow within; and a breast-high screen or earthen wall concealing the holy junk heap where broken or discarded holy articles, still imbued with magic, were flung to keep them from falling into ignorant or profane hands where the magic with which they were imbued might have been of dangerous consequence.

The arrangements of these furnishings appears to have been according to ritualistic pattern, the Fire mound occupying the center of the Temple floor, the Red Seat the northern end of the edifice, and the White Seat the southern

end. The "altar" — which must have been a flat-topped cup-
board, since mention is made of putting the articles of the
rituals into it, and of its being raised on crotched poles and
hung with painted skins — was built against the west wall.
The entrance to the Temple, according to most authorities,
was spaced in the center of the east wall, facing the Rising
Sun.

Reports from Louisiana and other areas state that the
bones of dead chieftains were kept in the most holy of the
Temple centers, sometimes laid out at length on a loft-like
shelf, and sometimes packed in baskets covered with painted
skins and ornamented with sprigs of gold.

The contents of the altars, as reported by Spanish missionaries in Texas, were musical instruments, feathers, vest-
ments, conch shell ladles, and little bowls shaped like birds
and animals.

The University of Texas Museum has on display a number of handsomely carved shell gorgets of the kind described
by early travellers as part of the priest's insignia; several
conch shell dippers like those said to have been used in the
Temples, and numerous effigy bowls and bottles typifying
ducks, doves, turtles, deer, and other animals — vessels tally-
ing with those described by the Spanish missionaries as
figuring in observed Indian ritual.

The Spiro Mound in Oklahoma, near the Arkansas River
and the state line, has yielded the greatest single treasure in
effigies and gorgets. If all the artifacts "recovered" here are
genuine, they indicate an infiltration from the far south —
perhaps *Mayan*. Potsherds show an intricacy of line drawings: geometricized birds, beasts, and men. Exclusive of
these designs, the findings closely relate to findings in East
Texas, Louisiana, Arkansas, and Missouri.

Standards surmounted by wooden Eagles carved with
outspread wings sometimes stood behind the *tapestles*, says
Adair; while Du Pratz and others mention three carved
Eagles perched, one in the center and one at either peak of
the roof ridge, on the quadrangular Temples. Adair also

speaks of seeing images of the Sun and the Half Moon inside the Temples — images similar, apparently, to those Espinosa saw raised during the funeral celebration of the Grand Death in East Texas, described in detail in ORIGIN AND IMMORTALITY.

COLOR SYMBOLISM

Quoting Adair again, we learn that white, among the southern agricultural peoples, was the sacred color, symbolizing holiness, peace, sanctuary — the beneficent aspect of the Sun to which both white and yellow were sacred — and that the White Seat, therefore, was the seat of the High Priest. This seat was recoated for every important ceremony with spotless, shining clay, and then covered with satiny buckskins, as pure and glistening as untracked snows.

The Red Seat might be painted in two ways, according to whether it was occupied by the Civil Chief or the War Chief. If the first should preside, the *tapestle* was stained with a dark red vegetable juice, but if the War Chief held forth, bright vermilion was applied, symbolic of war and of blood.

We are informed that when an assembly gathered in a Temple, the more important members sat on the west side facing the entrance and the Rising Sun; while the least considered ones sat with their backs to the East, facing the altar and the west wall. The floor, on these occasions, was covered with finely woven mats, which, at other times, were kept rolled and stacked against the wall. Women, children, and all men condemned as weaklings, appear never to have been permitted among Temple gatherings.

CONVENTIONS OF THE FIRE

Since Fire, whether Perpetual, New, or even the hearth Fire, was looked upon as the supreme medium of human communication with the spirit world, with the gods, and with the Sun, a special etiquette or set of conventions naturally grew up concerning it, exclusive of the ceremonial rituals by which priests and prophets thought to bend its supernatural power to human ends. Among these conventions or rules were the following:

To feed a Fire with rotten wood was sacrilege.

Special kindling materials were used in striking Fire.

Walnut wood had a special sanctity.

It was an act of irreverence to blow harshly on the Fire — an act sure to result in bad weather, since the scattering ash would return to Earth in form of snow.

Ashes were sacred and filled with magic, and, therefore, required special disposition.

No Fire was ever quenched with water, save death torches and war torches — the one symbolic of a life gone out, and the other indicative of the hope that enemy lives would go out with violence.

If a house Fire failed, more Fire was got from the Temple where the New Fire of the year was deposited.

Meat was passed through the Fire as a purification rite.

New-born children were passed over the Fire as a form of purifiation — a kind of baptismal ritual.

The first spoonful, or mouthful, of any meal was fed to the Fire. (Compare with the Christian act of saying grace.)

The most holy Perpetual Fire could not be touched for any secular purpose.

THE SACRISTANS

In order to insure the strict observance of these conventions in the Temples, and therefore to protect the populace against the evils that would befall through any disrespect to, or neglect of the Perpetual Fires and the New Fires, each Province had its group of sacristans, old men of special sanctity, ordained to tend the Sacred Flames for given periods; and its group of lusty young men, set apart to shape the holy wood into proper lengths for Temple use. Considering the tedium of manipulating hardwood timbers with stone tools, the reverence involved in the preparation of the fuel can be appreciated by even the most skeptical mind!

ADJUNCTS TO THE TEMPLE

Outside the Temples, indispensable wood piles were stacked in pyramids containing ceremonial fuel gathered when new forest areas were cleared for the planting of spring crops. Authorities say the proper size for Temple wood was two feet thick and the length a man could reach by spreading both arms.

Adjacent to the Temple was always a tremendous ash heap (*cenizario*) where cinders from the Sacred Fires were respectfully poured for generation after generation.

In East Texas, several of these huge ash heaps exist today, sole markers of the spots where Fire Temples once stood, crested with plumes of sentient, sacrifice-laden Smoke.

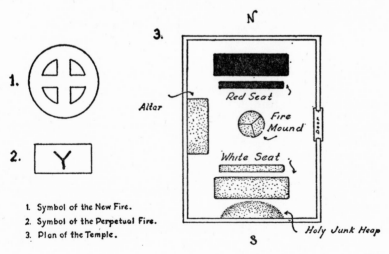

1. Symbol of the New Fire.
2. Symbol of the Perpetual Fire.
3. Plan of the Temple.

41

FOOTNOTES

Comparatively speaking, the *estufas* (stove rooms) of the *Pueblos* were a desert counterpart of the Mound Builder temples east of the Trinity River in Texas, except that they were exclusively entered by men. This limitation to protect the magical arts of war and the hunt from any possibility of feminine contamination would have been another natural accommodation to the open desert territory.

Smoke, birds (or plumage), and snakes were all divine messengers or "go-between-the-worlds" in the Indian pantheon, as in all nature worshipers' pantheons. The snake had exclusive entry to the Earth or Under World — hence the extreme prejudice against snakes in the Christian world; hence also the plumage of the angels, *angelus* being from the Greek word for "messenger."

To understand the Indian pantheon, it must be understood that the Day Sun was a masculine essence, one with Fire and with blood; and that both gold and red were the Day Sun's colors. The Moon or Night Sun was the feminine essence of the same spiritual being. White and silver were one with the Moon, as Albino Fetishism — the reverencing of naturally white objects and animals — was one with worship of the Moon. Out of the mass of symbolism here entailed we have derived our modern gold and silver coinage which is a relic of the use of these "precious" metals in Sun and Moon ritualism.

VI

The Indian Pantheon

"They were a people devotional to their beliefs which were founded alone upon the teachings of Nature — their only Light."

Cushman.

SUPREMACY OF THE SUN

Now that we have before us a picture of the Sacred Fires, and of the Temples in which they were maintained — this being the most conspicuous feature of Sun-worship among the southern Tribes and Nations — let us see if, by attempting to unravel the mysteries of the Indian's mind, we can gain something of the import of his faith.

In looking among his concepts, let us first consider the idea universally paramount among primitive peoples, that every natural object — every stone, every tree, every star — was supposed to be possessed of a life essence, a spirit thing; and was, therefore, capable of registering offense or pleasure; capable, also of dealing good or evil to the cause of man.

What more logical outcome of such an idea than the belief that the Sun, most noticeable of all natural objects, was supreme among the elements? Was it not apparently true that the movements of the Sun brought day and night, winter and summer? That the Sun dried up water from the Earth, or veiled its face and let Rain fall? That it was the source of light and warmth, and, therefore, of all life?

In the Indian's Pantheon, says Cushman, not only was the Sun looked upon as the Life Giver; but the Moon, called the Night Sun, was thought to be the Sun's wife.

THE BALANCE OF POWER

The second fundamental concept upon which the Indian based his religious practices, was the idea of eternal conflict between the forces of good and evil, an idea based on the two faces of Nature. Water, for instance, was necessary to man's life. Without water to drink, he would perish. Without water, the crops would wither and die. Yet, with too much water, the crops would be washed away. Man would drown. Thus there was good water — and bad water. So, to the Indian, all the forces of Nature were in an eternally balanced conflict — man filling the hazardous position of pawn in their colossal game of war.

According to Dodge, Cushman, Du Pratz, and numerous other authorities, the Indians, almost without exception, believed in two great spiritual Beings, one supreme among the Powers of Evil and the other supreme among the Powers of Good — the Captains of the Hosts — between which eternal warfare raged.

In *The Commerce of the Prairies,* published in the 50's by Josiah Gregg, we come upon this discussion of the matter with regard to the beliefs of the *Shawnee,* one of the great agricultural Nations of the Mississippi Valley: "But though the Shawnees consider the Sun the type, if not the essence, of the Great Spirit, many also believe in an evil genius, who makes all sorts of bad things, to counterbalance those made by the Good Spirit.

"For instance, when the latter made a sheep, a rose, wholesome herbs, etc., the Bad Spirit matched them with a wolf, a thorn, poisonous plants, and the like."

POWER OF DARKNESS vs. POWER OF LIGHT

Of evil phenomena, the eclipse was taken with the most

profound seriousness, says Cushman, for it was looked upon as a huge beast, threatening at intervals to devour the life giving Orbs and thus bring about the destruction of the universe!

When this phenomenon occurred, the Indians threw their every effort on the side of the Sun or the Moon. Into the open they rushed, the women and children screaming, shrieking, beating *tom-toms,* and urging on the frantic dogs; the men taking their stands with grim determination, firing flight after flight of arrows toward the monstrous terror — the great Black Squirrel — that was about to devour the Life Giver and plunge the world to darkness and death — the Indian "millenium." The Sun, with the help of the Indians, so the Indians thought, always won.

Hence, being human, and looking upon the Sun as having human emotions, when they found themselves in the pinch of any natural disaster, they expected aid from the Sun in return for their efforts expended at the time of the eclipse.

So it came about that when there was a flood or a drought, they made haste to send up the story of their trouble by the Smoke, or by feathers, which, resembling Smoke, and like it, able to mount the air currents, they looked on, also, as sacred messengers.

In spite of his awe of the Sun, the Indian considered it much more familiarly than does the modern American; for he was sure that it was not a tremendous way off. It might be as big as a small house, an Indian once conceded to a white visitor, after much argument, but he doubted if it were nearly so large! It was, in fact, a neighborly sort of Power, more distant than the World Quarters, perhaps, but by no means so distant as to fail to be cognizant of man.

SPIRIT KINSHIP THE BASIS OF MAGIC OR MEDICINE

The third fundamental concept upon which the Indian

based his religious faith, the concept upon which was founded all his tremendous practice of magic or Medicine, was the idea that *like* things were related things — *kin* things — and that, because they were related, they had a natural affinity, one for another, such as the affinity between Smoke and Fire.

With the Indian himself blood ties were the strongest of human bonds; consequently, when he credited the inhabitants of the supernatural world with the same sense of obligation, he was but creating gods in his own image — thereby proving himself as human as any other man.

Man, in order to know any peace of mind, must have, or think he has, some means of control over the elements. Consequently, the Indians, like all other peoples in the absence of scientific knowledge, found magic indispensable.

By magic, product of his own fertile imagination, the Indian explained the universe, and by magical inventions — divinations, auguries, occult contacts, and charms — he attempted to control his national or tribal and his personal destiny — a spiritual condition which caused the not more sophisticated Europeans who followed Columbus to brand the occupants of the new regions, one and all, as "hopelessly benighted savages."

The Serpent and the Flame

Second only to the worship of Fire, in the Americas, was worship of the Snake. Both, strange as the notion may be to the uninitiated, were phases of Sun worship — a relation explainable only through the great primitive doctrines of associative and sympathetic magic, or kinship Medicine.

Testifying to the extent of fanaticism with which various forms of Sun worship were regarded by their respective devotees, there stands today the mighty Temple of *Teotihuacan* in the Valley of Mexico — a Temple as tremendous in its import as any to be found among the ruins of Greece or Rome.

THE INDIAN PANTHEON

Here the *Aztecas,* worshipers of the Sun through Fire
and the blood of human sacrifice, the root worship of the
Tortures throughout America, knocked down the mighty
Serpents' heads raised by the beneficent *Toltecas,* covered
the onyx eyes and the stucco plumes with earth, and mounted the Temple pyramid with an altar for the running of
human blood. Clear to the eye stands the ravaged Temple
of the *Toltecas* who brought *Quetzalcoatl,* the Plumed Serpent, to Mexico from somewhere over the Gulf — Mediterranean of the Americas.

THE ALL-SEEING EYE

In Ohio, almost to the northern extremity of the Mound
Builder area, coils the Great Serpent, an effigy mound built
of tons of Earth carried into place by devout Indians who
sometimes, in their weariness, dropped their baskets with
the last load at the end of the day — leaving to be disinterred
by archaeologists, centuries later, the rotting fibres, still
encircling burdens of the past.

The true significance of the Snake in Indian religion remains as yet among the ancient Mysteries — we can offer
only a hypothesis. We do know, from Lawson, Bartram,
Adair, and other early travellers, that Snakes were respected throughout the Mound Builder area — never killed
or in any wise disturbed, lest others of their kind visit the
Blood Right on their destroyers.

Espinosa tells us the *Tejas* were promised by their
priests that they should most surely be bitten by Snakes, and
thus destroyed, if they touched a single ear of the new corn
before the harvest was offered in symbolic sacrifice to the
Sun at the Green Corn Festival.

Thus it would seem that with these people, the Snake
was accepted as another version of the Sacred Fire — another form of the jealously watchful, bright-eyed, all-seeing
Flame keeping tab on the conduct of its parishioners in
order to report their indiscretions to the Sun.

The Thunder God

So now we come to the matter of attempting to explain the kinship association between Snake and Fire. It is necessary first to discuss the Indian's attitude toward electrical atmospheric phenomena, seemingly the connecting link.

Adair tells us Thunder was called, in Louisiana, "the-great-chieftain-in-the-skies"; and that Thunderstorms were looked on, like the eclipse, as a celestial battle between the Life Giver and the Powers of Darkness — furnishing still another occasion for the allies of the Sun to seize their weapons and shoot repeatedly upward in an effort to drive away the evil spirits that were seeking, with Earth-shaking rumblings and furious, fiery darts, to overthrow the Light.

Many times repeated by chroniclers is the story of the Lightning Bolt that struck the *Natchez* Temple, setting it aflame — the story of the heroic conduct of the *Natchez* women, who hastily strangled their children and flung them into the blaze in an effort to appease the terrible wrath about to destroy the universe.

More than a dozen infants perished in the holocaust and many more, upward of two hundred, it is said, would have followed, but for the presence of European priests and soldiers (this incident took place in historic time) who restrained the sacrifice by force.

The Counterpart Hypothesis

Granting the laws of sympathetic and associative magic, we come to the possible assumption of the Indian that the Striking Death, the Rattlesnake, which reaches a length of nine feet in the coastal states, was the counterpart of the deadly Lightning Bolt.

Was not its flickering, forked tongue like the flickering forked-tongued Fire in the skies, and was not its rattling comparable to the roll of the Thunder Drums?

Again, was there not a resemblance between the sinuous, grey-blurred motion of the Snake and the sinuous, twisting grey Smoke plume?

Among a people imbued with the idea that like things were either the same or kin, Snake, Smoke, Lightning, and Thunder, could rise to any degree of significance.[1]

It could range, as it undoubtedly did, from the punitive characteristic of the Fire, its place among the *Tejas,* to the magnificent position of *Quetzalcoatl,* which, perhaps, superseded that of the Sun in the estimation of the *Toltecas.*

THE PART THE EAGLE PLAYED

Closely allied to the part Smoke played in Indian theology was the part played by birds, also denizens of the air. The higher a bird soared, and therefore the closer he came to the Sun, the more he was revered. For this reason, the Eagle held the place of honor among his kind in the Upper World, just as the Rattlesnake held the place of honor among the creeping things of the Under World. And perhaps, because of the supposed kinship of both to Smoke, the Snake, as it grew in popular esteem, was given plumes — eventually becoming, among some peoples, *Quetzalcoatl,* the Plumed Serpent.

Apparently the Eagle, unlike the Snake, did not inspire fear. What the Indian desired of the Eagle was to enslave its spirit by virtue of possessing its plumage so as to force it to become his messenger to the Sun.

Eagle plumes being among the most hallowed objects in the Indian world, Eagles' nests were guarded as tribal or national treasure; and, by the same token, peoples foreign to the territory where they were located sought to obtain access to them, as the Crusaders sought to gain access to the shrines of the Holy Land.

Among the agricultural Nations, to bring in an Eagle Tail, Adair declares, was equivalent in honor to bringing in a scalp; and if a young man wished to go in quest of one, the whole community would contribute to the value of two hundred deerskins toward outfitting him for the enterprise.

INDIANS OF THE SOUTHWEST

The Oracles

Feeling that the great spirit gods were too far away and too absorbed in their perpetual strife to attend the practical needs of the earthly tribes and nations, the Indian attempted to relay his prayers to the more neighborly Sun through the captive spirits of the Eagles, obtained by possessing their Tails — an instance of associative magic — and through fiery oracles he attempted to derive divine guidance in the conduct of his affairs.

FOOTNOTES

[1] A *Report to the Secretary of War*, 31st Congress Executive Document 64, 1850, shows an Indian drawing of the "emblem of Good Lightning." Plate 9 shows an *estufa* wall painting of "barbed zig-zag lightning" seen at Santo Domingo on the Rio Galisto by Lt. J. H. Simpson. Good Lightning is tipped with the symbol for earth and Bad Lightning with the symbol for war.

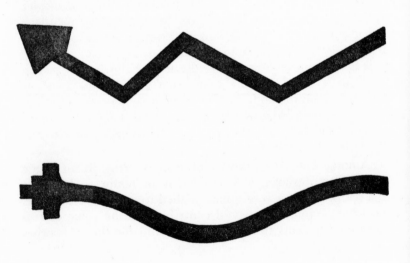

VII
The Peace Pipe

There was a tradition among the Indians that the sacred Pipestone quarry in southwest Minnesota was owned in common, and held as neutral ground, by all Tribes and Nations who met there to renew their Pipes under some belief "which stayed the tomahawks of natural foes always raised in deadly hate and vengeance in other places."

Catlin.

FUNCTIONS OF THE PIPE

One may say, without exaggeration, that among inventions symbolizing spiritual ideas, the Pipe was the most sacred and venerated object in North America. It epitomized Fire worship as a phase of Sun worship by combining within itself a sacrificial altar in miniature (the tobacco bowl) with a prayer conveyer (reed stem, or *calumet*).

There were special Pipes dedicated to all important functions of Indian life. These included: the Medicine Pipe, serving as an oracle in the prophetic Mysteries; the Council Pipe, serving as the symbol of justice and equity in local administration; and the Peace Pipe, with its counterpart, the War Pipe, serving as flag, passport, and Great Seal of any given Nation.

Under the Peace Pipe all diplomatic procedure was put forward, ranging from regularly interchanged visits of state, where the existing peace was ratified, to emergency compacts between semi-hostiles concerning unusual economic measures — such as an interchange of surplus products or the granting of special and temporary hunting privileges on foreign soil. Under the Peace Pipe, trade flourished; advancing behind it, stranger delegations entered foreign territory; and under the War Pipe, which was the Peace Pipe in another dress, negotiations were broken off and international conflict given official sanction. Within the great League of Mound Builder Nations, whatsoever transpired that partook of sovereignty brought forth the Peace Pipe; and its use as a symbol spread far out over the Buffalo Range.

THE HOLY OATH

Space, for the Indian, was divided into seven parts: East, West, North, South, Up, Down, and Middle — or Here. The *Here* was peopled with humans, but the other six divisions were inhabited by spirits, ghosts, demons, and gods — the Pantheon with which the Indian's imagination enveloped his own soul, or life spark.

Believing that Smoke was a magical messenger, carrying with it his thoughts and petitions, his very breath itself, the Indian, when he smoked a Pipe over a compact and blew the Smoke towards the seven different parts of space, took not only all men, but the whole spiritual universe, to witness his intentions.

Thus the Pipe became the great symbol of sincerity, and any pledge made under it a holy oath, equivalent in effect to the taking of vows on the cross of the sword hilt, on the Bible, or at the altar of the Christian faith.

THE PEACE PIPE — DANCING THE CALUMET

The Peace Pipe was called The Word and he who bore it, the Word Bearer. More than a yard long, it is described by Du Pratz: "It is trimmed with the neckskin of

52

a crested duck, the plumage being of many colors and very beautiful. At the bowl end, shaped in a quarter-circle, is fastened a fan of white Eagles' feathers. At the end of each feather is a crest, or tuft, dyed a brilliant red. Only the mouthpiece of the Pipe is left undecorated."

The purpose of the red tip was to accentuate the beauty and holiness of peace — the White Road — and to warn how easily it might be broken. For if the truce were broken, all the feathers must be dyed red; the Peace Pipe would thus be converted to the War Pipe; and the White Road would be exchanged for the Red Road of War.

From his observations of the ritual in Louisiana, Du Pratz tells us the members of the peace delegation, clad in moccasins, breech-clouts, shoulder capes (mantles of finely dressed skins or of native woven cloth), and coronets of feathers or tufts of plumes, the headdress of each signifying the rank of the wearer, invariably formed in single file. According to pen sketches, the mantles, which were square, and extremely graceful and picturesque, were passed under the left arm, and over the right shoulder, leaving both arms free.

The Word Bearer carried the long pipe extended in front, while the eleven followers carried a gourd rattle with which to mark time for the chant and the dance used in the procession.

The rhythmic steps by which the ambassadors proceeded, the grace of their swaying bodies and draped mantles, the brilliancy of the Pipe and the plumed headdresses, together with the solemn demeanor of the performers and the deep cadence of the chant, made a never-to-be-forgotten impression on all witnesses.

According to the Spanish Creole, Ramón, who observed the smoking of the Peace Pipe in Texas, the tobaccos of the various Tribes and Nations taking part in the ritual were mixed as a symbol of the mingling of their wills.

Ramón further tells us: "This ceremony was performed

53

with manifestations of joy because these natives (the *Tejas*) are a smiling, happy and agreeable people."[1]

DIPLOMATIC EXCURSIONS

Between the allied Confederacies of the *Caddo* and the *Asinai,* in East Texas, tribal visits were a matter of fixed policy. Espinosa gives the following account of the ceremonial grandeur of such excursions: "Upon occasions when the *Caddo,* who live towards the north, come forty leagues (a hundred miles) to the country of the *Asinai,* they send a messenger in advance to give notice of their coming.

"Hostages are immediately exchanged, and information is furnished to all the houses in the region so that necessary provisions may be prepared.

"Each household gives liberally, and all the officials go out on the road for several leagues in order to greet the visitors before they reach the settlements.

"Every one dresses in gala attire.

"After the company arrives in the settlements, the *Asinai* give dances and festivals and exchange gifts of whatever they have in abundance. Thus the allies renew their friendship and make treaties to defend each other against the enemies.

"They observe this same custom with the tribes that lie to the south," he continues, alluding to the *Karankawa, Tonkawa,* and others, "who are in the habit of coming to their aid. To keep these lesser allies well-dispositioned in time of war, the *Asinai* entertain them every year, after the crops are gathered."

How effective were the diplomatic policies of the great Mound Builder Nations is attested by further remarks: "The way in which they most clearly show their civilization is in the embassies they send to various settlements, especially when they wish to call their allies together for war.

"The chiefs receive with great honor the person who acts as ambassador. They assign him the principal seat (evidently the high *tapestle* in the Council House) and, following their custom, they make him a great many presents while preparing the reply they are to return by him to his people.

"So strict are they in the observance of their League pledges that they do not dally even a day in going out against the enemy, the most implacable of which is the *Apache*."

THE DANCE OF HONOR

Among ceremonials accompanying diplomatic festivities between allies, Adair describes the Dance of the Eagle Tails as the supreme function: In "renewing their old friendship, they (the allies) first smoke out of the Friend-Pipe and eat together; then they drink of the *Cusseena* (yaupon tea), (using the customary invocation *Yo He Wah*) and . . . wave their large fans of Eagle Tails; concluding with a dance."

The hosts to the visiting delegation, he goes on, "appoint half a dozen of their most active and expert young warriors to perform this religious duty," choosing those who have already been awarded swan feather caps — a mark of high rank in THE WARRIORS AWARD. "These performers paint their bodies with white clay, (symbolic of peace) and cover their heads with swan-down."

They approach the leading representative of the strangers who, by way of honor and strong assurance of friendship, is placed on the White, or Holy Seat (in the Temple or the Council House, or perhaps, the public square) and wave the Eagle Tails backward and forward over his head.

"Immediately they begin the solemn song *Yo He Wah, Yo He Wah* with an awful air, and presently they (begin to) dance in a bowing posture." They then raise themselves so erect that their faces are turned partly upward, waving the Eagle Tails with their right hand towards the Sun, sometimes with a slow, at other times with a quick, motion. At the same time they touch their breasts with small calabash-and-pebble rattles fastened to a stick about a foot long, which

55

they hold in their left hand, keeping time with it to the motion of the Eagle Tails.

"During the dance they repeat the usual divine notes, *Yo He Wah,* and wave the Eagle Tails now and then over the stranger's head, not moving more than two yards backward and forward before him. They are so expert in this office, and observe time so exactly with their particular gestures and notes, that there is not the least discernible discord.

"The Indians cannot show more honor to the greatest potentate on Earth than to place him in the White Seat, invoke *Yo He Wah* while he is drinking the *Cuseena,* and dance before him with the Eagle Tails."

What this dance actually amounted to, ritually, like the presence of the Eagle Tail on the stem of the Peace Pipe, was to send the spirit of the Eagles aloft to notify the Sun of the supreme affection expressed by the people supporting the dance for the people honored by the attention. The basis for this assumption was made clear in the preceding chapter, supplemented by THE MAGIC ART.

TRADE AND BARTER

"It is at the time of their annual visits," says Espinosa, "that they trade with each other for all the things they lack in their own country."

The existence of this form of interchange, or primitive international commerce, supplemented by constant gambling, explains the appearance in Texas graves of articles which obviously are not the products of the immediate south or southwest. Such, for instance, as thin copper sheeting on ear plugs and other ornaments. Copper, in pure form as the Indians used it, was not to be found in localities close to Texas.

According to the findings of Sibley, one time Indian agent on the Red River, and of De Mézieres, a French gentleman once in the employ of the Spanish government, there was a day when the *Tonkawa* brought deerskins, together with other products of the deer, the principal game animal of their central Texas hunting grounds, to trade by the thousand on the border of the civilized or agricultural region.

The Mound Builders were accustomed to use deerskins for breechclouts, for the garments and bed-clothing of their womenfolk and for ceremonial purposes, particularly in the garb of the priests and in the Temple trappings. In return for bales of deerksins, they gave baskets of corn and *faons* of bear oil. How they obtained the latter is told in THE PRODUCTS OF THE CHASE.

INDIAN MONEY

Facilitating trade, which flourished under treaty pacts sealed by the Peace Pipe, was a primitive monetary system based on beads. The American Indian, in the development of his civilization, had not yet come to the use of metals — except as just stated, in their softer forms — when the Spaniard arrived to pound the capitals of the southern Empires to fragments with an iron mace. All that the Indian valued, save for intrinsic worth, were "core beads," spoken of ordinarily as *wampum,* or as *peag* and *roanoke.* According to Lawson, the use of these beads was common to the entire Atlantic coast; and there are statements that they passed in exchange far inland, even to the Plains Tribes.

Adair describes the coin of the realm as follows: "They had great quantities of wampum made of conch shells by rubbing the shells on hard stones (till only the ground-down cores remained). With these they bought and sold at a stated current rate. . . .Four deerskins was the price of a large conch shell bead about the length and thickness of a man's forefinger; which they fixed to the crown of their head as a high ornament — so greatly they valued them."

These beads were of two colors, dark blue and white. The dark ones were the rarer and more valuable. Adair speaks only of the white, saying they bore a strong resemblance to ivory.

INDIANS OF THE SOUTHWEST

From Indian burials in East Texas, the University of Texas archaeology crew has removed a number of the beads described by Adair: "corebeads" ranging from three to six inches long, one of which still adheres to the skull of the Indian who counted it a treasure. A gorget, or shell medallion, removed from another burial, is carved with a human head showing the single long bead ornamentation on the brow. Thus does archaeology check the truths of history.

LIQUID MEASUREMENT

While on the subject of trade and barter among the Indians, it may be interesting to note the method of liquid measurement described by Lawson. When an Indian intended to acquire a small amount of liquid goods, *metheglin,* or mead — the fermented product of honey and water — or some other native "home brew," he brought a bowl to the place of exchange; then looked around for the largest man present and besought him to act as measurer. This the accommodating bystander did by sucking up the liquid in mouthfuls and transferring it from the main container to the bowl. Payment was made by number of mouthfuls. The customer was allowed to choose the mouth to his own advantage, but it was also up to him to see that no liquid was swallowed in transit. Over this matter bouts of fisticuffs sometimes resulted between customer and measurer, says Lawson.

John Dunn Hunter tells us that for larger quantities, regular measures of gourd or skin were kept in the public squares.

THE AMERICAN ESPERANTO

In order to maintain the system of intertribal and international trade existing under the peace pacts, it was necessary for the Indians of the Americas to develop a general trade language independent of their numerous dialects. What they evolved was a very nearly universal sign or

gesture language; making communication possible from the
Mohawk Valley to the Valley of Mexico, and on through
the Empires far south.

According to American army officers who had dealings
with the tribes in the chill desert mountains of the southwest, the Mexican Indian, when manual signs were impeded
by the comfortable enclosure of his hands in the folds of
his *poncho,* used his stuck-out lips, twisting them from side
to side to indicate directions, while employing various other
facial contortions for conversational purposes.

THE INDIAN FRONTIER

Not only did their allies under permanent peace pacts
come to trade with the *Asinai;* but also, under semiperma-
nent trade treaties, came the *Kiowa* and the *Comanche,*
fierce outlanders of the Plains, drawn to the border of the
civilized nations by the lure of bear oil, indispensable Indian cosmetic; of plumes plucked from the water fowl on
the eastern marshes; of sweet gum, the "liquid amber" of
the Spanish scribes; and of tobacco, cultivated product of
the village gardens. For these, and other Indian luxuries,
particularly corn, even the fierce *Apache,* rival of the *Comanche* for control of the Texas Buffalo Range, laid down the
tomahawk for a day to smoke the Peace Pipe with its fan of
snow. In exchange, the Plainsmen gave buffalo hides; horns
and hoofs for glue; worked flint; and, it may be, vermilion.

Red paint found in the Indian graves of East Texas is
always a mineral product, (colored earth, in fact) but
chroniclers often mention powdered vermilion in common
use among the southern peoples, both on the Plains and in
the agricultural area. Kennedy, a British citizen who made
a survey of Texas at an early date, says cochineal of good
quality was parasitic on the *opuntia* or prickly pear of West
Texas, and that it was customary to remove the insects from
the plants by means of a rabbit tail brush. All early observers comment on the brilliancy of the dyes used by the

Apaches and *Comanches* of the San Saba and Llano districts, especially the blues and reds. Consequently there is room for the supposition that blue and green mineral dyes and vermilion may have been among the trade products of the Plains nomads. The Casparis shield described in THE WINTER SOLSTICE appears to have been decorated with such dyes.

Besides the other items mentioned, turquoise found its way from west to east, as did iridescent abalone shells from the far Pacific coast, greatly prized as ear drops.

Whatever was brought, we are assured by the early Spaniards that it was not the policy of the civilized Nations to permit the denizens of the Plains to penetrate into the garden lands. It was a case of "so far shalt thou come, and no farther," with the Confederacies of the *Caddo* and the *Asinai* forming the frontier outposts of Indian civilization. In other words, the Mississippi was the boundary line. Beyond the "Great River" or "All Waters" was forbidden territory, except to League Members.

THE BUFFALO TREATIES

Apparently the *Asinai* never went trading on the Plains; the *Kiowa* and *Comanche* came to the *Asinai*. So long as the Plainsmen left their stone-edged weapons behind, in custody of a small contingent, and advanced upon the villages with the *Calumet* or Peace Pipe to the fore, they were made welcome, according to the laws of Indian hospitality; and feted and feasted for the sake of their trade goods — though, say the Spanish Fathers, the *Tejas* sometimes complained of the *Comanche* that they stole more than they bought!

A considerable amount of pilfering and imposition could be borne with, however, for the sake of the Buffalo Treaties by which the *Tejas* were permitted excursions at stated intervals into the buffalo country, to obtain a dried meat supply.

These treaties seem to have been strictly with the

Comanche; fear of the *Apache,* according to old accounts, invariably turning buffalo hunts into nerve-wracking experiences for the gardeners. Accustomed to fighting only in forests, and totally unskilled in the procedure of Plains warfare, the *Tejas* were almost certain to lose their scalps and other properties if surprised by *Apaches* while curing or transporting meat in the clear, level spaces of the *Comancheria.*

LOWLANDER *vs.* HIGHLANDER

And so we come, among the Indians, to the age-old romantic contrast of the lowlander and the highlander — the man of crops *versus* the man of herds — except that in this case the herds were totally unadapted to domestication; for which reason the Indians on the American "highlands" remained forever on the hunting plane.

THE INTERNATIONAL CULTURE LINE

Running through Texas from north to south is one extremity of what W. P. Webb sets forth in THE GREAT PLAINS as a tremendous and eternal cultural boundary line, bisecting the continent. In Texas this line extends between the *mesas* and the prairies of the southwest, or the Buffalo Range of the Plains nomads, and the fertile forests of the south, the Indian garden lands.

THE SHIELD OF WAR AND THE PIPE OF PEACE

Though they made no permanently intimate compacts across this natural boundary which forced their civilizations into such widely different forms, the Tribes of the Buffalo Range and the Nations of the timber-surrounded garden patches, profited immeasurably from their casual relationships. The merest acquaintance of each with the customs and inventions of the other could but result in an interchange of ideas as well as of goods.

61

So it came about that, though the Plains Tribes, in all probability, achieved the invention of the North American *aegis*, the tough buffalo bull's hide shield that would turn the stoutest arrow, that type of shield was in demand by Indians everywhere. Likewise, though Charlevoix says the *Pawnees* claimed to have had the *Calumet*, the sacred Pipe, as a gift direct from the Sun, that supposedly divine invention was the symbol of ambassadorship, of peaceful intentions, and of sincerity throughout most of the continent.[2]

FOOTNOTES

[1] See CONVENTIONS OF THE PIPE, Chapter XXIII.

[2] No evidence has been found of the use of a Pipe south of San Antonio. Smoke and tobacco were sacred, but the ritual was confined to the "wrapper" form — the *cigarillo* — through Mexico, Central and South America.

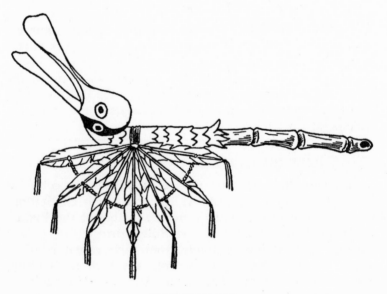

THE CALUMET

VIII
The Magic Art

"The Medicine Men have their own particular insignia of feathers which they wear upon their heads, and curious necklaces of serpents, skins, and a seat in the house which is higher than the seat for the chieftains."

Espinosa.

THE MEDICINE MEN

The early Spanish who came into the Southwest as soldiers and missionaries tell us the Indian nations of the agricultural area were priest-ridden to the last degree. They also tell us the priest caste, the most popular profession in the area, was roughly divisible into four groups — Prophets, Rain Makers, Witch Doctors, and Herbalists. Of these, the Prophets were the most respected and the Herbalists the most practical.

THE PROPHETS

It was the business of the Prophets to consult the Temple oracles, which were the Temple Fires — either the Perpetual Fire or the New Fire — divining from the patterns of the Smoke, or from such other idiosyncrasies as the Sun's servants should exhibit — after being duly cajoled with sacrifices — what the elements had in mind for the coming year with regard to crops, abundance of game, and the like; and then to make known to the people what to expect in these directions. In other words, their chief function was to consult the oracles and, through divine revelation, to compile the Almanac.

THE GO-BETWEEN

Since Smoke was the familiar of the elements, it was assumed to be able to divulge the intimacies of their minds to man, just as it was supposed to be able to divulge the intimacies of man's mind to the elements.

THE ALMANAC

Says Father Morphi, with regard to prognosticating the future among the *Tejas*: "They forecast the events of the year in a solemn festival held during the New Moon of February. The men provide rabbits, mountain cats, deer, turkeys, badgers, and dried buffalo meat. The women provide cornmeal, fruit, roots and other products of the Earth.

"All the chieftains, together with the oldest and most venerable Medicine Men, enter the Temple.

"The Medicine Men begin the ceremony at daybreak by drinking *Cassena* (yaupon tea). They spend the entire morning doing this (a purification rite by which they made themselves fit to commune with the gods), giving the drink from time to time to the chieftains. They then, with uplifted faces, address their deities, after which they take an elaborately decorated Eagle wing and, with it in their hands, begin to dance and chant. Without interrupting this performance they salute the Fire, offering it ground tobacco, while the Pipe is passed from mouth to mouth."

For this purpose they would have used the most sacred of all Pipes, the Great Medicine Pipe.

"After the dance," Father Morphi continues, "they demonstrate that the Eagle, whose feathers they have in hand,

64

ascends to heaven to consult the 'Great Chieftain' with regard to the coming events of the year.

"In the meantime the elders, with much show of reserve, compute the Almanac; then, the ceremony being complete, they leave the Temple to communicate their findings to the people."

It is to be noted that the good *padre* leaves us with no information as to what was done with the articles of sacrifice brought to the Temple. He was perhaps of the same mind as another Spanish missionary who said: "Even to recount the acts of these Indians would be blasphemy!"

GIFTS FOR THE GODS

However, C. C. Jones, in ANTIQUITIES OF THE SOUTHERN INDIANS, quotes for us the following description of a sacrifice which must have had similar import: "Toward the latter part of February in each year, the Indians of Florida, taking the skin of the largest stag they had killed, stuffed it with the choicest fruits and matters which chiefly delighted them. The horns, neck, and body were encircled with vines and fruits most rare. Thus attired, the stag, with music and parade, was carried and placed upon the top of a tall tree with its head and breast turned full toward the Rising Sun. By the King and high priest — who stationed themselves nearest the tree — prayers were addressed to this celestial luminary, and petitions offered that he would be pleased to reproduce the good gifts which were then presented. The members of the Nation assembled in a circle, and, at a little remove, repeated these supplications, (possibly employing the circle dance). When they were finished, all having saluted the sun (probably by bowing three times), departed, leaving the stuffed and garlanded stag until the recurrence of the same season, when, on each ensuing year, similar ceremonies were observed."

THE CALENDAR

It was the priests, among these peoples, as among all other primitives, who evolved the calendar — a scientific outgrowth invariably following from the experiments of an agricultural people attempting to forecast a planters' guide or "almanac."

Du Pratz tells us the southern agricultural Indians divided the year into thirteen Moons, based on the waxing and waning of that Orb. The last of these was a Short Moon, thus making the time divisions fit the seasonal round. Says he: "At each New Moon they celebrated a fete that took its name from the fruits or crops that had just been gathered, or the animals that had just been hunted, according to their season." The year began in March, ended with the Short Moon, and ran in the following series: The Deer, Strawberries, Small Corn (June corn), Watermelons, Fish, Mulberries, Green Corn (the period of the great harvest festival), Turkeys, Buffalo (dried meat), Bears, Cold Meal (a favorite corn preparation), and Nuts (chestnuts, pecans, and walnuts).

The Indians counted time, says Adair, by Sleeps and Moons. He also names the seasons, saying they were called: THE SUN (Summer); THE BONE (Winter); THE BUD (Spring); and THE BUZZARD (Autumn).

Farther to the northward among the Mound Builders were Nations who spoke of the passage of years as so many "Cohonks" (Winters) because of the sound of geese flying overhead at the turn of the year.

The southern Nations, like most other Indians, kept their simple accounts and their date records by bundles of sticks, a stick being added or removed each day; by means of notched sticks, a notch being added or cut off each day; and by means of strings in which a knot was tied or untied each day — thus we arrive at a consideration of the "little alcoves containing small mounds of stones" over the doors of East Texas homes. These, in all probability, were devices representing the "almanac" or calendar.

ESTABLISHING SPIRIT GUARDIANSHIP

Besides consulting the Fire Oracles; making auguries from the flights of birds, the movements of animals, and the shifting of stars; interpreting dreams; and conducting rituals; the Prophet of the south directed parishioners concerning their selection of and their conduct toward personal spirit guardians — an almost universal Indian practice described in detail under THE MEDICINE BAG of the Plains Indians.

THE PALLADIUM

The Prophets also dealt with the Mysteries of the tribal or national Medicine, which, when typified by some outstanding object, has been compared to the possession of the Ark of the Covenant among the Jews, or of the Pallas Athene among the Greeks; the general term "palladium" being derived from the latter to denote that which is the peculiar protection or safeguard of a given people.

According to Adair and Dodge, the Indian palladium, wherever one existed, was kept in a sacred box of painted skins and specially guarded, so that it might never be subject to the touch of profane hands.

It always was venerated as a mystic and holy object, from which magic powers emanated, and to which sacrifices were a pleasant savor. In time of war it was carried before the fighting file on the back of a warrior consecrated to the task. When the "big" Medicine of any people was captured, war came to an end — there was no fight left in those whose Medicine deserted them!

At the University of Texas now rests an ancient palladium ascribed to the *Wichita* — though probably only secured by them through capture from the *Comanches* — which was obtained at Fort Belknap when the remnants of the Texas Tribes and Nations were crowded onto northern

67

reservations. This once deified object is a meteorite that fell centuries ago, hissing and flaming, to strike a great hole in the Earth before the eyes of the startled Sun worshipers. Taking it for a thing of true divinity, the Indians, despite its weight, carried the awesome object over the Buffalo Lands for generations, to lose it at last, and with it lands, buffalo, and tribal sovereignty.[1]

Most magnificent of all palladiums in North America, perhaps, were the Perpetual Fires described in Chapter Five.

The Rain Makers

It would appear from old reports that second in importance to the Prophets, or diviners, were the Rain Makers — Rain being equal with the Sun and the Earth in fundamental human values.

The Rain Maker was a magician, pure and simple. He did not consult the Pantheon to find out what was going to happen; he essayed to *make* happenings.

Adair tells of such a miracle worker whose power lay in a flashing jewel picked up near a dead Snake — presumably expelled from its forehead. Adair did not see this marvelous stone, which was eventually buried with its master, but was told by the magician's clientele that it sparkled with such amazing lustre as to illuminate the darkness like strong flashes of continued Lightning, so that they dared not approach the dreadful Fire-darting place where it was kept "for fear of sudden death." The relation between the Snake and Lightning has already been explained in THE INDIAN PANTHEON. Naturally this relationship was associated with Rain.

The Witch Doctors

Just as the Rain Maker presumed to bring moisture from heaven by means of magical charms and incantations, so the Witch Doctor professed to heal the sick. Sickness, like death, could not exist, thought the Indian, save as a matter of witchcraft — the entrance of evil spirits into the person of the sufferer — and all remedies were applied with the sole idea of routing the undesired tenant from "the temple of clay" — again showing that the religious and scientific development of the American Indian was like that of all other peoples, the development of medical science being rooted in religion the world around.

Lest we should feel that the Indian was unduly backward in these matters, it may be well to remind ourselves that the germ theory of disease did not permeate the Christian world until after the Civil War — our own progenitors being divided in their minds as to whether sickness was caused by God for purposes of chastening the soul, or by the Devil for his own delectation.

AID OF THE OWLS

The Witch Doctors of the *Asinai,* according to the Spanish Fathers, seem to have had an especial fondness for attributing to their neighbors, the *Bidai,* the shooting of invisible "witch-darts" which were reputed to pierce the vitals of the denizens of the Piney Woods with sharp and frightful pains.

The home talent magicians claimed not to be able to remove these inconvenient darts unless the *Bidai* Witch Doctors would lend a hand by appearing nearby in the woods, disguised as owls. The woods were full of owls advertising their presence all night long with hoots and screeches from which the cries of the transformed visitors were indistinguishable. The shrewd Witch Doctors of the Red Lands had an excellent alibi.

If the patient recovered, they could claim success in relieving his ailment by means of their supernatural abilities — and thereby harvest a rich reward; whereas, if he died, then the *Bidai* wizards had refused to co-operate!

HOME REMEDIES

Remedies for illness, outside of magical practices similar to those to be described under *The Healing Art* of the *Comanche,* were of three varieties: sweating; dry-cupping or sucking; and the use of medicinal herbs, applied both externally and internally. Favorites among the latter were vomitories and purgatives, both of which were given for the purpose of expelling evil spirits, rather than for ordering the functions of the body.

Sweating, says Cushman, was performed in a special low edifice made of chinked logs. A Fire was used to superheat this little house and then taken away, the patient being instructed to crawl in immediately thereafter, while the Medicine Man in charge of the cure sealed the door behind him. When the cure was thought to be fully accomplished; that is, the evil spirits causing the sickness having been sweated out, the director of exorcism opened the door and brought forth the patient. There are many observers who declare that when the patient was too ill to move about, a Fire was made under his bed and kept burning until he either died or recovered.[2]

Espinosa informs us that since sucking proved to be an efficacious remedy for Snake bites and boils, the Witch Doctors attempted to apply it to all other sorts of disease, even going so far as to introduce into their mouths foreign objects which they spat out during the course of operation as evidence that the cause of the ailment had been extracted.

THE HERBALISTS

However much humbuggery went on, there are, nevertheless, a number of statements from early explorers to the effect that among the Indian Medicine Men were frequently found persons, some of whom were women, possessing a very considerable knowledge of the properties of native plants — albeit the Herbalists, like the other magicians, supposed the law of Nature under which they operated to be the ousting of demons rather than of disease germs.

The Major Ills

Malaria and poisonous Snake bites are reputed to have been the major scourges of the southern agricultural area. Since sweating, purging, and sucking are effective methods of dealing with these ills, it would seem that medical practices of the Witch Doctors, despite their basis of magical control, were fairly adequate to the situation before the Europeans arrived bringing measles, mumps, and smallpox to mow down families, villages and whole peoples. An evidence, one English explorer informs us, of God's love for the white man — these diseases not being fatal to those who spread them, due to their long-standing immunity.

What Price Glory?

The Rain Maker sought to produce rain and the Witch Doctor to heal the sick through supernatural power with which each was supposed to be mystically imbued. In order for either to rise to prominence and to reap the harvest of his extraordinary genius, it was necessary to create a strong belief in that genius among the multitude — yet here lay supreme danger. So great was the confidence of the gardening Indians in their priests, that when no relief was apparent from the efforts of the latter, they were liable to be put to death as traitors who cold-bloodedly withheld their talents from the public good.

Thus it behooved the priestcraft to encourage belief in the "all-seeing eye of the Fire," and in the punitive functions of the Snake, as described in THE INDIAN PANTHEON. Certainly it was more convenient, in case of a magical failure, to set the citizens scanning their own conduct than to have them criticizing that of the holy men.

Category of Sin

Thus we come to the necessity for a definition of "sin"

71

according to the Indian view. "Sin," as simply as it may be defined, was one form of "bad" Medicine — the reverse, so to speak, of beneficent magic.

There were three broad classifications of sin among the gardening Indians of the south: the eating of unclean food, the breaking of stipulated fasts, and unclean sex acts.

THE BLOOD PRINCIPLE

The idea of transgression paramount in the first and third classes apparently was derived from the "spirit in the blood" principle.

The Indians, like primitives in general, believing sincerely that every natural object was filled with a spirit essence, a *life thing,* communicable to human beings, lived in mortal terror of tainting their personalities with the tenantry of evil spirits acquired through unclean food.

According to the discussions of Adair, the southern gardeners seem to have considered that in no way could these transitions of the spirit take place so readily as through blood contacts.

Not on penalty of starvation, he declares, would one of them have profaned himself by swallowing a single drop of the blood of a slain beast — except, perhaps, in some magic ceremonial conduct under the auspices of the Medicine Men.

So careful were they in this regard in Louisiana, that when the game was brought in, women cleaned the flesh of the fish, the fowls, and the four-legged creatures until it was tasteless before offering it for the consumption of their families and their guests.

In the *Tejas* country the Spanish explorers report that no slain animal was touched by the hunter until the nearest priest could arrive in hot haste to perform the necessary ritual over the carcass for the "laying" of its vengeful ghost.

The student of ethnology can but surmise that these peoples believed the "life essence" of every creature to be

72

contained in its blood stream — a logical deduction, since, with the draining away of the blood, the spirit or "life essence" ceased to animate the body. This principle of the "spirit in the blood," incidentally, is bound up with the practice of human sacrifice, and the Tortures, to be discussed under customs of capture in THE WARRIOR'S AWARD.

Not only did man fear to pollute himself with the blood of beasts, lest his body become inhabited by the spirit of a beast, but he feared to pollute himself with the blood of woman, lest his person become imbued with the weakness of woman, thereby diminishing not only his own strength, but the man power of his Nation.

So it came about that menstrual lodges, as described by Joutel, were provided for women to which they were not only expected but compelled to retire, and special houses were dedicated to *accouchement* where women retired for stipulated periods preceding and following childbirth.

THE HOUSE OF NATIVITY

Says De Solis: "The women go through childbirth in this manner: on the bank of the river or creek where they are living, they make some wigwams in which to dwell. In the midst of one they put a low forked pole which is strong and well placed in the ground; and in the hour when they feel the birth pangs, they go to that little wigwam, and, by helping themselves with the pole, they bring forth the child — and afterwards throw themselves into the water to bathe both their own persons and the baby."

Says Adair concerning the menstrual lodges: "Here the women are obliged to stay during the required period at the risk of their lives. Should they break this law they would have to answer for every misfortune that befell any of the people, for it would be taken as a supposed effect of the Divine Fire" — another evidence of belief in the all-seeing eye. Lawson tells us that a woman, while in this condition, was not even permitted to prepare her own food lest she contaminate it.

73

EXPIATION OF SIN

For the sake of men who had unintentionally or undetectedly profaned their persons, either by unclean sex acts or by eating unclean food, regular expiation ceremonies were conducted by the priests. These involved sweating, blood-letting, and the taking of emetics and purgatives — all of which were looked upon in the usual way; that is, as mediums for the exorcism of demons and evil spirits from the bodies of the devout. Women performed entirely separate expiation rituals of a minor character.

HUMILIATION OF CONFIRMED SINNERS

According to Adair, those men who were known to commit profanities willfully were driven from the Temples and from the Sacred Squares, where the New Fire was made, and forced to perform their devotionals with the womenfolk and children. These renegades were further humiliated by the old women's doling out to them green tobacco pellets — the form of vomitory used by women and children — and by being given only a half portion — as indication that they were so low in the social scale their pollution could not be very serious regarding sex acts, since no woman would be interested in them. However, it is not to be understood that violation of the marriage bond came under the category of sin — contact with menstrual blood, whether in wedlock or out and failure to remain continent during fasts, were the only sex transgressions serious enough to require formal expiation.

SERVING THE SPIRITUAL NEEDS OF THE SICK

The spiritual needs of the aged and the infirm among the righteous were not neglected, Adair states, for they, and those who attended them, were sent special messengers bearing consecrated conch shell dippers filled with foaming *Caseena,* the sacred Black Drink of the southern Indian.

THE BLACK DRINK

The leaves of the Yaupon, a form of holly, *Ilex vomitoria*, are said to have served three purposes: they were brewed into a sacred drink or vomitory for the ritual of the purification of the flesh; they were used as sedatives, both by novitiates during puberty rites and by Prophets, when seeking dreams and visions; and they were chewed as a stimulant by the couriers, or long distance runners.

Adair describes, as follows, the method of brewing the Black Drink: "The Archi-magnus (high priest) sends a religious attendant to pull some *cusseena* or *yopon* belonging to the temple; and having parched it brown on the altar, he boils it with clear running water in a large earthen pot, about half full; it has such a strong body, as to froth above the top by pouring it up and down with their consecrated vessels which are kept only for that use."

The description of the vomitory rite as given by John Howard Payne will be found in the next chapter of this book.

THE THIRD SIN — CONTEMPT OF THE GODS

Rites of purification invariably involved the sex segregation of the adult public. Fasting was also obligatory at these times. To fail in abstinence was to transgress under the third classification of sin, namely, to commit blasphemy — an expression of complete contempt for the most holy service of the Indian to his gods.

Such an act, according to Indian theology, would be sure to result in national disaster — defeat in war, loss of the harvest, or total destruction by cyclone or tornado. Thus, whenever a crisis faced the people, the priests were certain to cry out that blasphemy was the cause — disclaiming, before they were accused, the charge of having erred in "the magic art."

FOOTNOTES

[1] Compare the Black Stone in Mecca, Sacred to Mohammedans.

[2] An artifact found by Morris A. Fry of Houston, working with army engineers between the Rio Grande and the road from Laredo to Dolores, appears to be a stone fire carrier. It is 5½ inches long, 1 to 2 inches in total diameter, and is drilled to form a cylinder with the hollow an inch in diameter. It was a surface find, washed over by the river and trodden into the earth by cattle. Despite these abuses it shows a length of approximately 50 finely scratched tally marks and very dimly, several finely scratched serpent-lightning symbols running its full length. When found it was packed with fine ash flecked with carbon. It compares with a similar object in the Texas state capitol and also with a picture of Old Woman Hicks in the Cunningham collection of frontier photographs in Stillwater, Oklahoma. She is drawing on an object of similar shape and size which is wrapped with thong, shaped into a mouth piece at one end. One assumes that this artifact indicates the mode of transferring the sacred New Fire from temple to household and that the tally marks indicate the number of New Fires struck within the time of its usage. It indicates, also, the existence of a high culture along the lower Rio Grande. (See page 234.)

IX

The New Fires

"The Green-eared Moon is the most beloved, or sacred —
when the first fruits become sanctified, by being annually offered
up; and from this period they count their beloved or holy
things."

Adair.

REMISSION OF SIN

All agricultural Indians celebrated the eating of the first
fruits of the corn as their supreme religious festival. The
Nine Nations of the *Asinai* celebrated together, according
to Espinosa's account. This occasion was the spiritual New
Year when every sin, save murder, was blotted out, and man
"born again" with the birth of New Fire.

Espinosa tells us the East Texans conducted themselves
with such strictness regarding the proprieties of this event
that the very dogs were hobbled lest they profane the harvest — even the unwitting blasphemy of a canine, according
to Indian theology, being sufficient to cause the indictment
and destruction of an entire Nation.

Throughout the garden lands the "Green Corn Dance"
occupied eight days in September, immediately prior to the
Harvest Home. The major points of the ceremony were
the same, though there was considerable variation in minor
detail.

Epitome of the Green Corn Dance — Festival of the Busk

The making of New Fire by the priests, ordinarily occurring on the first day, followed by a Dance of the Ancients in which both men and women took part.

The purification rites, occupying two nights and a day, including purging, fasting and the segregation of the sexes.

The breaking of the fast with "old corn," and the thorough cleansing of the Sacred Square, thereafter, in preparation for:

The distribution of New Fire among the women, and the sacrifice in the Sacred Square of the first ear of corn from the new harvest.

Mimic wars, pantomimic dances, and awards of honor, on the part of the men, and the contribution of food to the Temple supplies, on the part of the women.

A ceremonial hunt for the purpose of securing a sacrifice.

The salutation of the Sun at Dawn by the whole populace on conclusion of the segregation period, and the Dance of the Olden Time, celebrating the reunion of the sexes.

The initial step in preparation for this great religious event was the proclamation of the date. Issued on affirmation of the Council, by the chief herald, or town crier, it was dispatched to outlying districts by couriers bearing bundles of sticks numbering the intervening days.

The Barbecue

Concerning the hustle and bustle that followed, Adair tells us the men hastened into the woods immediately on receipt of the announcement and spent the intervening time hunting and barbecuing game, filling vast pits in the forests with savory roasted meats in anticipation of the feast to come.

The Fall House Cleaning

At home the women worked unceasingly, cleaning house,

burning old clothes and mattings, constructing new raiment, weaving new mats, molding fresh pottery, and baking every conceivable form of breadstuff in an effort to use up all old food supplies, every particle of which had to be disposed of in time for the reception of New Fire.

No doubt this vigorous housecleaning, which included calcimining the walls with fresh clay, was a most hygienic procedure, especially with regard to the extermination of insect pests and other vermin, particularly fleas. Such a nuisance were the latter that Adair suggests the raised bed of the gardeners, as opposed to the floor bed on the Plains, was devised for the express purpose of inconveniencing these parasites "which could not then reach the occupants at one jump!"

Be that as it may, every woman in the celebrating province had her house immaculate, her larder replete with cooked provisions, and her "thank offerings" for the Temple in readiness when the great day arrived on which the priests struck New Fire.

THE SACRED SQUARE

In the meantime, while the hunting and barbecuing, the housecleaning and baking, were going full blast, the priests and war leaders were not idle, for upon them fell the task of preparing the Sacred Square — the holy spot where purification rites were to take place round the New Fire.

Once again the reader must be warned not to confuse the New Fires with the Perpetual Fires. Regarding the latter Du Pratz tells us: "The guardians of the Perpetual Fire do not leave the Temple during this festival, but are served in the Temple with the feast" — (presumably, also, with the Black Drink).

According to Payne's description of the Sacred Square, supplemented by observations of other witnesses, the holy dance floor, which adjoined the village cornfield, was surrounded by four rectangular houses, or pavilions, open at the front and covered with peaked roofs. The backs of these houses were also open, above the height of an adult's chest, thus leaving transoms through which interested spectators might gaze on performances within the hallowed space. The floors were of banked earth, sloping forward, and spread with mats of cane. Entrances to the Sacred Square were at the corners, beyond one of which stood the round thatched public granary, or storehouse.

In the angle before another opening was the "outer square" which contained the conical refuse heap. This space was flanked on one remaining side by a terraced embankment and on the other by a waving cornfield.

Among details of construction, Bartram tells us the supporting pillars in front of the pavilions were upstanding serpents; while Payne declares that vines of the rattling calabash were laced across the open fronts. Bartram's description

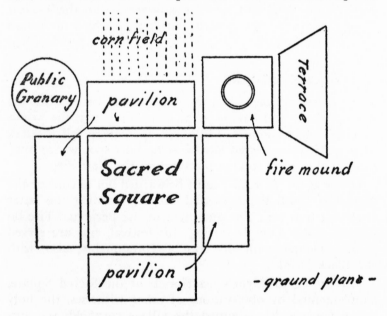

The Sacred Square.

may well be compared, ideologically, with the ruins of the Temple facade in *Chichen Itza.*

Preparation of the Sacred Square, according to Adair, to Payne, and to others, consisted of scraping away the past year's earthen floor and removing the ashes of the past year's Fire from the central Fire pit — both Earth and ash being added to the conical mound in the outer square, where debris accumulated from season to season.

After it was scraped clean, the Sacred Square was covered for a depth of several inches with fresh clay or "dobe," and then sprinkled with water to make a firm surface. Armed guards were now set at the entrances to destroy any creature, though it were no more than a squirrel, that should attempt to set profane foot in the holy rectangle before it became the seat of the New Fire.

THE ROYAL PALANQUIN

To hands equally as sanctified as those that prepared the Sacred Square, says Du Pratz, was assigned the task of decorating the palanquin in which the Great Sun, or Chieftain of the Province, was conveyed to the Festival grounds.

This imperial litter, made on a frame of four red-painted bamboo poles, had a padded seat, canopied with awnings of elaborately painted skins lined with magnolia leaves. The floor at the front of the seat was covered with three rows of flowers, red ones forming the two borders and white ones the center strip. These were the colors of royalty.

At the opening of the Festival, the Great Sun was borne to the Sacred Square on the shoulders of his most distinguished warriors, who, running at full speed, relieved one another, two by two, so skillfully that there was no cessation in the rapidity with which he traveled.

SALUTATION OF THE GREAT SUN

Arrived at the point of entry to the outer square, he greeted the multitude with three cries of *Hou! Hou! Hou!*

81

to each of which the multitude answered with nine shouts of *Hou!*, bowing to the ground with every shout, since the Great Sun was looked on as divine. At the last resounding *Hou!*, he set foot to earth and made his way to his pavilion, one of four rectangular structures surrounding the Sacred Square. Another of these pavilions, says Du Pratz, was especially dedicated to the leading War Chief.

GOLDENROD — THE FLOWER OF LIGHT

The opening act in this tremendous ceremonial, according to most authorities, was the striking of New Fire, an act which took place, not in the Sacred Square, but in the outer square, the conical mound of refuse Earth and ash serving for an altar.

Of the kindling of this Fire, Payne tells us, regarding the *Cherokee*: "A circle was drawn around the top (of the conical mound) to receive the Fire of sacrifice. Upon this (circle) was laid, ready for use, the inner bark of seven kinds of trees. This bark was carefully chosen from the east side of the trees, and was clear and free of blemish. . . . Early in the morning seven persons who were commissioned to kindle the Fire commenced their operations. . . . A round hole being made in a block of wood, a small quantity of dry goldenrod weed was placed in it. A stick, the end of which just fitted the opening, was whirled rapidly until the weed took fire."

Buttrick, for many years a missionary among the *Cherokee*, tells us goldenrod was called the "Light Bearer."[1]

To other details concerning the kindling of New Fire, Adair adds that friction-ignited sparks falling from the sacred fire drill were gently fanned to Flame by a snowy swan's wing in the hands of officiating priests.

When the Fire was well alight, according to Adair and Payne, it was removed to the Sacred Square where pots of Yaupon Tea were set to boil over its fresh pure Flame.

DANCE OF THE YAUPON BOUGHS

The next act in the prolonged ceremonial seems to have been a performance of twelve selected ancients, six men and six women, which, according to Adair's description, might well be termed the Dance of the Yaupon Boughs. Says he: "A religious attendant is (now) ordered to call six of their old beloved women to come to the Temple, and dance the beloved dance with joyful hearts to the old beloved speech." These six women, he tells us, enter the Sacred Square in solemn procession, "each carrying in her hand a bundle of small branches of various green trees; and they join the same number of old . . . priests who carry a cane (a bamboo wand) in one hand, adorned with white feathers, having likewise green boughs in the other hand which they (have) pulled from their holy arbor, (the Temple grove of transplanted Yaupon.) Those beloved old men have their heads dressed with white plumes; but the women are decked in their finest, and anointed with bear's grease having small tortoise shells, and white pebbles fastened to a strip of white drest deerskin, which is tied to each of their legs."

This group forms in three circles about the Fire, the description continues, and "the eldest of the priests leads the sacred dance, ahead of the innermost row, which . . . is next to the Holy Fire.

"He begins the dance . . . by invoking Yah! on a bass key and with a short accent"; then he sings Yo! Yo!, which is repeated by the rest of the religious procession; and he continues his sacred invocations and praises, repeating the divine word, or notes, till they return to the same point of the circular course where they began; the leading priest then exclaims He! He! while the procession goes around again; the priest now concludes the invocation with Wah! Wah! accompanying the circling motion as before. As the procession encircles the altar each performer strikes the ground with right and left foot alternately, "very quick but well timed."

83

"Then the awful drums," pots with water in the bottom and covered with thin wet skins, "join the sacred choir, which incite the old female singers to chant their pious notes and grateful praises before the divine essence, and to redouble their former quick and joyful steps, in imitation of the leader of the sacred dance and the religious men ahead of them. What with the manly strong notes of the one, and the shrill voices of the other, in concert with the bead-shells and the two sounding, drum-like earthen vessels, (together) with the voices of the musicians who beat them, the reputed holy ground echoes with the praises of YO! He! Wah!"

PURIFICATION RITES

After this performance all women, according to various reports, were expelled from the vicinity of the Sacred Square, since the solemn purification rites were about to begin. These led off with the imbibing of the Black Drink. Says Payne, having already told us the assembled chiefs were standing like chiseled figures, one opposite to another, along the walls of the rectangular buildings: "The first sounds I heard were a strange low, deep, wail, a sound of many voices drawn out in perfect unison, and only dying away with the breath itself. . . . This was followed by a second wail, in the same style, but shrill, like the sound of musical glasses, and giving a similar shiver to the nerves. And after a third wail in another key, the statue-like figures moved and formed diagonal lines opposite to (facing) each other, their backs to opposite angles of the square.

"One by one, they then approached the huge bowls in which the black drink was boiling, and, in rotation, dipped a gourd, and took, with a most reverential expression, a long deep draught each.

"The next part of the ceremony with them was somewhat curious; but the rapt expression of the worshipers took away the effect which such an evolution would be apt to

produce on a fastidious stomach if connected with an un-
interested head. In short, these dignitaries, without moving
a muscle of the face, or a joint of the body, after a few
seconds, and with great solemnity, ejected what had been
swallowed upon the ground. It seemed as if given forth in
the spirit of a libation among the ancients. The chiefs having
afterwards tasted, each replacing the gourd and returning
to his stand before the next came forward, they all went to
their seats, and two old men approached and handed round
gourds full to the other parties present who had remained
stationary. The looks on each side were as full of solemn awe
as I have ever seen at any Christian ceremony; and certainly
the awe was much more universal than usually pervades our
churches."

ADMONITION OF THE MEN

Payne next tells us the supreme dignitary at the celebration — The Great Sun, if he were there — harangued the
crowd. This, according to other reports, was an admonition
to continue in proper deportment during the coming year.

"One chief," Payne continues, "then walked around,
and, in short, abrupt sentences, seemed to give directions;
whereupon some whitened, entire gourds, with long handles,
and apparently filled with pebbles, were produced; and
men took their stations with them on mats, while those who
had been seated all arose, and formed in circles round the
fire, led by a chief, and always beginning their movement
toward the left. The gourds were shaken — there arose a sort
of low sustained chant as the procession went on; and it was
musical enough, but every few seconds, at regular intervals,
a sound was thrown in by all the dancers, in chorus, like the
sharp, quick, shrill yelp of a dog. The dance seemed to
bear deference to the Fires in the center. Every time they
came to a particular part of the square, first the head chief
turned and uplifted his hands over the Flame, as if invoking
a benediction, and all the people followed his example in
rotation.

"The dancers never crossed their feet, but first gave two taps each with the heel and toe of one foot, then of the other, making a step forward as each foot was tapped on the Earth; their bodies all the while stately and erect, and each, with a feather fan — their universal and indispensable companion — fanning himself, and keeping time with his fan as he went on.

"The dance was quickened, at a signal, till it became nearly a measured run, and the cries of the dancers were varied to suit the motion, when, suddenly, all together uttered a long, shrill whoop, and stopped short, some few remaining as guards along the Sacred Square, but most of the throng forthwith rushing down a steep, narrow ravine, canopied with foliage, to the river, into which they plunged: and the stream was black on every side with their heads as they swam about, playing all sorts of antics."

Still following the observations of Payne, who tells us the men at once returned to the Sacred Square, we find that the dances now took on the form of boasting pantomime, recounting feats of strength and deeds of prowess, while awards were made for special honors achieved in ball play or other public-spirited activities. "Each dance," says Payne, "seemed to have a special form and significance, and . . . the close . . . was invariably sudden. . . .after a long general whoop."

THE COMIC SKIT

One of the pantomimic dances is described by Timberlake, another of the early travellers, who saw a performance in which two actors, disguised in bear skins, appeared in the Square, followed by two hunters. Arrows brought down the two bears, but one arose and gave fight. The subsequent scuffle before the beast was finally conquered by the hunters afforded much amusement to the audience.

MINOR PURIFICATION RITES

While the men had their purification rites in the Sacred

Square, according to Adair, the women had similar, though less strenuous rites on the outside. "In order that none might be left godless," says the trader, a very old woman was permitted to come to the edge of the Sacred Square and receive pellets of green tobacco from the priests — these to be distributed among children according to age, the women, and those men considered unfit to enter holy ground. Payne tells us, however, that any man entering the Sacred Square unobserved and partaking of the Black Drink was forgiven his sins and reinstated in the life of the community.

He tells of a ritual participated in by boys and youths below the warrior age: "The last of the ceremonies of the day consisted of a sort of trial of fortitude upon the young.

"Old chiefs were seated at the back of the . . . four houses of the Square. They had sharp instruments . . . awls and flints. Children of from four to twelve and youths and young men, presented their limbs and the . . . instrument was plunged into the thighs and calves of their legs, and drawn down in long, straight lines.

"As the blood streamed, the wounded would scoop it up with bark or sticks, and dash it against the back of the building; and all the building thus became clotted with gore. The glory of the exercise seemed to be to submit without flinching, without even consciousness. The youngest children would sometimes show the most extraordinary self-control. All offered themselves to the experiment voluntarily. If a shudder were detected, the old chiefs gashed deeper. But where they saw entire firmness, an involuntary glow of admiration would flit across their stony faces."

This ritual, which Gatschet, the ethnologist, says was common throughout the agricultural area, can, perhaps, be explained on the hypothesis accorded by Frazer, author of THE GOLDEN BOUGH, to the *Aztec* practice of human sacrifice — namely, the idea that blood was necessary to the life of God; in other words, that the strength, or life essence, which was poured out by human sacrifice went into the spiritual power, or life essence, of God, the beneficent; continually renewing the power of that deity, and giving fresh strength for the eternal struggle against the sources of evil. This is also an explanation of the sacrifices of their children on the part of the gardening Indians whenever some terrible catastrophe overtook their Nation. Believing that the Power of Evil was gaining ascendancy over the Power of Good, they sought to resuscitate the Power of Good by dedicating to it the life stream of their children — an idea closely related to that of the "spirit in the blood," previously discussed as part of THE MAGIC ART.

THE FEAST OF OLD CORN

The thirty-six hour fast, in the Green Corn Dance, Adair tells us — and Espinosa indicates the same thing in Texas — was broken with old corn. The Feast of Old Corn began with the appearance of one of the most respected and aged women, one especially assigned to the part, at the corner of the Sacred Square where she offered all manner of dishes baked from corn of the preceding harvest.

Sanctified attendants reached out to receive these viands so that it might not be said that any female foot, even though it were that of the oldest and most withered, or the most venerated woman in the province, had profaned the Holy Earth during the period of abstinence.

Du Pratz tells us that to him the feast now assumed a gluttonous aspect. The public granary was emptied amid much hilarity, and runners were sent out to learn if there were any more corn to be had, owners of much corn hanging an ear in the doorway to indicate a supply on hand. A comparison of reports on the Festival leads to the conclusion that these activities were but the effort of the populace to rid itself of the surplus of the old crop. Any that was left over uneaten, Adair assures us, would have to be burned in preparation for the new harvest which must, under no circumstances, be contaminated by contact with the old.

While the men were eating the old corn within the

Sacred Square, the women and children were served in their encampment without. Both Payne and Espinosa have left us descriptions of the multitude gathered about the holy place during the period of the supreme religious Festival.

Following this feast after the fast, the Sacred Square was most scrupulously cleaned of every crumb of old food, of every shred of old matting and clothing, of every scrap of pottery of the past year's manufacture; and all was set in readiness for the sacrifice on the following, or fourth day — the sacrifice of the first ear of new corn; after which only new corn might be eaten, only new clothes worn, and only new pots cooked in or drunk from. In the meantime, the stomachs of the participators were again cleansed with vomitories and purgatives.

And now — all old corn being righteously disposed of — another proclamation, according to Payne's account, echoed throughout the province, and every Fire was extinguished simultaneously. Then, according to Adair, priests came forth issuing to each woman a torch with which to relight her hearth, accompanying the torches with a lecture advising against touching of New Fire by an individual not free from sin and ready to live properly through the coming year. This over, the women set off at once to kindle their cold hearths, returning to the festivities immediately thereafter.

To continue with Adair's story, while the majority of the women were away, one very aged woman, previously set apart for the service, was ordered by the supervising priests to bring forth a basket of fresh-plucked corn and other field products. This she set down at the corner of the Square, where she was permitted to stand, if she wished, and watch the completion of the most holy of all sacrificial rites among the gardening Indians — the consumption of the first fruits of the new harvest by the pure and uncontaminated Spirit of the New Fire.

Anent this sacrifice, Adair says: "The (high priest) or Firemaker rises from his White Seat and walks northward

89

three times around the Holy Fire, with a slow pace and a very sedate and grave manner, stopping now and then, and speaking certain old ceremonial words . . . which none understand but a few of the (other priests) who equally secrete their religious Mysteries that they may not be profaned. He then takes a little of each sort of the new harvest . . . rubs some bear oil over it, and offers it up . . . to the bountiful, holy Spirit of Fire, as a first fruit offering, and an annual oblation for sin." He likewise pours a little of the *Caseena* into the Holy Fire.

Payne states that during the latter part of the Festival the men went on a ceremonial hunt, urged forth by cries from the women, returning with the first animal procured to be sacrificed by the priests over the New Fire.

Payne also describes the mimic war among the *Creek,* when a chorus of fifty women singers, accompanied by men musicians with calabash rattles, marched out through the Sacred Square and took their places on the conical mound in the outer square, while the terraced embankment filled with excited spectators. The mournful song of the female choir, says Payne, was symbolic of the weeping that occurred when men prepared for war. Answering shouts from the cornbrakes where the mimic army was assuming war-paint, affirmed the determination of the men not to be swayed from their patriotic duty.

From opposite sides of the cornfield, the contenders came rushing, armed with rattling cornstalks. After belaboring one another, they fell to the carnival buffoonery of belaboring the spectators, who fled in mirthful excitement before the farcical attack.

Of the final episode in the prolonged ceremonial, Adair tells us the priests shouted forth the glad tidings that the old year was at an end — that the old sins had been forgiven, that the New Fire now burned with a pure and holy Flame on every hearth in the land — and that the harvest, already sanctified, was waiting in the fields for willing hands to gather grain.

With this proclamation, the women were summoned to take their places with the men in the final act of pageantry — The Dance of the Olden Time.

SALUTATION OF THE TRUE SUN

Among the *Tejas,* says Espinosa, before Dawn of the last day of the ceremony, scouts were sent out to watch for the first faint glow of the Rising Sun. With its discovery they set up a joyous shout of salutation which was echoed by the populace. Then the races of the youngsters began. First, the young men lined up and ran to a tree at a given distance, whirling round it and returning to the starting point, continuing this exercise till exhausted. They were followed by the young boys and girls who did the same thing.

In Espinosa's own words: "All the relatives are intent upon seeing who gains the advantage, and this person is the one that carries off the laurels of the occasion. The wives and female relatives of the man who is left behind, or becomes tired out, all set up a great weeping because they say that when he goes out to war he will be left behind — either as a captive or dead — for his lack of speed.

"This ceremony lasts about an hour."

Following the foot races came the "grand march" concluding the performance. Again quoting Espinosa: "They then take hollow logs covered on top with green branches, bury the ends of them, and select eight strong Indian women, who, seated at intervals with sticks in each hand, use the hollow logs as drums to the accompaniment of the calabash which the old men play, and to the songs of more than twenty men and women singers.

"This music is for the dance in which all engage, old men and women, young boys and girls, and little children. They dance in a circle, the men facing the women, keeping time, moving only their feet. They do this until midday when, tired and sleepy, each goes home to rest from his strenuous exercise."

Du Pratz adds that the men and women moved in opposite directions about the Fire, while Payne declares that in this dance the sound of terrapin rattles on the women's leg bands, which they were able to keep silent when needed, was like the tinkle of sleigh bells.

Even today, about El Paso, and probably in many other districts, the Indians separate the boys and girls, sending them in opposite directions in the dances. The Spanish families practicing the same custom declare it serves the purposes of chaperonage, but it would seem to be the direct result of old Sun worshiper influences. The reverse circular motion is especially noticeable in the *paseo* or courtship promenade on the Mexican *plazas* where the young gather without their elders to enjoy an evening of decorous flirtation.

THE ORIGINAL AMERICAN THANKSGIVING

Says C. C. Jones, in ANTIQUITIES OF THE SOUTHERN INDIANS, a book which is concerned mainly with the Georgia Nations: "This happy institution of the 'Boos-ke-tuh' (the 'Busk,' or 'Green Corn Dance') restores man to himself, his family, and to his nation. It is a general amnesty which not only absolves the Indians from all crimes, murder excepted, but seems to bury guilt itself in oblivion. In ancient times this Festival was celebrated at the appearance of the first New Moon during which the corn became fully eared. Subsequently, however, it was regulated by the season of the harvest. From the time consumed and the formalities observed in its solemnization, it is manifest how important and sacred this Feast of the Busk was in the estimation of the agricultural tribes of the South. The ingathering of the matured maize crop was preceded by an extinguishment of former Fires and the kindling of one consecrated New Flame, which was to prove the parent of light and heat for the coming year. This was the season of physical and moral purification, of general forgiveness, universal amnesty and united thanksgiving. Then was the blotted chapter of the old year closed and sealed, and a new, clean page opened in the life of every one."

Bartram, the traveller, now takes up the tale to inform us that not only was every private harvest immediately gathered, following the conclusion of religious festivities, but that the public granary described in THE GARDEN PATCH was filled for the relief of the needy, for the entertainment of guests, or for any other emergency which should arise during the coming year — a fitting and appropriate close to the original American "thanksgiving."

FOOTNOTES

[1] This use of goldenrod as "the flower of light" can be compared to the *planta de genista* or Scotch Broom from which the Plantagenets took their name, and to the Lily of Florence, Italy, from which we have the *fleur de lis*, originally *fleur de luce*.

DANCING
THE
CALUMET

X

The Garden Patch

"Indian corn, maize, the *elote,* was developed from the *teo-centli,* a wild grass indigenous to the Valley of Mexico."

Note from a lecture on Mexican Archaeology, University of Mexico.

THE STAFF OF LIFE

The staff of life among Indians of Central and North America was maize — the "Indian corn" of the Pilgrims' first Thanksgiving — presumably acquired through past eons in the high Valley of Mexico where the prehistoric gardeners took to their hearts the *teocentli,* a wild grass of that region, devoting their lives to its perfection as a cereal.

So well did these patient horticulturists perform their self-set task that they produced a grain, which, since the discovery of America, has been passed round the world in the ever-flowing tide of cultural exchange. Nor is this a single contribution to the world's luxuries.

The American Indian, though he had few domesticable animals — none, in fact, save the turkey, the bee, the guinea pig, and that weakling camel, the llama — had a tremendous wealth of domesticable plants — among them corn, or maize; tobacco; the "Irish" potato; the yam, or "sweet potato"; tomatoes; beans; pumpkins; cushaws; watermelons; chile pepper; chocolate; vanilla, and innumerable others. With these, he made the best of his opportunities. The development of civilization in the western hemisphere, based on plants, paralleled the development of civilization in the eastern hemisphere and surpassed the European civilizations which were based largely upon animals — until Eurasia forged ahead in the use of metals — bronze and iron.

At least two-thirds of the garden truck produced in the United States today, and a large part of that in Europe, originated in the gardens of the agricultural American long before Columbus presented the most famous egg in history at the court of Isabella and Ferdinand of Spain.

THE MAIZE MOTHER

Corn being paramount over all other agricultural products in America, and Nature filled with spirit creations for the Indian, the *teocentli* or "god grass" inevitably became the "maize mother" of his Pantheon — the epitome, the very essence of benevolent fecundity — and the Green Corn Ceremony the most sacred event of his calendar.

THE SOOTHING WEED

After corn, perhaps tobacco held the most distinguished place, since it was the almost universal Indian incense, medium of good fellowship between man and the gods. Introduced into Spain from Mexico some thirty years before Sir Walter Raleigh made the Virginia brand fashionable in England, tobacco, like corn, has circled the globe.

SANCTITY IN THE CANEBRAKES

After corn and tobacco, cane, or bamboo, the dense "bottom land" growth of the southern river valleys and the Gulf region, was possibly the most important botanical feature in the garden lands. The tender shoots were edible. Cut to a point and the tips hardened in Fire, the tough canes became spears and harpoons, while the naturally sharp edges made knives. Cut in joints, the larger sections were cups to drink from or tubes in which to carry precious plumage for coronets or fans. Sections of joints, properly appended with legs, arms, ears, necks, heads and other parts of the anatomy, made toys for the youngsters — such toys as may be bought, made to hand, in Mexican curb markets today.

Split into shreds when young and pliable, these canes were woven into mats, platters, sieves, baskets, and carpets. Lined with tough clay, receptacles woven of cane were converted into water jugs. The largest and driest bamboo stalks required little labor for conversion into bedrails, into frames for sedan chairs, and into pole racks for the suspension of heavy carcasses when carrying home the "kill" from the forests. Bound into bundles, they made *balsas* for ready transport along the bayous or across the rivers.

The canebrakes themselves offered refuge from the cold or for the pursued, and spots of sanctuary for the seclusion of the religiously minded, retiring in pursuit of divine inspiration.

NUT AND FRUIT TREES

Sylvan nut trees were, like the bamboo, of tremendous value to the Indians. Says De Solis, speaking of the *Asinai*: "They gather quantities of thick-shelled nuts (pecans and black walnuts) and acorns to last a year." He also mentions the extensive use of persimmons among the *Tejas;* while other writers speak of seeing quantities of dried fruits, including persimmons, grapes and wild plums in the Indian store-houses. These were dried, says Lawson, either over the Fire or in the Sun.

BREAKING THE SOIL A COMMUNITY ENTERPRISE

In Louisiana, according to Du Pratz and Adair, and in East Texas, according to Joutel and Espinosa, breaking the soil for planting was a community enterprise. Here where

96

there was reasonable security from surprise attack, the basis for the division of labor between the sexes was totally different from that on the Buffalo Range. Constant readiness to spring to arms being unnecessary, men did the heavier work. Methods of performing certain tasks among the *Asinai* have given rise to the idea that men and women were not permitted to work together — a mistake, as can be readily discerned by considering the "Building Bee" in THE HOUSE OF STRAW. However, in gardening, men and women did have separate functions — the whole process amounting to a ritual.

Du Pratz tells us the first act toward planting, after the weather prophets, or priests set the "time of the Moon," was to burn over the ground selected for cultivation during the coming year. All wood of proper size, prepared by hacking with stone axes and girdling with Fire, was laid aside and stacked in pyramids for Temple use, or as other ceremonial fuel.

Next, the able-bodied men of the community were called together for the purpose of breaking ground — a difficult task, and one achieved, say Joutel and Espinosa, with wooden "picks" — made by splitting the end of a walnut bough and inserting a sharpened point of the same hard material. With these implements, the men trenched light furrows which the women of each household, using their interlaced fingers for seed-drills, planted, sometimes later, to corn and beans.

Before the women started their part of the work, however, it was their business to furnish the ground-breaking crew with a bountiful repast. The official herald, says Espinosa, gave the women of each houshold due warning as to when they might expect their turn at serving refreshments. Any woman who was pregnant, he continues, was allowed to have nothing to do with the planting — not for her sake, but because her presence might spoil the crops — a magical provision which harks back to the "spirit in the blood principle" of THE MAGIC ART.

97

The work of the crew began with the fields of the civil chieftain and the high priest, and continued until every citizen's plot was in shape to receive seed.

Of the seed corn, Espinosa tells us: "For this purpose each man selects the quantity needed for two years' planting, so that if the first year be dry, no lack of seed shall exist for the second year. They will not touch a grain of this reserved seed, (carefully stored in the House of Straw) even though all the food corn they have is used up. Instead, they hurry out to hunt for and trade with those whose crop was more abundant."

The most complete picture of planting operations seems to be that given by Adair: "Every dwelling house has a small field pretty close to it: and, as soon as spring of the year admits, there they plant a variety of large and small beans, peas, and the smaller sort of Indian corn, which usually ripens in two months, from the time it is planted.

"Around this small farm, they fasten stakes in the ground, and tie a couple of long split hickory or white oak saplings, at proper distances to keep off (the larger animals.)

Their fields lie quite open with regard to fencing. . . . because, as they say, they can cultivate the best of their land here and there, as it suits their convenience, without wasting their time in fences and childishly confining their improvements, as if the crop would eat itself!

"The chief part of the Indians begin to plant their outfields when the wild fruit is so ripe as to draw off the birds from picking up the grain. This is their general rule which is about the beginning of May.

"An old beloved man (priest) warns the inhabitants to be ready of a prefixed day. At Dawn of it one by order (a herald) goes aloft, and whoops to them (the populace) with shrill calls 'that the new year is far advanced — that he who expects to eat, must work, — and that he who will not work must expect to pay the fine according to the old custom, or leave the town, as they will not sweat themselves for an healthy idle waster!'

98

THE GARDEN PATCH

"At such times may be seen many chieftains working with the people.

"About an hour after Sunrise, they enter the field agreed on by lot, and fall to work with great cheerfulness; sometimes one of their orators cheers them with jests and humorous old tales, and sings several of their most agreeable wild tunes, beating also with a stick in his right hand, on the top of an earthen pot covered with a wet and well-stretched deerskin: thus they proceed from field to field, until their seed is sown.

"Corn is their chief produce and main dependence. Of this they have three sorts; the early or six weeks corn, which has already been mentioned. The second is yellow and flinty, which they call 'hominy corn.' The third is the largest, of a very white and soft grain called 'bread corn.'

"They plant a sort of small tobacco . . . and frequently use it on the most religious occasions.

"The women plant also pompions (pumpkins) and different sorts of melons, in separate fields, at a considerable distance from the town, where each owner raises an high scaffold, to overlook this favorite part of their vegetable possessions; and though the enemy sometimes kills them in this their strict watch duty, yet it is a very rare thing to pass by those fields without seeing them there at watch.

"This usually is the duty of the old women who fret at the very shadow of a crow, when he chances to pass on his wide survey of the fields; but if pinching hunger should excite him to descend, they soon frighten him away with their screeches.

"They plant their corn in straight rows, putting five or six grains into one hole, about two inches distant. They cover them with clay in the form of a small hill. Each row is a yard asunder, and in the vacant ground they plant pumpkins, watermelons, marshmallows, sun flowers, and sundry sorts of beans and peas, the last two of which yield increase.

"Their old fields abound with larger strawberries than I have seen in any other part of the world.

99

"They have a sort of wild potatoes, which grow plentifully in their rich lowlands. . . . There grows a long flag, in shallow ponds, and on the edges of running waters, with an evergreen, broad, round leaf, a little indented where it joins the stalk; it bears only one leaf that always floats on the surface of the water, and affords plenty of cooling small nuts which make a sweet-tasted and favorite bread, when mixed with Indian corn flour (meal). It is a sort of marsh-mallows, and reckoned a speedy cure for burning maladies, either inward or outward — for the former by an application of the leaf; and for the latter, by a decoction of it drunk plentifully."

Among other horticultural notes, Adair states that Yaupon was transplanted to sacred groves about the Temple sites.

Espinosa says of the *Tejas*: "When they plant their bean vines they stick a forked cane in each hill so that they (the vines) may run up it and be protected from small animals and the mildew. When they gather the crop they pull up the cane and carry the whole thing home."

Of the various kinds of corn, Espinosa tells us these Indians always planted an early crop — the "small corn" of the calendar — which, in East Texas, was gathered in June; and a later crop of "large corn," gathered in September. The latter was the crop celebrated by the Green Corn Festival, as described in the preceding chapter.

He says also: "The *Tejas* plant quantities of sunflowers which grow to be of enormous size, having a seed in the center like the piñon."

Of the harvesting of these carefully tended foodstuffs, we are told by Bartram that among the southern Nations, immediately after the Green Corn Festival, the entire citizenry gathered at the cultivated area and brought in, each man his own produce, from his own allotted garden space.

THE COMMUNITY CHEST

Bartram also informs us that where he traveled there

100

was, in each neighborhood, a public storehouse, — the "community chest" of that day — which was filled at harvest time by voluntary contributions from public-spirited citizens. The issuance and apportionment of these stored supplies was at the discretion of the civil chieftain.

The storehouse is said to have been always a round, thatched building, set in some secluded and shady spot beside a running stream. Its contents, besides the surplus vegetable products of the surrounding fields, included every possible variety of dried meat — thus providing insurance against embarrassment or want in any civic emergency.

Of the *Tejas,* Captain Ramón tells us: "They are very charitable among themselves, and assist one another in their emergencies."

Many of the Indian recipes for preparing their wild and cultivated crops will be given in the chapter on ARTS AND CRAFTS — in the meantime, it is necessary to look to their method of obtaining meats and fats with which to season these numerous and excellent vegetable products.

XI

The Products of the Chase

"The buffalo is distant more than forty leagues (an hundred miles) from the *Tejas* country."

Espinosa.

BRINGING HOME THE BACON

"Bacon," with the southern agricultural Indians, consisted, in the main, of buffalo meat, venison, and bear oil. The first they were obliged to secure through commercial treaties with the Plains Tribes — notably the *Comanche*. The second they had in plenty at home. The third, which was a great trade commodity, both at home and abroad, was confined to certain sections within the forested area.

BIRNAM WOOD ON TEXAS PLAINS

The *Tejas* of East Texas, as was mentioned in THE PEACE PIPE, had a treaty with the *Comanche* by which they were permitted to hunt buffalo within the *Comancheria* at given intervals. Nevertheless, when they sallied forth from the shelter of the Piney Woods on such a mission, they were obliged to keep a sharp eye for interloping *Apache* Bands — the *Apache* being the deadly foes of all other Texas Tribes and Nations, including the *Comanche*, with whom they contested the control of the Buffalo Range.

THE PRODUCTS OF THE CHASE

The first act of a party of gardeners setting forth for buffalo and arriving at the Timberline, says De Solis, was to send a scout up the tallest available tree, that he might look out over the open country for evidences of hostility. If he reported the coast clear, his comrades below fell to twisting off tree branches for screens as they advanced upon the Plain — a classic camouflage. Shakespeare's army, it will be remembered, moving out of Birnam Wood, employed a similar strategy.

"The *Tejas* go well-armed," says De Solis; "for if they fall in with the *Apaches* at this time, the two murder one another unmercifully!"

It was necessary to be even more cautious and wary a few weeks later, when the party returned to the Timber Lands loaded with hides and smoked meat. Though scalps were a sufficient inducement for attack at any moment, scalps plus plunder offered an irresistible stimulus to the everlurking *Apache*.

THE DECOY

On setting forth to hunt the deer in their own woods, the *Tejas* were accustomed to put a deer's head on a post inside the house of the hunters, and then to pray to their gods, by medium of the Fire, to permit many animals to be killed, accompanying these prayers with the customary offerings of tobacco and bear oil.

Having concluded their invocations of the Sun and of the spirits of the wood, the gardeners removed the deerhead, still on its post, to a position outside the house door. They then covered their faces with white Earth, signifying that they came into the wood in peace and not in war, and departed on the hunt, carrying another deerhead, mounted like the first.

Cushman enlightens us very fully as to the use of this second head and the method of the chase. Says he, concerning the more easterly nations where he was reared: "They made a very ingeniously constructed instrument for calling deer to them, in the use of which they were very expert. In connection with this call they used a decoy made by cutting the skin of a deer clear around the neck, about ten inches from the head, choosing a buck with huge horns. The skin was then rolled in one entire section up to the head and (the bone) cut off at the neck where it joined the head. The skin, thus made hollow from the head back, is kept in its natural position by inserting upright sticks. The skin is then pulled upward from the nose to the horns and all the flesh and brains removed; then the skin is repulled to its natural place and laid away to dry.

"In about a year it has become dry, hard, inoffensive and fit for use. All upright sticks are then taken out except the one next to the head which is left as a hand hold.

"Thus the hunter, with his deer caller and his head decoy, easily enticed his game within range of his weapons. Secreting himself in the woods he began to imitate the bleating of a deer. If within hearing distance, one soon responded, but, catching the scent of the hunter, perhaps, would stop and look around. The hunter then inserted his arms into the cavity of the decoy, and, taking hold of the upright stick within, held it up to view, attracting the attention of the doubting deer by rubbing it against the bushes or a tree; seeing which the deer no longer suspected danger but continued to advance till it met death."

According to the Spanish in East Texas, a priest ordinarily accompanied the hunting party, and, whenever a deer was killed, performed the duties of his office by whispering propitiatory words into its ear, beseeching its spirit not to be angered because of its violent death.

As to the "bleats" or "calls" — there were various kinds of such implements in use for various kinds of game — American army officers tell us their use by a skilled performer often resulted in bringing down, literally upon his head, a hungry mountain lion or timber wolf, which, startled at the seeming transformation of its prey, might give him more of an adventure than he bargained for — thus it did not pay for a man to go out alone equipped with such an apparatus.

JACK O'LANTERNS ON THE CHASE

While discussing the chase, it seems fitting to introduce the method of catching waterfowl seen by Major John Cremony, while stationed in the *Apacheria* — a method probably in use throughout the Americas. He tells us large numbers of gourds were set adrift on the windward side of the lagoons, whence they were gradually propelled by the wind until they reached the opposite side, where they were recovered, carried round to windward, and again set adrift. At first the ducks and geese exhibited dread and suspicion of these strange, floating objects, but soon grew used to them, and paid them no further attention. Having brought the fowls to this stage, the Indians fitted the gourds on their own heads, furnishing holes for eyes, nose, and mouth. Next, armed with bags, the hunters entered the water, not over five feet deep anywhere, and, exactly imitating the bobbing motion of the empty gourds upon the water, succeeded in getting close enough to the birds to seize them by the feet, drag them under, and stuff them in the bags. "The dexterity and naturalness with which this is done," says Cremony, "exceeds belief, yet it is a common thing among them."

BAITING BRUIN

Buffalo were hunted in the summer or fall when fat, and deer at any time; but bears were hunted in the winter while hibernating in hollow trees.

Few bears came to Texas, says Espinosa, except when the acorn crop was scant towards the north, but the *Tejas* traveled in the country of their allies, the other gardening Nations, searching for Bruin wherever they spied a cavity in a tree trunk.

When hunting bears, Du Pratz tells us, the first act of

105

the Indians was to locate a hollow tree and examine the outside for claw marks. If such were found, the hunters beat a violent tattoo on the resounding trunk with a handy limb. A bear within was sure to move about, and would, perhaps, show himself before relapsing into his disturbed slumbers.

Once he was at rest again, the spying Indians piled dry bamboo about the foot of the tree and stuffed a bundle of the same combustible material into the handiest opening leading down to his winter couch. They then stood off and threw lighted flares at these improvised targets until one caught and a blaze sprang up about the hidey-hole. Resulting Smoke and Flame brought the bear forth, singed and raging, to meet a barrage of arrows beneath which he often dropped dead without having escaped from the base of the sheltering tree.

CASING THE DEER

The next step in taking care of the bear was to kill a deer. The hide of the deer was then "cased"; that is, drawn off, as Du Pratz explains, by being rolled down from the neck "as one would roll hose." The skin was then cut around the knee joints and the resulting "leaks" stopped with a cement made of cinders from the camp Fire and tallow from the animal itself. Meanwhile the fat of the bear, which was precious because it formed a non-congealing oil, was rendered out in large earthen pots and poured from them into the cased skins. Such a skin of oil, tightly fastened at the neck, was known to the French-Indian trade as a *faon* of oil.

According to Espinosa, when the *Tejas* happened to find bears near home, they brought in the meat and the unrendered fat wrapped in moss.

THE HUNTING HOUND

To help them in the hunt, say the early Spanish, the

Tejas had a wolf-like, thin-nosed breed of dogs — the *ju-bines*.

The dogs of the agricultural Nations were badly spoiled, says Charlevoix. They had a habit of sleeping with their masters and liberally sharing fleas — moreover, he complains, he could not even read his breviary because the unduly familiar canines jumped over him if he squatted down, knocking it out of his hand; and if he were spared this indignity, while walking, he could not keep his mind on holy things because of the continuous necessity to scratch!

FISH STORIES

"When warm weather comes," says Espinosa, "the *Tejas* go with their families to certain spots where they stay for some days, living on fish; . . . they carry quantities of cooked fish back home with them." He explains that due to sudden rises in the rivers, fish were not always to be found in the same lagoons.

Adair says of Indian fishermen: "If they shoot at fish . . . they aim at the lower part of the belly . . . which seldom fails of killing. In a dry summer season, they gather horse chestnuts, and different sorts of roots, which, having pounded pretty fine, and steeped awhile in a trough, they scatter this mixture over the surface of a middle-sized pond, and stir it about with poles, till the water is sufficiently impregnated with the intoxicating bittern. The fish are soon inebriated and make to the surface of the water, with their bellies uppermost. The fishers gather them in baskets, and barbecue the largest, covering them carefully over at night to preserve them from the supposed putrifying influence of the Moon. It seems that fish catched in this manner are not poisoned, but only stupified; for they prove very wholesome food. . . . By experiments, when they are speedily moved into good water, they revive in a few minutes."

Adair also describes fish nets, fish traps made of canes, and stone dams behind which the fish were driven by whooping swimmers carrying interlaced grapevines weighted with pendant stones. These vines were stretched across the river, from swimmer to swimmer, and carried swiftly along to rake the bottoms of the streams. Of such fish drives, Adair says; "With this draught, which is a very heavy one, they make a town feast, or feast of love, of which everyone partakes in the most social manner, and afterward they dance together, singing . . . praises to the Divine Essence, for his bountiful gifts to the beloved people."

Harpooning with sharpened canes was a favorite method of acquiring fish; while crayfish, which, according to Lawson and Adair, were very popular with the southern Indians, were taken in bushels by threading chunks of half-cooked venison about six inches apart, on stout bamboo stakes, and driving the stakes into the mud bottoms of the lagoons. These stakes were watched, and as often as they were weighted with crustaceans, pulled up, and the "haul" shaken off into baskets.

Du Pratz tells us that when fish were to be taken home fresh — that is, unsmoked or unbarbecued — the fishers took a limber and leafy branch, bending the leaf end around into a loop, and weaving it into a sort of racket, with vines or grasses. The fish were then bound into layers in this contrivance, and the whole kept under water until the fisher left for home, when the pole, with its burden, was lifted and slung over his shoulder.

According to C. C. Jones, fish were so popular as food in the agricultural area that the Indians maintained well-stocked fish preserves.

The Alligator Hunt

Besides the sport of fishing, the southern Indians, according to old narratives, had still greater adventures in their streams and bayous when they set forth on alligator hunts. The booming roar of these great lizards seems to have punctuated the peaceful forests with an eternal series of

108

threats — for the alligators hunted the Indians more assid-
uously, perhaps, than the Indians hunted them — it being
much easier for an alligator to make off with a man than a
man with an alligator.

The method of capture was hazardous in itself. A pole
was rammed down the alligator's throat and several men,
using it as a lever, turned him on his back. In this position
he was, with considerable labor, clubbed to death. However,
before he met his end, he was very liable to get the pole
loose from his tormentors and swing it about in such a
manner as to batter them violently before their accomplices
were able to batter him. Of forest denizens, the alligator,
armored except for his eyes, was perhaps best able to hold
his own against all comers.

Conventions of the Hunt

Like every other feature of their civilization, hunting,
among the Indians, had its special conventions, and to ignore
them was to bring down individual if not national disaster.

No pregnant woman, says Lawson, might eat of the first
catch from a fish trap.

No snake was to be killed or disturbed by hunters.

A huntsman must never step over a fallen log, but always
go around its end.

A man might never eat of his first childhood kill. When the
first animal fell, by his arrow, he must present it to someone else.

Hunting a Fundamental

Since they possessed no buffalo and few bears, the *Tejas,*
had they been without other incentive to trade, would probably have been drawn into commercial contacts with their
neighbors in order to acquire proper seasoning for their
garden truck, and a pleasantly varied meat supply.

Certainly, without the products of the chase, their diet

109

would have lacked much of its attractiveness as described by Adair in the next chapter but one, ARTS AND CRAFTS, and their life much of its zest, not only as incident to the hunt, but as expended in rituals and religious festivals designed to bring success to the hunters or to increase the abundance of the game supply.

RITUAL OF THE BUFFALO HUNT

" (Whilst I was among the Southern Nations toward the Mississippi), their old men, six days before the hunting of the wild bulls (buffalo) sent four or five of their most expert hunters upon the mountains to dance the Calumet with as many ceremonies as amongst the Nations to which they are wont to send embassies to make some alliance. At the return of these men they openly exposed for three days together one of the great cauldrons they had taken from us. They had wreathed it about with feathers of divers colors, and laid a gun (also secured from the French, replacing native bows, arrows, and spears). For three days together the chief wife of a captain carried this cauldron on her back, with flowers in great pomp, at the head of about two hundred hunters. They all followed an old man who had fastened one of our Indian handkerchiefs (bandannas) to the end of a pole like a banner; holding his bows and arrows he marched with great gravity and silence. This old man made the hunters halt three or four times to lament bitterly the death of the bulls they hoped to kill.

"At the last stay where they rested, the most ancient of the company sent two of their noblest hunters to discover wild bulls. They whispered softly to them at their ritual before they began the hunting of these beasts. Afterwards they made a Fire of bulls' dung dried in the Sun, and with that Fire they lighted their Pipes to smoke the hunters which had been sent to make the discovery."

"Every Nation adorns the *Calumet* as they think fit according to their own genius and the birds they have in their country" — thus runs the account of Father Hennepin.

XII
Vanities of the Villagers

"The *Tejas* are fair-complexioned, handsome, and well-proportioned. The women . . . are most beautiful."

De Solis.

TURKISH AND COLD BATHS

The Indians of the southern agricultural Nations are described as not only extremely comely, but extremely clean — Turkish, or vapor baths in specially dedicated structures, and cold baths in convenient creeks and rivers, constituting regular purification rituals.

THE FASHIONS

Their garments were ordinarily scant because they occupied a semitropic region where there was no necessity for conserving body heat; where, indeed, the main problem was to keep cool, except when blizzards, at irregular intervals, blew suddenly and briefly from the north. The anticipation of such erratic temperatures, however, brought about some borrowing of styles from the chill Plains to the northwest, thus causing the local "wardrobe," on occasion, to partake of the nature of that area as well as of the tropic countries far to southward.

What the natives lacked in actual clothing, to the great

scandalization of the armored and sweating Europeans who first stared upon their peaceful and well-ordered society, they made up in adornment, setting great store by dangling ornaments and bright colors, every object and every color having, for them, symbolic import.

Since extensive spaces of skin were left free for pictorialization, they employed tattooing to excess, both as a decorative feature and a magical device, continually plastering themselves with varitoned earths and dyes over the tattooed work.

Save for "bobs" or queues, as the style might run in particular communities, men, using clam, mussell shell, or wooden tweezers, or singeing with hot stones, removed every portion of hair from their persons, including eyebrows and eye lashes. This almost universal practice, profoundly concerned with magical and religious Mysteries, gave rise to the supposition, on the part of the explorers, that the tribes and nations of America were beardless.

People of all ages and social stations went barefoot except when on journeys, in bitter weather, or for specific ceremonials. Departing from the common practice among weaver Indians, who ordinarily wore straw sandals, these Indians, according to all accounts, wore moccasins like the Plains people — of buffalo hide for hard travel, and of fine, decorated deerskin for ritual purposes. Not only were they accustomed to go barefoot, but they invariably went bareheaded except when bedecked with chaplets of plumes or coronets of flowers.

FABRICS AND TEXTILES

They had three varieties of fabrics, besides furs: perfectly tanned leathers, lacy textiles woven from bleached mulberry or other vegetable fibres, and feather cloths made from a combination of these fibres with plumes or down — cloths similar to those famous in the Indian Empires across the Gulf.

112

VANITIES OF THE VILLAGERS

Detailed information concerning the manufacture of fabric is given in ARTS AND CRAFTS.

Regarding the picturesque qualities of leathers, frequently referred to in old writings as "shammies," (chamois skins) we are told by Captain Ramón and others that women's garments often bore the appearance of rich black velvet, while canopies and awnings afforded a sheen and lustre equal to old world taffetas.

CAPES AND FALDAS

According to the early Christian Fathers in Texas, when women made *faldas,* or "wrap-around" skirts, from straight lengths of the rich black stuff, they cut the edges to deep fringe and sewed them with thousands of tiny pearl-like seed beads (thought to be hackberry seeds) — to shine like infinitesimal Moons and make a faint musical clattering with the movements of the wearer. The black stuff, it is said, was reserved to the wardrobes of royalty.

In summer a skirt was all a woman wore, with tattooing for a bodice; but during winter "cold snaps," a waist-length, sleeveless upper garment was added, of the same material as the skirt, and, like it, made from a single straight piece. A vertical slit in the middle permitted the head to pass through. If the costume was of the black stuff, bordered with seed beads — often referred to as "berries" in the chronicles — the borders of the straight, unsashed tunic were finished in the same manner as the borders of the skirt.

Myriads of seed beads, recovered from kitchen middens and burials, some still strung in patterns, are among the archaeological exhibits at the University of Texas.

For extremely cold weather, garments heavier than the soft tunics were worn, garments made of skin with the hair left on. Du Pratz describes a semifitted shoulder cape worn by the women of Louisiana cut to a pattern still used by native women in parts of Mexico today — a one-sided creation drawn over the right shoulder and under the left arm,

113

fitting snugly about the waist, but leaving one shoulder and one breast bare.

THE OVERCOAT

As a final protection against the cold, both men and women wore whole buffalo skins with the hair on, letting the robe fall from the shoulders, hair side in, and drawing it close about the body. The smooth, or outer surfaces of such robes were customarily emblazoned with a single great Sun symbol, the rays completely enveloping the wearer in multicolored splendor.

THE MANTLE OF NOBILITY

For festive occasions in general, and in particular for the ceremonial affairs attending each New Moon, the men and women of nobility wore glimmering feather mantles, to make which, says Du Pratz, they took feathers from turkeys, wild ducks, and other native birds — the women of high social rank delighting in snowy, floating shoulder capes of swansdown.

The ceremonial mantle was purely an expression of dignity, floating under one shoulder and knotted over the other. With men, it hung to the left side; with women, to the right, which may have been influenced by the dances, men moving always to the left and women to the right.

A drawing in Lafitau shows the regal mantle, made of handsomely painted skins, as falling to the knees — most mantles fell only to the waist. From a decorative standpoint, this garment, balanced by three great strands of beads dropping from the left shoulder and draped round the opposite hip, was superb. The royal attire was completed by strands of beads in pairs about the arms and legs; pairs of inflated fish bladders, possibly representing the Sun and the Moon, suspended from the imperial ears, and a tuft, or coronet, of plumes.

Hariot, arriving with the earliest English colony that

essayed to settle on the Atlantic seaboard, describes quilted rabbit skin mantles worn regularly by the Medicine Men. These mantles, contrary, apparently, to all others, had two arm holes, hung straight round the body, and tied at the center front instead of on the shoulder.

AMERICAN NETHER GARMENTS vs. EUROPEAN

Though the woman of the gardening region wore her wrap-around skirt so as to cover the lower body completely, the man, not only of that area, but of practically the whole continent, had a particular aversion to covering his hips, his seated toilet habit being opposite to the standing habit of Europeans. Adair tells us Indians designated white men by the contemptuous term of "tied rumps" because the latter followed the genteel habit of wearing seats in their trousers — a practice looked on by Indians, both men and women, as too profoundly "sissy" for words!

THE TAPARABO

The single essential and universal nether garment of the Indian man was the breechclout, a narrow fold of mulberry cloth or finely tanned deerskin, passed between the legs, drawn over a belt, back and front, and allowed to hang loose for half a yard or so at each end. Even this he might dispense with on occasion — as when, if it happened to be dyed red, he took it off and dangled it in the haunts of inquisitive and unsophisticated trout. Such impromptu fishing tackle, according to Adair, was a customary means of securing dinner in an emergency, and embarrassed none, save, perhaps, the unfortunately deluded fish.

The breechclout, used in Spain long before the discovery of the Americas, was called the *taparabo* by the Spaniards.

LONG BOOTS OF BUCKSKIN

When it was sufficiently chilly to make nakedness uncomfortable in the garden lands, men wore loose tunics like the women, and, under them, leggins which must have been in one piece with the moccasins, since Adair calls them "long boots of buckskin." Leggins were kept in place by suspender-like straps attached to the belt. They were fitted tightly to the leg, and a wide flap left beyond the outer seam was slashed to fringe sewn with all manner of trinkets, classified by Adair as "turkey cocks' spurs, fauns' trotters, and Snakes' rattles." Such garments were extremely practical, protecting the wearer against Snakes and thorns, as well as frost.

THE MATCHCOAT — A MAN'S SKIRT

Though, as has been several times repeated, the gardening Indian wore little or nothing, in warm weather, save his own oiled and painted skin, Lawson's HISTORY OF SOUTH CAROLINA describes a man's skirt, extremely short, made of mulberry cloth, feather cloth, or fur; and an old sketch of a *Wichita* village, published in Marcy's EXPLORATIONS OF THE RED RIVER, shows men so attired. These skirts, referred to as "matchcoats" from the Indian word *matshigode*, were sometimes a mosaic of mallards' neckskins, brilliantly green and exquisitely beautiful.

MISSES' SKIRTS

Tiny children and boys in the gardening area, as elsewhere, went naked — at least for every day — but young girls in Louisiana wore ankle-lengths skirts — a kind of *hula-hula* fringe — attached to wide, lacy girdles fitted tightly round the stomach and edged, above and below, with heavy braided cords. As described by Du Pratz, the four ends of these cords were brought together and tied in one knot at the back, streamers, ended with acorns, dropping from the knot.

THE ACORN

The acorn had a magical significance for women concerned with fertility. Note the importance of the acorn in the legend of the Birth of God and compare with its several uses in women's dress.

Tattooed Charms

The faces and breasts, and sometimes the entire persons of the gardening women — not the Plains women — were often elaborately tattooed, the underjaws bearing particular designs thought to ward off toothache. Patterns on the bosom, as pictured in old books or described in old chronicles, invariably consist of circles and rays — evidence that the breasts symbolized twin Suns, or Moons.

Charlevoix says of the gardeners in Louisiana: "They covered their bodies, both men and women, with figures of birds, animals, leaves, and flowers," by holding the skin stretched tight and tracing the design with coloring matter, then pricking it with fish bones "till they drew blood." The perforations thus achieved were filled with charcoal and other pigments. The tiny wounds swelled and formed scabs, which eventually dropped away, leaving the design clear and everlasting on the anatomy — though the operation often resulted in fevers and sometimes in death.

Espinosa comments of the *Tejas* women that they "had a line down the middle of their faces" — a line appearing in the descriptions of nearly all southern women. Joutel carries the description of tattooing among the *Tejas* much further, practically repeating Charlevoix: "The men are generally handsome, but disfigure themselves by making scores or streaks on their faces from the top of the forehead down the nose to the tip of the chin, which is done by pricking the skin with sharp implements till it bleeds, whereupon they strew the pricked places with finely powdered charcoal which sinks into the skin and mixes with the blood. They also make, after the same manner, the figures of living creatures, of leaves and of flowers, on their shoulders, thighs, and other parts of their bodies, tinting themselves with black or red, and sometimes both."

117

"The women are generally well-shaped but they disguise themselves as much as the men, not only with the streak they make, like the men, down their faces, but by other figures they make on it — at the corners of their eyes, and on other parts of their bodies, whereof they make most particular show on their bosoms, and those who have the most tattooing on their persons are reckoned the handsomest!"

Adair tells us "tattooing was practiced by the Indians generally"; the ink differing — some peoples using charred box-elder, and others the dripping of rich pine roots; the pricking was done with sharp flint points, sharpened bones, or gar's teeth; and, in the west, with cactus spines, most tribes boasting at least one person expert in the art.

Du Pratz informs us that with the masculine portion of the population, military honors were recorded on the skin, tattooing setting forth a man's rank; and Adair assures us that those who secretly assumed insignia to which they were not entitled by the Warrior's Award were invariably apprehended and forced to undergo the discomfort of having it removed.

De Solis, whose observations among the *Karankawa* tally in detail with those of Charlevoix in Louisiana and Joutel in East Texas, interprets the designs worn by women as indicative of virginity, or the reverse, increasing elaboration signifying the development of sex life.

MAGIC IN THE PAINT POT

Besides tattooing, the Indian, on occasion, covered his face and limbs with dyes and colored earths, worked up like startling carnival masks. The uses of this overlay were several:

The designs were magical, intended to secure success in the hunt or other project.

The colors were evidence of intent, whether peaceful or war-like.

Color and design disclosed to what Tribe or Nation a man belonged.

The overlay served as a foil for mosquitoes, ticks, and other insect pests.

It hid the emotions.

It concealed personal identity — a possible means of escape from the Blood Right defined in THE LAW OF THE LAND.

"Paint" was applied with the use of a mirror if one were obtainable, and C. C. Jones suggests that the blocks of mica often found in burials served this purpose. It is also possible that thin sheets of copper served as reflectors.

Outsiders residing among Indians say the natives invariably calcimined their countenances when strangers were known to be approaching; and, needless to remark, never left home without the protection of such disguise.

LANGUAGE OF COIFFURE AND PERIWIG

After tattooing and painting, perhaps hairdressing spoke most eloquently of achievement and position among the gardeners. The women of these Nations — unlike the Plains women who were obliged to crop their hair on their marriage day — took pride in abundant locks, oiling and ornamenting them, wearing them "banged" across the front, long and loose, or braided, according, probably, to age, maidenhood, matronage or widowhood.

Braids, among the *Tejas,* were held in place by tie-backs of red-dyed rabbit skin, say the Spanish; while Du Pratz describes lace bands of mulberry fibre, ending with acorn tassels, in Louisiana. Charlevoix says women wearing their hair loose on fete days powdered it with vermilion, and those wearing long single braids sheathed them in shining, iridescent Snake skins.

Men's headdresses are described with even more elaborate detail. "They cut their hair in many different ways," says Sanchez, a Spanish traveller, speaking of Indians seen at a great assembly in East Texas; while Espinosa tells us of the *Tejas*: "They do not wear their hair long, but bobbed to two finger-lengths, all very much alike and carefully combed. They leave a thin lock long in the middle to which they tie certain very beautiful plumes in a very curious manner. In this way each one looks like a sprout! They keep these plumes most carefully in a chest, so as to wear them always at their brightest."

Du Pratz says it was a mark of special distinction when a man was allowed to wear the beautiful plumes of the egret attached to his long, thin "top-knot" — plumes that, now, would be worth more than their weight in gold at Paris shops.

Powdering the hair with swansdown was a favorite ceremonial device.

TAIL PIECES

Not only did a man's headdress and make-up serve to set forth his position and fame, but, according to the old chroniclers, feather medallions or bouquets of flowers attached to the back flaps of breechclouts also indicated achievement or social position.

PENDANTS AND OTHER ORNAMENTS

The *Tejas* "hang long, smooth bones from the lobes of their ears," says De Solis; while Adair states that both men and women in Louisiana wore coarse native "diamonds," such as quartz crystals from the Arkansas Hot Springs, each having "a bit of stone fastened with a deer's sinew to the tying of their hair, their nose, ears, or their moccasins." Similar crystals are found in Texas burials.

"The Indian females," Adair goes on, "continually wear a beaded string round their legs made of buffalo hair . . . and they reckon it a great ornament, as well as a preservative against miscarriages, hard labour, and other evils."

120

Charlevoix informs us that though women wore ear-drops, necklaces, bracelets, anklets, and rings, nose pendants were worn only by men. Adair also comments on the moderation of women's vanity saying that they contented themselves with piercing the earlobe in several places for the reception of bone pendants, crystals, and pearls; but that ambitious young men frequently cut almost entirely around the ear — so that the extended loop actually flapped on the shoulder with its weight of tooth, claw, and feather trophies.

Occasionally these ear-loops were torn from the head in hunting accidents or in rough play, and then the distressed victim was hard put to it for a means of repairing his dis-figurement. Sometimes his elders succeeded in mending the torn lobe with deer sinew, if only one end were loose; but where they could not, it was necessary to shear away the fragments, leaving an everlasting deformity.

Says Sanchez, speaking again of the Indian assembly seen in the Red Lands: "Some wear a bunch of silver rings joined with lead and suspended from the nose, hanging over the mouth. The *Caddo* commonly wear a medal more than two inches in diameter, and they have the entire lobe of the ear pierced with holes in which to place beads or feathers. Others, in place of ornaments, wear well-cured heads of birds." An effigy from the Spiro Mound, on display at the Philbrook Museum in Tulsa, Oklahoma, shows a buffalo horn inserted in each ear-loop. The smoothly closed cut end is toward the face, with the horn turned down and back.

There were, according to some chroniclers, persons so extreme as to thrust live and wriggling serpents through the perforations in their ears — small, bright-colored snakes that constantly contorted themselves about the faces of their wearers!

Caddo, according to Hodge's HANDBOOK OF THE AMERICAN INDIAN, means "pierced nose" — the verbal name having grown out of a gesture in the sign language indicative of a people distinguished by their nose ornaments.

121

Adjuncts to the Dance

At fiesta time, particular mention is made by all observers concerning the terrapin shell rattles used by the women and the feather fans used by the men as adjuncts to ceremonial dancing, especially during the Green Corn Festival.

Of the women's rattles, Adair says: "They wear also a heap of land tortoise-shells with pebbles or beads in them, fastened to pieces of deerskin, which they tie to the outside of their legs, when they mix with the men in their religious dances."

He also mentions the brand new pair of white buckskin moccasins always fashioned by the priest who actually struck New Fire — moccasins for use on this occasion and never to be donned again, destined to become, thereafter, relics in the holy junk heap, alongside other broken or discarded articles still too full of magical essence to be idly scattered among an uninsulated laity. These moccasins, supplementing the snow-white sacerdotal costume that "tied like a figure eight" behind, were painted red for about three inches on the toes and further ornamented with a cluster of clicking "turkey cock spurs."

Says Bartram, continuing the story of "women's wear": The "leather stockings" of the *Creek* women were "hung full of the hoofs of the roedeer, in form of bells, in so much as to make them sound exactly like castanets." One witness counted as many as four hundred and ninety-three pairs of "horn-bells" attached to one pair of "dancing stockings." Terrapin shells, like those described by Adair, containing beans, pebbles, or dried corn, supplemented these dancing stockings, but were worn suspended from the waist. Outdoorsmen today still ship the *Pueblos* turtle shells from the Gulf Coast for their dances.

Payne says of the performance he witnessed: "A selected number of the dancers wore under their robes, and girded upon their calves, large squares of thick leather, covered all over with terrapin-shells closed together and perforated and filled with pebbles, which rattled like so many sleigh bells."

The men taking part in the ceremonial dancing kept the time with wide-spread, feather fans, which, according to Payne and other authorities, it was their custom to carry on all occasions of a dignified nature.

The museum collections of the University of Texas contain a number of the perforated tortoise shells that once lent liveliness to the festivals of the Piney Woods as well as many other items of significance of the unlimited "vanity" of the ancient villagers; but the lovely, graceful feather fans that pointed the measures of the *mitotes,* despite the care bestowed upon them by the Indians, have long since shattered into dust. However, one such specimen, recovered in another state, is minutely described under ARTS AND CRAFTS.

ASINAI CACIQUES'S ROBE OF STATE AND WOMAN'S MOSS REBOSA

XIII
Arts and Crafts

An Indian chieftain visiting in Washington, D. C., once said:

"I revere the ingenuity of the white man's mind, but I loathe the avarice of his heart!"

No Monopolies

Knowledge of any invention among the Indians was immediately distributed, use of the technique spreading through Tribe or Nation, and on to strangers. Only the priest caste had its secrets. Other men who obtained more than ordinary wealth did so through ability in craftsmanship — which enabled them to trade with neighbors or visitors — and not by a monopoly obtained through the invention of a particular process.

The southern nations were primarily gardeners; but, besides horticulture, they were skilled in pottery-making, in tanning, in weaving, and in featherwork. They did some woodwork, and a small amount of carving on bone.

Fire the Principal Tool

Carving and wood-shaping were achieved principally through erosion of Fire — the charring followed by gouging and scraping with tools of stone, shell, or bone. Since there was little rock suitable for cutting edges in the Gulf area, and no metals at all except a small amount of pure copper secured in trade for ornamental purpose, Fire was the sole available medium for felling trees and shaping heavy timbers.

THE BOAT BUILDERS

Hariot tells us the Indians "mashed" the fibres at the tree base with their blunt tools, rather than "cut" them, and then built a bonfire about the bruised section. Du Pratz tells us the ground stone celts with which such work was done often cost a lifetime of labor and were handed down as heirlooms from father to son.

Such axes were hafted by binding them into the slit stems of growing saplings so that the living wood was forced to clamp down on them through natural growth. When the hafting was complete, a matter of months, or perhaps years, the handle was cut away, top and bottom, and the celt ready for use. Many of those secured by the University of Texas show the effect of constant sharpening; and much used grindstones — flat slabs with abrasive surfaces — frequently accompany them in the burials.

Getting back to boat building — once the tree was down, according to Hariot, the limbs were burned off by Fires kindled next to the trunk. Says Bartram, "I have seen trunks of these trees (cypresses) that would measure eight, ten, and twelve feet in diameter for forty and fifty feet straight shaft." Hariot tells us that when the trunk was free of branches, it was mounted on trestles made of boughs laid across crotched uprights; there it was worked into shape with Fire and scrapers. The Fire, built on top of the log and forced to eat out the wood till the proper hollowness appeared, was controlled by mud packs, so that no part of the shell became too thin.

Of the worth of such craft, Bartram says; "These Indians (near Tallahassee) have large handsome canoes which they form out of the trunks of cypress trees, some of them commodious enough to accommodate twenty or thirty warriors. In these large canoes they descend the river on trading and hunting expeditions on the neighboring islands and keys, quite to the point of Florida and sometimes across the gulf, extending their navigations to the Bahama Islands and even to Cuba."

This description compares with that given by the Gentleman of Elvas and by Father Membres in THE LEAGUE OF NATIONS.

The Mortars

Having a scarcity of flat stones for *metates* such as were commonly used in west Texas, and no stone ledges in which to bore "potholes," the agricultural Indian made mortars from sections of logs, using a technique similar to that for the canoes, or *pirogues*. Fire was started on top of a log block or a length of log — there seem to have been two patterns — and forced to eat downward, with the rim of the log protected by packed earth. Once the wood was charred, it was a simple matter to scrape out the "bowl" with stone or shell tools. In this burned-out chunk, grain was crushed with wooden pestles and sieved through a colander of woven bamboo splits. The Spanish explorers, say one of their chroniclers, indignified themselves to the extent of sieving meal with their chain mail. Of the use of mortars, Lawson says: "The . . . men never beat their corn to make bread, but that is the women's work, especially the girls, of whom you shall see four beating with long great pestils in a narrow wooden mortar, and everyone keeps her stroke so exactly, that tis worthy of admiration."

The Four-Legged Stools

Presumably the small, four-legged stools, "made all in one piece," that were seen in both Texas and Louisiana received the same treatment as the canoes and the mortars — the legs taking shape from a log by means of Fire.

THE COLOSSI

Due, presumably, to their lack of adequate cutting implements, the southern Indians did very little decorative carving, though several of the early travellers express great amazement at the sight of colossal wooden figures seen in and about the Temples. Sometimes these were simply columns; sometimes they were human or Serpent forms, crudely shaped; none of them seem to have survived till the present time.

MASKS

Masks used in religious ritual were often made from mosaic of gourd chips, Adair and Lawson tell us. The Spanish missionaries mention cowls and face coverings of leather employed by Indian priests.

Collections of wooden masks, assembled to make up the characters in portrayal of Nature Myths — ritualistic theatricals with a deep underlying philosophy — still exist. Such a treasure of antiquity has been produced in color film by courtesy of the Museum of Natural History in Ottawa, Canada. In this pantomimed story, THE LOON'S NECKLACE, the music is as "other world" as the mimicry depicting the blind Indian philosopher; his victory over his tribal enemies, the wolves; and his achievement of sight through association with his guardian spirit — or his Totem Animal — the loon.[1]

THE BOW AND ARROW

Going from articles of religious ritual to weapons — a natural sequence — war being a part of religion in Indian society, as well as elsewhere — we find that flint usually had to be acquired in trade; hence, the arrows of the southern agriculturalists were generally tipped with some other material. The smallest arrows, those used for birds, were of sharpened bamboo; again, the tips of wooden arrows were hardened in the Fire and scraped to a point. Du Pratz tells us war arrows were tipped with the sharp, enameled scales of alligator gars abounding in southern waters; and also that fish glue was used to hold the points and the feathering in place.

The bows were long, as compared with the Plains bows used later by "horse" Indians. Bows in Louisiana are said to have been made of acacia wood, and bowstrings woven of bark from the same tree.

Although many Indians themselves look upon the "stone age" of flint chipping as far back in their ancestral history, quotations given in Chapter XXIX indicate that the use of flint arrowheads was an emergency measure outside the timbered areas so long as the bow and arrow was in use as a defensive weapon.

POTTERY

Pottery was moulded by hand or shaped in clay coils on a basket foundation and the basket burned away. Designs on bowls, bottles, and jars — all known by the common name of "pots" in the archaeology laboratory where they are mended and restored — were cut in with the finger nail or a sharp bit of shell, or were appliqued with rolls of soft clay put on before firing. *Asinai* and *Caddo* pottery differs from the *Pueblo* of today in carving on of the design in preference to painting with colored earths or "slip." A good pottery smoothing stone was a household treasure. Such stones are frequently found in women's burials. Presence of pots in burials, often deliberately smashed to "let the spirit out," is explained in ORIGIN AND IMMORTALITY.

BASKETRY

Basketry, though none has been found in the burials, due to its perishability, was made in plenty by the southern Indians, including large panniers, which, when loaded, were attached to headbands or to collars of bear skin painted white. The uses and beauty of the matting produced have been amply demonstrated in THE HOUSE OF STRAW. Further discussion of this art occurs in uses of bamboo listed in THE GARDEN PATCH.

LA BARBA ESPAÑOL

Prime among raw materials from which the Indian constructed necessities and luxuries was the gray southern moss, christened by incoming Europeans *La Barba Español* — Spanish Beard.

Women made a graceful shawl, or *rebosa,* of this material, a kind of fringed garland worn over the left shoulder and draped round the opposite hip, a pattern shown to be customary in VANITIES OF THE VILLAGERS. They also invariably wore, as much for decent covering as otherwise, a vaginal pad of moss secured with a string belt.

Moss, in packs, was used on the babies' cradle boards in lieu of diapers; and both Adair and Lawson comment on the rigid cleanliness observed in child care. Head-flattening, performed on the infants of many Nations, was accomplished by wooden frames attached to the cradle boards and kept from bruising the forehead by means of moss padding. According to Du Pratz, the mosspadded "cribs" in Louisiana were regular bassinets, woven of cane, with canopies over bamboo bows. They were made to rock from end to end, instead of, as was the European fashion, from side to side.

Mattresses and cushions, covered with ticks of softly tanned deer skin or of buffalo hide, were stuffed with the inner black fibre of Spanish moss — presumably prepared by burying quantities of fresh moss until the silvery gray outer covering rotted, leaving a material similar to horse hair. Such mattresses, with cloth ticks instead of buckskin, are in constant use in creole New Orleans today; and it was once a regular duty of plantation slaves along the Atlantic seaboard to prepare moss fibre for wrapping young fruit trees in winter — one of many useful practices acquired from the Indians.[2]

129

INDIANS OF THE SOUTHWEST

CLOTH

As to the production of cloth in the Gulf region, a white fibre from young mulberry sprouts was a basis of mantles, breechclouts, and skirts.

Several persons have left us detailed descriptions of the weaving process. Says Du Pratz: "Many of the women wear cloaks made of the bark of the mulberry tree, or of the feathers of swans, turkeys, or ducks. They take the mulberry bark from sprouts rising from the roots of cut trees. They are very careful to clip these sprouts before the sap rises. After the bark is dried in the sun they beat it to make all the woody part fall off, and they give the threads that remain a second beating, after which they bleach them by exposing them to the dew. When the threads are well whitened, the women spin them to about the coarseness of pack thread and weave them in the following manner: they plant two stakes in the ground, about a yard and a half asunder, and having stretched a cord from one to the other, they fasten to it double threads of bark which they then interweave in a curious manner to make a cloak of about a yard square with a wrought border round the edges."

Another observer tells us a rope run through the warp, ahead of the shuttle, was used to facilitate weaving.

FEATHERWORK

Feather cloth, used for both mantles and blankets, was the most sumptuous of Indian manufactures, commanding the wonder and admiration of all European beholders. Of its production, Adair says, concerning the *Choctaw*: "They twist the inner end of the feathers very fast into a strong double thread of hemp, or the inner bark of the mulberry tree, of the size and strength of coarse twine, as the fibres are sufficiently fine, and they work it in the manner of fine netting."

True gorgeousness in Indian attire was invariably achieved with feathers. Though feather articles and ornaments ranged from martial headdresses and banners to fans, the technical construction of all was fundamentally the same, Feathers were attached to cords, or to stitches in foundation material, by sharpening the quill ends below a slit, softening the quills, and turning the points back over the cord, or over stitches, then inserting the points in the slits, thus forming loops. The connection formed by the point and slit was then bound with fibre, and the feathers further tacked or bound in place as required for a given pattern.

C. C. Jones tells us of a fan found in a Tennessee burial: It was "formed of the tail feathers of a turkey. The points of these feathers were curiously bound by a buckskin string, well dressed, and were thus closely bound for about one inch from the points. About three inches from the point they were again bound by another deer skin string, in such a manner that the fan might be closed and expanded at pleasure. Between the feathers and this last binding by the string, were placed, around each feather, hairs which seem to have been taken from the tail of a deer. This hair was dyed of a deep scarlet red."

It is to be assumed that these Indians, like other Indian craftsmen, wore one fingernail long and sharpened. The Indians of southern Mexico used this long, sharp nail to cut patterns in lacquer. It would serve as well to trim and slit feather quills softened in hot water.

DYESTUFFS

Speaking of colors, "They obtain vermilion," says Captain Ramón, "and use it freely in decorating their tanned leather. They have excellent dyes which they use for their clothing, the blue in particular being very fine. The green comes from a cuprous metal. They know of an herb or wood (probably black walnut) so good and so strong that the deerskins they color with it have the appearance of black velvet."

Commonest in use among the Indians for coloring their goods were red and yellow ochres and white clay from local

Earth pits. These, together with charcoal, they applied as calcimines. They also had innumerable vegetable dyes with which to color their goods, such as the vivid yellow of the *Osage* orange.

TANNING

Tanning, being the principal art of the Plains women, will be discussed in connection with the *Comanche,* except for a trick or two mentioned by Lawson. The gardening women, says he, baked deer brains into bricks among the embers, laying them aside to be dissolved in water when needed for preparing skins. If this substance was exhausted, green corn, beaten to a pulp, was used for the same purpose.

THE CULINARY ART

Besides their ability as potters, weavers, and tanners, the women of the southern villages were particularly ingenious cooks, devising all manner of recipes for their wide variety of foodstuffs. Lawson says they cooked all day long; while Adair pays a glowing tribute to the cuisine: "It is surprising to see the great variety of dishes they make out of wild flesh, corn, beans, peas, potatoes, pompions (pumpkins), dried fruits, herbs, and roots. They can diversify their courses, as much as the English, or perhaps the French cooks; and either of the ways they dress their food, it is grateful to a human stomach.

"In July when the chestnuts and corn are green and fullgrown, they half-boil the former, and take off the rind; and having sliced the milky, swelled long rows of the latter, the women pound it in a large wooden mortar, which is wide at the mouth and gradually narrows to the bottom; then they knead both together, wrap them up in green corn blades of various sizes, about an inch thick, and boil them well as they do every kind of seethed food.

"This sort of bread is very tempting to the taste, and is reckoned most delicious by the Indians themselves.

"They have a great deal of fruit, and they dry such kinds as will bear it. At the fall of the leaf, they gather a number of hickory nuts, which they pound with a round stone, upon (another) stone, thick and hollowed out for the purpose.

"When they are beat fine enough, they mix them with cold water, in a clay basin, where the shells subside. The other part is an oily, tough, thick white substance, (which the Indians call the 'fat' of hickory nuts) with which they eat their bread.

"They have another sort of boiled bread, which is mixed with beans, or potatoes (tubers). (To make this) they put on the soft corn till it begins to boil, and pound it sufficiently fine. . . . When the flour is stirred and dried by the heat of the sun or fire they sift it with sieves of different sizes, curiously made of the coarser or finer cane splinters.

"The thin cakes mixed with bear oil were formerly baked on thin stones placed over a fire or on broad earthen bottoms fit for such a use. . . . When they intend to bake great loaves, they make a strong blazing Fire, with short dry split wood, on the hearth. When it is burnt down to coals, they carefully rake them off to each side, and sweep away the remaining ashes: then they put their well-kneaded loaf, first steeped in hot water, over the hearth, and an earthen basin above it, with the embers and coals atop. This method of baking is as clean and efficacious as could possibly be done in any oven; when they take it off, they wash the loaf with warm water and it soon becomes firm, and very white. It is likewise very wholesome, and well-tasted to any except the vitiated palate of an epicure.

"When the pompions are ripe, they cut them into long circling slices, which they barbecue or dry with a slow heat. And when they have half-boiled the larger sort of potatoes, they likewise dry them over a moderate fire, and chiefly use them in the spring season, mixed with their favorite bear oil.

"As soon as the larger sort of corn is full-eared, they half-boil it too, and dry it, either by the Sun, or over a slow Fire. . . . This they boil with venison, or any other unsalted flesh."[3]

Of the "cold meal" which gave rise to one of the regular feast days among the southern gardeners, W. B. Parker says, "cold flour is a preparation of corn. It is first parched, then pounded, and according to taste, a little sugar mixed with it. A handful of this will make a pint of gruel upon which a man may subsist for twenty-four hours." (The Indian had no sugar, but perhaps used "sweetening" of honey, maple sugar acquired in trade, or dried fruits.)

It was from the Indian that the white American learned the use of hominy, "cold meal" and other corn preparations, which, together with venison and honey, kept many a pioneer family alive through months on end.

American life of today, having passed through several centuries of close association with the "red man" and the Red Man's country, is infinitely more obligated to him for the free use of his ancient methods and his inventions than the average citizen can be brought to realize.

FOOTNOTES

[1] See Bibliography — LOON'S NECKLACE — for securing picture in 16 mm film.

[2] An entire moss industry was bequeathed to the Gulf Coast through Indian uses of Spanish moss. The Louisiana "Cajun" (the French-Indian Acadian driven by the English from the Canadian province of Acadia) has a laddered *pirogue* specially built for moss gathering, and the "moss gin" is of frequent appearance through the Texas Big Thicket and all the way to Hallettsville, in South Texas. After the "green" (uncured) moss has been wet down and buried to rot off its grey covering, the remaining black fibres are put through a cleansing blower and then baled, like hay, for sale to upholsterers. Trucks from the best firms in Houston and other cities can be seen any time waiting to load this

product. Their experts declare moss fibre to be equal with
horse hair in fine furniture making. Wisps of the stuff
strung on barbed wire fences around Liberty, Texas, to dry
remind the traveler on the highway of Amy Lowell's poetic
fit:

> I cannot bear
> This dead man's hair
> Hanging everywhere!

Flower beds in local towns covered with the uncured
moss are reminiscent of Indian gardens protected from the
cutting edge of the coastal "norther" — an adaptation (for
a northwind) of the Spanish term: *El Norte!*

[3] In using a mortar, two women stood opposite each
other with it between them. Each operated a wooden pestle
as tall as herself, that looked like an ear. Their standing
position and cooperative labor made a far less toilsome task
of preparing breadstuff than the use of the flat *metate* and
mano (tablestone and handstone) which women west of the
Trinity, exclusive of the Pueblos, used, kneeling on the
ground.

The "bread line" between the *tortilla* as the staple bread
form, cooked on the *comal* or heated flagstone, and the
oven-baked "pone" (adopted by the Anglos as "cornbread")
ran between the two-mile-long Comal River (on which
New Braunfels is located, and which is said to be the shortest
river in the world) and the Trinity River; always keeping
in mind that the *Jumana*, as ex-patriate timber Indians,
occupied the small, fertile valleys all the way down to the
mouth of the Rio Grande, and built their beehive ovens
there. (See Footnote 1, Page 190.)

XIV

The Law of the Land

"They owned this vast continent, and had possessed it for ages exceeding in time the ability of the human mind to conceive."

Cushman.

THE VILLAGE HIERARCHY

The *Caddo* Nations west of the Mississippi and the Nine Nations of the *Asinai* were gathered into two confederacies which were, in turn, interleagued through permanent treaty under the Pipe. All nations had their petty chieftains *(caciques)* who were subject in rank to the overlords or "Suns" of the confederacies.

Acting as an advisory body to the petty, or national chieftain, and to the high priest, who, in the social whirl, stood second, if not actually first, in civil authority, was the Council of Elders, or "old beloved men," in whom the Mound Builders, like most other American Indians, believed to be concentrated the wit and wisdom of their communities.

C. C. Jones, in ANTIQUITIES OF THE AMERICAN INDIAN, tells us this body convened every forenoon in the public square for the consideration of civic problems, both foreign and local, administrative and judicial.

Under the petty chiefs, say the Spanish Fathers, were

heralds and sub-heralds, or town criers, who made the official rulings of the Chief and Council known to the populace; while under-ranking the heralds were two grades of police whose especial duty was the enforcement of announced ordinances. A part of the work of these individuals has already been set forth in chapters dealing with community projects, namely, THE HOUSE OF STRAW and THE GARDEN PATCH.

It was the extreme privilege of the highest ranking herald, according to the early French and Spanish in Texas and Louisiana, to hand the civil, or hereditary chieftain his lighted Pipe each morning as he appeared in his doorway to greet the Dawn — the official salutation to the Sun which included bowing, chanting, and the customary smoke ritual as discussed in detail under THE PEACE PIPE.

"The peace and harmony among the officials is so great," says Casanas, in his LETTERS, "that during the year and a quarter we have been among the *Tejas* we have not seen any quarrels, either great or small; but the insolent and lazy are punished!"

THE FUNCTIONS OF THE COUNCIL

The Council, which was the hub of the government, just as the public square was the hub of the village, served, in foreign affairs, as an executive cabinet, and, in local affairs, as the village tribunal.

Acting with the hereditary chieftain who ordinarily presided over its deliberations, except in the case of a minor heir, when the Body of Elders acted as regent, the Council considered all diplomatic procedure with other Tribes, Nations, and Confederacies, deciding such questions as the making of peace, war, or proposed treaty connections.

Acting with the high priest, who was Weather Prophet and interpreter of the divine will, as set forth in THE MAGIC ART, the Council decided all questions of community welfare such as when to make foreign hunting excursions, when to plant crops, and when to bring the harvest in.

137

Acting as the local tribunal, the Council arbitrated all disputes between citizens, received reports of marriages, and assessed fines and punishments.

The most common activities of the two classes of police, according to the early Christian Fathers, were the overseeing of public works ordered by the Council and the administering of punishments affixed by the Council — the latter usually comprising public whippings applied with plaited lashes, so many strokes for each misdemeanor.

INDIAN COMMON LAW

Common law, as it existed among all the Indians of North America, Plains Tribes and agricultural Nations alike, may be summed up under three main heads: the Land Law, Tribal Law and the Blood Right.

LAND LAW

The universal Land Law is simple enough to define. The land belonged to the tribe or nation as a whole; and the tribe or nation was sovereign over its land. No member of another tribe or nation might set foot thereon save at his own risk unless he came with the proper signals, particularly the Peace Pipe, in hand.

Among the agricultural nations, a man's holdings in real estate, consisting of a homesite and gardens, were definitely secured to him by what amounted to an unwritten lease, the tenure dependent upon acceptable civic conduct. So long as he chose to occupy the land where he was settled, he could not be removed therefrom, except by banishment. To remove at his own pleasure, however, according to Cushman, meant instant termination of his unwritten lease; and the spot was open for other occupancy.

The Indian attitude toward the ownership of land, forever irreconcilable with that of the invading white man, is best expressed in the word of Tecumseh, the great *Shawnee* sage: "What! Sell land! As well air and water! The Great

Spirit gave them in common to all — the air to breathe, the water to drink, and the land to live upon — you may as well sell air and water as sell land!"

TRIBAL LAW

Tribal Law, tantamount to ethics in modern legal systems, varied with the people concerned, having developed, in each case, largely from the relation of a given group to its habitat. It may well be separated into two parts, one dealing with magical relations and having all the force of law, but better considered under the head of religion; and the other dealing with political and social organization, or local government.

Among the gardening nations, Tribal Law, aside from magic, seems to have been mainly concerned with public works, including the building of houses and the planting of fields; with marriage; and with the awarding of distinctions and honors, particularly military awards.

THE MARRIAGE BOND

A description of the formal marriage ceremony (a woman's first marriage, or the putting aside of virginity) was given in THE SOCIAL WHIRL. So far as continuity of the marriage bond was concerned, both men and women seem to have been free to break away at will, each taking another companion with no further obligation than announcement to the Council. In such cases, according to Lawson, "all the children go along with the mother, and none with the father" — so, presumably, if it were the man who deserted, the woman returned to her father's house, accompanied by her offspring. And if it were she who acquired a new mate, she and the children removed to his abode.

Polygamy, though allowable by the law of the land, appears to have flourished only in the highest caste of the social system.

Infidelity to the marriage bond, among the agriculturists,

seems to have been taken with little seriousness; far less so, indeed, than among the "wild" or nomad tribes of the Plains. Espinosa declares: "Not only are the women of these nations loose in their conduct, but their husbands appear to take little notice of the fact." However this statement, though confirmed by many witnesses, is usually qualified to the effect that among better class people the standard of marriage was on a different plane — was, in fact, as high as marriage standards anywhere, polygamy notwithstanding; for polygamy, it will be remembered, flourishes in many aristocracies.

THE BLOOD RIGHT

Ranking in universality with the communistic Land Law of North America was the Blood Right, the only established form of criminal law among Indians. Says Cushman, speaking of the southern Nations: "It was their ancient practice to leave the murderer in the hands of the murdered man's relatives and friends; and, as 'an eye for an eye and a tooth for a tooth' was their inviolable custom, he was sooner or later most certain to fall by an unseen hand."

By this reckoning, the death of the first murderer at once laid upon his blood kin the unshirkable duty of destroying those who punished the original crime. Thus, in spite of a sincere love for peace, there was eternal strife going on in one quarter or another of the Mound Builder League day in and day out — as may be better understood from THE WARRIOR'S AWARD.

In order to put a check on this disastrous feudism, various specific measures were resorted to by the Councils — measures very similar to those in vogue in Europe prior to the development of criminal law.

First among these, says Adair, was the alternative of material compensation, or, as the Indians expressed it, "wiping away tears with gifts." If the relatives of the man whose blood was spilt could be satisfied in this manner, well and good, the feud was at an end.

140

Second among efforts at pacifism, also according to Adair, was the establishment of White Towns — villages especially set aside for refuge — where it was forbidden to shed human blood. A hunted man, entering these sacred precincts, was safe so long as he remained within the walls.

Totemism

To understand the working of the Blood Right or *Lex Talomis,* it is necessary to understand some special terminology, and particularly necessary to understand the term Totemism.

Spanish discoverers of America used the Indian term *Cacique* (cass-sée-kay) to distinguish the hereditary ruling rank among highly civilized gardening nations from the more or less competitively selected chieftains of the Plains tribes. This was true through Mexico and the Caribbean area as well as through our own Deep South. The related term *Montesuma,* or Over Sun, corresponds exactly to the European term "Sun King," which was last flaunted by Louis XIV of France. In southwestern terminology, *cacique* applies correctly to all villagers, or sedentary Indian peoples, from the *Pueblos* to the Mound Builders; and "chieftain" applies correctly to the nomadic peoples of the Plains, particularly those Buffalo Hunters, or *Ciboleros,* who are also referred to by the Spanish as *Los Indios del Norte.*

A note is appropriate here to the effect that *tecas* is a term meaning "the people" and that when affixed to a folk name, as *Toltecas* or *Aztecas,* it refers to a people as a whole — a feminine concept deriving from Totemism, which was once the world-wide religious concept of human reproduction; in Totemism, only maternal descent was humanly recognized — the "spirit" of the to-be-born was assumed to have entered the mother's body from some supernatural source. Thus a child always had a human mother but its "father" might be a star, a duck, a flower — or even the Sun. In the case of a ruling *cacique,* the spiritual ancestor or

141

Totem of the clan, as several times pointed out, was assumed to have been the Wind. Now, though *teca* is a feminine ending, and *tecas* refers to a whole people, *teco* is masculine and *tecos* refers to the manpower of a people, so that the *Toltecos* were the organized military of the *Toltecas*. By the same linguistic reckoning, *Ciboleros* refers to Plains military described in Chapter XV.

Totemism must always be kept in mind in dealing with any set of culture traits, including our own. For we, like the American Indian, who was also aware of paternal procreation, are the inheritors of primal social patterns that evolved before mankind made the tremendous, truly scientific discovery of "natural" procreation. Do we not continue to say, "Blood is thicker than water"? The Indian continued to recognize and honor his traditional totemic ancestor even though he knew perfectly well his own biological function as a human father.

How the Blood Right operated so as to involve whole Nations in war and break down old alliances is shown in the following chapter.

XV

The Warrior's Award

"There is no such thing among the Indians as desertion in war, because they do not fight . . . for hire, but for wreaths of swans feathers."

Adair.

SOUNDING THE TOCSIN

Adair says of armed conflict in the agricultural area: "The Indians are not fond of waging war with each other. . . . They consider with the greatest exactness and foresight all the attending circumstances of war. Should any of the young warriors, through forwardness, or passion, violate the treaty of peace, (with another nation) the (executives in the nation of the) aggressing party usually send, by some neutral Indians, a friendly embassy . . . (praying the injured ones to accept retribution equal to the injury), and to continue their friendship, assuring them that the rash, unfriendly action did not meet with the approbation, but was highly condemned by the head men of the whole nation (of the offending party.) If the proposal be accepted, the damage is made up, either by sacrificing one of the aggressors, (choosing one) of a weak family (in order to keep down the blood right feud) or by the death (of some adopted captive.)"

But if the injured nation refused to be appeased, Adair

tells us, a war chief in the nation of the offending party, having secured permission of the Council, at once set about to raise an invading host with which to make a counter-attack before the injured nation could put recruits on the vengeance trail. It was the purpose of each, once war was formally declared, to invade the other's territory rather than be invaded and suffer consequent destruction of personal and community property.

The War Pole

From constant references made to the War Pole by old writers, it would seem that every warrior who had attained the rank of chieftain or leader had such a pole, described by Adair as a small peeled tree, painted red, from which the limbs were lopped, leaving stubs.

When a chief was ready to enlist recruits for the sake of adding to his military renown, he hung his weapons and trophies, including scalps, on this pole and set it outside his door, together with the banner of war, described by Adair as a skin dyed red and raised on a pole — the "bloody colors marked with large strokes of black — grand war signal of blood and death!"

Having publicly and officially declared the opposing nation "a common enemy," and set forth the emblems of war to the public gaze, the ambitious leader marched three times round his house, going opposite to the direction of the Sun, beating upon his war drum and loosing from his lungs his war cry, in an effort to stimulate interest in his enterprise and to attract volunteers.

As he made his circular one-man-march, those among his audience who thirsted for martial achievement, rushed forward to strike his War Pole with their war clubs in token of desire to follow him upon the danger trail.

In the meantime, within the boundaries of the injured nation, a similar scene was being enacted, and even more vigor and eloquence poured out. Here, a war leader from the family of those slain by the original offenders was delivering, from beneath *his* War Pole, a speech to the effect that though their nation had consistently continued in friendly offices toward the offending people, these kindnesses "have been ungratefully returned with the blood of his kinsmen," and that "therefore as the white paths have changed their beloved colour, his heart burns within him . . . to tincture them along, and even to make them flow over with the hateful blood of the base contemptible enemy!"

Thus it came about that the Nations involved in the coming unpleasantness fell to purifying their warriors at the same time, each group betaking itself to the home of its acting chief who called in a Medicine Chief to supervise the magic ritual intended to frustrate the enemy before actual fighting began.

GETTING THE SPIRIT

Though bravery was greatly lauded among the southern Indians, Charlevoix tells us the outcome of war was entirely with the gods; hence, establishing the spiritual sanctity of the warriors was looked on as much more important than their keeping physically fit, for which reason almost the total preparation consisted of fasting, prayer, and magic ritual, intended to frustrate the enemy before actual fighting began.

Before starting the purification rites, says Du Pratz, the volunteers were treated to a very special feast intended to endow them with proper spirit for the enterprise. The magic viands served up in his presence were a great platter of cooked corn to give them strength, a haunch of venison to lend them fleetness of foot, and a baked dog to instill in them the instinct of following their leader with unquestioning loyalty.

This feast over, purification rites like those described in THE MAGIC ART took place, and pantomimic dances began,

145

under the direction of the Medicine Man. While the drinking of Yaupon Tea was in progress, the Medicine Chief tended the Fire on the hearth, offering it incense of tobacco and anointing it with bear oil. In the meantime the War Chief smoked his War Pipe to the World Quarters, to the Earth, and to the Sun in an effort to derive prophetic information concerning his martial project.

The Spanish Fathers located in East Texas tell us the dancing and fasting warriors gathered great handfuls of Smoke from the Fire and anointed their bodies on the assumption that this made their flesh impervious to the arrows of their enemies.

All the religious and magical dances of the Indians were pantomimic, often involving the use of masks calculated to replace the personality of the actor with that of the deity or spirit he imitated. Moreover the invariable accompaniment of these dances seems to have been the rhythm of the rattling calabash and the rolling of the drums — sounds reproductive, perhaps, of the infernal castanets of the tremendous rattlesnakes infesting the Gulf region and the thunderclaps of the frequent tropic storms. That both were regarded as extraordinarily dynamic supernatural phenomena is set forth in THE INDIAN PANTHEON.

Says Casanas, speaking of the *Tejas*: "In these dances — (the magical or pantomimic war dances) — they pray for strength to fight, for fleetness to run, and for valor to resist. They pray to the Fire, to the Air, to the Corn, to the Buffalo, and to the Deer. Every time a dance begins they are told what to pray for in that particular performance. They ask the game to permit itself to be killed for eating, (while they are on the trail). They ask the Water to drown their enemies, the Fire to burn them, the Arrows to kill them, and the Wind to blow them away!

" On the last day of such a meeting the chief comes forward and says to the warriors 'Think of your parents, and your children, but I charge you not to let them be a hindrance to our victory.' "

The nights, says Charlevoix, were spent in singing war songs and recounting deeds of valor; every man, as a part of the preparatory ritual, being obliged to chant from time to time his Death Song — the bold saga with which he steeled his spirit to meet the Tortures, should he fall, alive, into the hands of the enemy.

CAMOUFLAGE

Acting under the several restrictions necessary for military success — that is, partaking only of ceremonial food, purifying the flesh with fasting and vomitories, and fortifying the soul with eloquence, magic, and prayer — the candidates for military honors, having refitted their weapons, purged from them also, by rites and incantations, the unhealthful and weakening effects of female association received in the living quarters. They then set forth on their sacred expedition — the man with the smallest feet walking ahead, says Charlevoix, and the man with the largest feet bringing up the rear; each one carefully treading in the steps of the one before him, thus disguising the trail.

Adair tells of other maneuvers by which the trail was blurred. One was for the war party to spread out fan-wise, each member occasionally sounding the given "password" — the hoot of an owl or the bark of a squirrel — so, keeping in touch with those on either side, while leaving only a single trail to be discovered by an enemy scout. Again, the invaders, on reaching enemy territory, might put panther paws, bear paws, or deer hoofs over hands and feet, going through all the hunting or grazing motions of those animals, in order to throw the enemy off the scent.

THE WRATH OF GOD

The moment enemy territory was reached, Adair continues, a blazing torch was flung over the border, thus indicating the wrath of the Holy Fire toward the opposing people —and thus proving that the Indian's god was a tribal god whose maledictions were sure to descend upon the head of the tribal foe.

THE TOTEM AND THE ARK

Ahead of the war party went the Nation's palladium, carried in a chest of skins fashioned to fit the back of the individual designated and sanctified as assistant to the war leader. Following this all-important Medicine, according to Charlevoix, came the personal Totem of the War Chief, the emblem of his family or clan; and after it the Totems of all the other families in the party, each Totem suspended from or mounted on a lance sashed to the waist of a family representative.

Since the food of the crusaders had now to be regarded with extreme care, lest they take into their persons some unclean element, only that might be eaten or drunk which was prepared by the hands of the assistant appointed to perform this service, as well as to carry the powerful palladium.

Nor could rest be taken during the day save while standing bolt upright, lest the Medicine in the Ark, or the Fire, or the Sun take offense. Thus the consequence of going upon the war path, in the southern agricultural area, was to suffer as many "mortifications of the flesh" as a medieval monk in the most fanatic holy orders.

IN THE HANDS OF FATE

No guards were set over the camp at night, says Charlevoix, the outcome of the enterprise being out of man's control. Nevertheless, the participants were most earnest in the reading of auguries — natural signs and omens — by which they thought to keep in touch with the supernatural Powers; and a single discouraging dream or the sight of a scurrying animal was enough to send them all home again, pell-mell and posthaste, only too thankful to have escaped what would surely have been a disaster but for the timely warning sent from the gods.

THE WARRIOR'S AWARD

SATIATION OF THE BLOOD LUST

Once a killing was made, Adair declares, the blood lust was satiated, and the invaders ready to return home triumphant, refusing to pause for another attack, unless forced, even though the enemy should appear directly in their path.[1]

There was, indeed, says Adair, something thought to be distinctly unholy and unclean about the act of shedding blood, even in war; and those who were in the attacking party, on their return home, immediately underwent a purification rite lasting three days before they could mingle with the unsullied populace.

THE TORTURES A FORM OF SACRIFICE

Success in war usually meant captives, it being always the purpose of the attackers to secure captives if possible, rather than to slay outright, the result of taking captives being burnt offerings to the Sun who gave the victory. Says Cushman, "the odor of the sacrificial flesh of the tribal enemy was sweet to the nostrils of the tribal god!" Thus was human flesh, flavored with the condiments of tobacco and bear oil, the all-important sacrifice which the worshipers of the Sun offered to the object of their adoration.

The ancient chroniclers state that one of three destinies awaited the captive, depending on the age, the sex, and the personality of the individual. A child or a youth might be adopted into the Nation, and a woman taken to wife; but a man, a warrior, was almost certain to be put to the Torture. Contrary to the practice of the Plains Tribes whose warriors are said to have embraced every woman captive at the earliest opportunity, woman's chastity, due to the stringent laws concerning abstinence, was left undisturbed by the warriors of the agricultural area. Furthermore, the claim is made by persons who lived among the Indian Tribes and Nations that *Indian women* were never scalped — a custom, whether chivalrous or religious, not adhered to

149

after the terrible struggle for survival of the fittest began between the Indian and the white man.

The Torture most commonly practiced in the south — though not ordinarily by the Plains Tribes — seems to have required an upright square frame made with two poles crossed by bars at the top and bottom. On this rack the naked captive was stretched in the form of an X, or, as Du Pratz says, a St. Andrew's cross, feet bound to the poles at the lower corners and hands at the upper corners.

In position on this crucifixional contrivance, the captive was seared with flaming torches in the hands of his captors. Pieces of his flesh were torn away and eaten in lieu of the deity who was supposed to be devouring the spirit of the bound one. In other words, the feast was pantomimic, a dramatization of the spiritual feast of the Sun.

The scalp of one undergoing the Fire was always carefully preserved from injury by a daub of wet clay, so that it might be finally added to the trophy collection of the warrior responsible for the capture.

Where enemies were slain on the battlefield, it was customary with the gardening Indians to remove, not the scalp alone, but the whole head, which then became the object of peculiar ceremonies, or, in the words of Espinosa, who witnessed such rites in East Texas, "of ceremonies designed to prevent the angry ghosts from haunting the captors."[2]

He continues: "On occasions when these Indians gain a victory over their adversaries, they bring back the skulls as trophies and keep them hanging in a tree until they bury them. For this burial ceremony they gather on an appointed night, men and women, at the place where the skulls are.

"They build a number of bonfires, and having provided their sad and mournful instruments, (among them presumably the cayman described under THE CANNIBAL OF THE COAST) they arrange their singers and their bands of musicians painted black, seated on the ground with bowed heads, covered from top to toe with buffalo robes. These all sing together. The other performers dance without moving from the spot, the men and women in separate files. This dance lasts the greater part of the night.

"A very decrepit Indian, together with certain young Indians, forms a circle round the tree where the skulls are. Each has an arrow drawn in the same direction. They give a shout in unison. They turn and shout in the four cardinal directions, shooting from time to time toward the skulls.

"When morning comes they cover their faces and arms with white dirt (clay) and take the skulls to the Temple Ash Heap (cenizario) where they inter them. They spend the rest of the day celebrating at the Fire Temple. They offer food to the skulls which they eat themselves" — pantomimic eating, indicating that the spirit of the eaten thing was being spiritually devoured.

PENALTY OF DEFEAT

The Indian's philosophy had nothing to explain the loss of a battle except Bad Medicine, just as it had nothing to offer as a natural cause for death. Consequently, a defeated war leader was suspect of having personally profaned the war path, of having allowed the warriors to profane it, or of having failed to read auguries aright — hence he was in grave danger. If he did not lose his life on his return to the home community, he was certain to be reduced to boy's status, stripped of his War Pipe, drum, and other material insignia, with every step in rank to take over again if he were to recapture his lost prestige. A hazard which made a man think long before entering on, or continuing, upon the war path.

THE WIDOW'S PART

Somewhat illogically, it seems, should the leader lose his own life in conflict, he was honored as a national defender, and his widow required to sit in public mourning under his War Pole a whole Moon, remaining in seclusion for a period of years thereafter. She might be released from the latter obligation, Adair states, by becoming temporarily the wife of her husband's brother, after which she could legitimately and respectably become the wife of any man.

Even with these restrictions, the lady was lucky to have escaped being strangled and placed in the grave with the dead in order that her spirit might accompany his to the Other World.

THE CROIX DE GUERRE

The function of the warrior within the Nation, says Adair, is to "protect all, but not to molest or injure the meanest." Furthermore, "Every warrior holds his honor, and the love of his country, in so high esteem, that he prefers it to life, and will suffer the most exquisite tortures rather than renounce it."

Thus, the members of a war party, having brought any material venture to a successful conclusion, having performed the required purification rites, and attended the Tortures, eventually came to a day especially set aside for the making of military awards.

This celebration, as described by Adair, was participated in by the whole populace, while the red flag of war was displayed, and the war drums sounded the rhythms of the day. We may suppose that the Great Chieftain and the Council took their high seats, or squatted, according to rank, in pavilions under canopies of skin "with a sheen as resplendent as shimmering taffetas," whence were handed down the merited coronets of feathers, the feathered sceptres, and the chaplets of Eagles' plumes.

On this great occasion, which they are said to have attended with leaping and rejoicing, the "candidates for honors" all wore new, ceremonial moccasins of deerskin painted red.

Leaders were given coronets worked with Eagle feathers standing some three inches higher than the swansdown coronets of the warriors which were about fifteen inches.

Sceptres were awarded with the simpler feather head-dresses, evidently being the insignia of rank a step below that of "leader." It is also well to note that the "train" of Eagle feathers on the "war bonnet" appears to have been an ornament confined to the Plains region, developed only after the adoption of the horse.

Tattooed Heraldry

Du Pratz adds to Adair's account of the making of awards and honors the statement that a man who actually killed an enemy and brought in the scalp had the right to have tattooed on his left shoulder a war club with the national or tribal emblem of the slain one under it.

To guard against the infirmities consequent upon the act of tattooing, previously described in VANITIES OF THE VILLAGERS, the candidate for military honors had once again to perform the rites of purification — thus ending his achievement as he began it, by fortifying his spirit with mortification of the flesh, with magic, and with prayer.

FOOTNOTES

[1] See Smithwick's description of the instant cessation of hostilities on the part of the *Tonkawa* when a *Comanche* was slain, Chapter XX.

[2] See also SCALPING VS. HEAD HUNTING, Chapter XXII.

THE TSANTA OR SHRUNKEN HEAD

XVI
Origin and Immortality

"The final admonition of the *Tejas* priest in each dead ear, just before interment took place, was: 'Work hard in that other house until all have assembled.' "

Castañeda.

THE BIRTH OF GOD

In order to arrive at the Indian's attitude toward death and the reason for his burial customs, we must first investigate his ideas of origin and immortality.

From Espinosa's reports, Mrs. Mattie Austin Hatcher, Texas State Archivist, translated the following legend expressing the belief of the East Texas Indians concerning the birth of the Great Spirit and his removal from the Earth to the Upper World.

In the beginning there was a woman who had two daughters; one was pregnant, the other was not. Presumably this was a virgin conception, since there were said to have been only three people in the world at the time, all women.

The daughters wandered into the wood beyond the house and sat down to rest, the pregnant one laying her head in the lap of her sister.

As they reposed thus, there came upon them a mighty monster with horns on his head towering to the sky. The sister who was about to bear a child was seized upon and immediately devoured; but the other, being more agile, climbed into a tall tree. When the monster attempted to dislodge her by tearing the tree down, she plunged into a lake glimmering at its base, and swam under water to the house where her mother was, reaching the place in safety, despite the fact that the monster drank up the lake in an effort to secure her for the finish of his meal.

When they were sure the monster had left the neighborhood, the bereaved mother and sister returned to the scene of the disaster. There, while diligently searching for the footsteps of the victim, they came upon a tiny drop of blood in an acorn shell — the single remaining trace of the slain girl.

The mother capped the precious shell with another shell, placed the tiny container in her bosom, and carried it home.

She set the acorn casket in an earthen jar, covered the jar and set it in the corner of the room where she slept. Then she went to bed.

In the night she was awakened by a sound from the acorn shell. On examination, she found the tiny drop of blood had evolved into the body of a boy child, very beautiful and perfectly formed. Already it had grown the length of her finger. She covered the jar again and returned to her rest.

The following night she was awakened by the same sound — a scratching on the jar.

Rousing up once more she found the boy grown into a man. Presumably the jar had grown in proportion, since he was not yet out of it.

The woman at once set to work to make for this miraculously born grandson a bow and many arrows, which she presented to him before ever he set foot out of the cradling jar.

Having asked for his mother and learned the horror of her history, and that the horned monster still lurked about the wood, the youth went forth, armed with his new-made weapons, to give battle to the beast.

Such was his valor that the wounded demon fled the Earth, was, in fact, flung off the Earth by the strong-armed boy, never to return.

Then the boy and his mother and his aunt, deciding that Earth was a poor place in comparison with the Sky, went heavenward where he became the Great Spirit.

What happened to the womenfolk thereafter, we are not told, except that Espinosa reports another belief, current in East Texas, to the effect that an old woman in the sky daily gave birth to the Sun, the Moon, and the other elemental Powers. There is no real proof, however, that she was a member of the original feminine trinity.

TRIBAL ASCENSION MYTH

As to their own advent upon the Earth, most of the American Indians claimed to have come from regions underground, though the *Comanche* are said by federal army officers stationed among them to have believed *they* sprang from the Sun.

"The Earth," said Tecumseh, "is my mother, and the Sun is my father." — a statement broad enough to cover the claims of both Earth children and Sun children, and to span the entire Indian creed concerning human origin.

Lewis and Clark, returning from their famous exploratory expedition, (1803-04-05) give us the following legend from the *Mandan,* an agricultural branch of the Sioux located to the north of the *Caddo*: Once the whole Nation resided in a single village underground near a subterranean lake. A grapevine extended its roots down to their habitation and gave them a view of the light. Some of the more adventurous climbed up the vine and were delighted with the sight of the Earth, which they found covered with buffalo and rich with every kind of fruit.

Returning with the grapes they had gathered, their countrymen were so pleased with the taste of them that the

156

whole Nation resolved to leave their dull residence for the charms of the upper region.

Men, women and children ascended by means of the vine, until, when about half the Nation had reached the surface of the Earth, a corpulent woman clambering up the vine broke it with her weight, closing upon herself and the rest of the Nation the light of the Sun.

W. B. Parker, who accompanied Marcy's expedition into Texas in 1854, tells us the Texas *Caddo* believed they issued from underground to Earth by way of the tortuous vent passages of the Hot Springs of Arkansas; while the Spanish Fathers record the views of the *Tejas*, (presumably the *Asinai*) to the effect that they reached the Earth's surface at a spot somewhere near the junction of the Red River with the Mississippi.

According to one of the versions of tribal ascension found among the *Caddo,* and quoted by Hodge, the first man coming up to Earth carried a lighted Pipe in one hand and a drum in the other, while the first woman brought up the Indian corn or maize in one hand and pumpkin seeds in the other.

Thus did the new inhabitants of the Earth arrive supplied with the elements of their ancient civilization — corn, the staff of life, the great Maize Mother; Fire, the oracle, the supreme gift of the Sun; the drum or *tom-tom,* instrument of magic with which to set the masculine rhythm of their rituals; and the pumpkin or pompion, beloved delicacy of the womenfolk, symbol of fertility.

THE UNDER WORLD

However much they varied as to the location of the exact spot of tribal ascension, all the agricultural peoples seem to have been fairly well agreed on the route of the dead by which those in ghostly guise returned to the Under World.

This route, say the authorities, was the path of the Setting Sun.

157

INDIANS OF THE SOUTHWEST

When the Sun sank below the world's rim, Cushman tells us, it was the belief of the agricultural Indians that it went to light that other ancient region whence their ancestors rose by means of the miraculous grape vine, or the winding of the Hot Springs, or long lost, traditional caves — all analogies drawn, perhaps, from the tedious process of human birth.

THE HOLY PILGRIMAGE

Gatschet tells us that among the *Creek* it was considered a matter of holy pilgrimage to visit the Bay of Mobile at least once in a lifetime to watch the Sun sink into the waters, spreading a path of gold across the sea. He also quotes a woman, long a resident of the Texas coast, who affirms that it was the custom of the *Karankawa* to stand, as still as chiseled statues, contemplating the glory shed by the Setting Sun on the blue expanse of the Gulf.

THE AMERICAN STYX

"When the *Mandan* die," Lewis and Clark said, "they expect to return to the original seat of their forefathers, the good reaching the ancient village by means of a lake which the burdens of the sins of the wicked will not enable them to pass."

Cushman elaborates upon this idea, from his experience among the more southerly gardeners, stating that the watery barrier was a rushing river where witches lurked and demons crowded the depths.

This American Styx was spanned, according to his findings in legendary lore, by a slippery peeled log over which evil spirits hovered, ready to lend a hand in the downfall of unlucky ghosts about to attempt the hazardous crossing. Those among the dead who had "made good Medicine" during their lives had nought to fear, but those who had perpetuated evil deeds were now at the mercy of their own "bad Medicine" — and sure to slide hopelessly from the log to join the foul throng below.

158

THE OTHER HOUSE

The *Tejas* priests explained to Espinosa that unless the proper incantations were spoken at the burial of the dead, the spirits of the departed could never hope to reach "that other house" where the *Tejas* ghosts gathered to await the millenium, at which time, according to their beliefs, the entire assembly would set forth for some other world, as yet unknown.

UNIVERSAL BELIEF IN IMMORTALITY

The testimonials of all recorders of Indian beliefs and customs give evidence of a universally deep-seated faith in immortality and their statements are invariably borne out by archaeological findings.

In Texas, as elsewhere, every Indian grave opened shows with what care the occupant was provisioned for its spirit journey. From some of the individual graves — there are group burials as well as single burials — as many as a hundred articles have been removed, articles placed there for the convenience of the flitting ghost. According to the Indians, as explained in THE INDIAN PANTHEON, these articles themselves had ghosts, and it was their spirit essence rather than their material substance that was expected to be of value to the dead.

The body, Espinosa tells us, was always carefully washed and dressed, while a continuous howling went up around it from the moment of demise till the beginning of the funeral feast which followed the burial.

In order to announce the coming of a new ghost so that the doors of "the other house" would be opened to it, he continues, clouds of arrows were sped toward the Sun from the bows of surviving friends and relatives.

Beside or over the bodies in the grave were always placed the necessities of long travel — food, tools, and weapons — assorted according to the age and sex of the individual concerned.

159

In Texas, from the child graves, come toys, among them miniature vessels and weapons, and even baby rattles made of terrapin shells. From women's graves come ornaments, pottery-making tools, and fleshing tools for the preparation of hides and skins. From men's graves come beads by the thousand; beautifully carved gorgets, or fancy breast plates; grindstones; axes; arrow points; and paint.

Some of these recovered items now lending themselves to the study of ancient Indian life by archaeologists and anthropologists may have been among those Espinosa saw placed in fresh graves during his missionary residence among the *Tejas*.

To give a different point of view, from Espinosa's (an anthropological view,) and one that coincides with anthropological findings, in respect to the "continuous howling" over the dead, let us quote from Julia Lee Sinks of Giddings, Texas: "The ceremony of calling back the spirit of the dead was witnessed by a friend of mine who was present in a Tonqua (*Tonkawa*) camp at the death of one of the tribe. Without knowing the Indian custom of using on such occasions a secret name (sometimes known only to the parents or godparents) he described the calling or shouting of the name as one of the most impressive things he ever heard. He regarded it as a kind of mourning ceremony, the constant calls being kept up all night." (Actually, this was the calling of the departing spirit in an attempt to delay its departure from Earth — the crucial purpose for which the secret or *real* name was given — an art as holy in the Indian ritual as the sacrament of extreme unction in the Christian ritual.[1]

In Honor of the Absent

For the honor and comfort of those who died away from home, very special funeral rites were observed among the East Texas villagers.

The first step, according to Espinosa's account, was the building of a pyramid of wood and brush, in the open, but near the house of the departed one.

With the appearance of the Sun at Dawn, a terrific howl-ing began within the house, set up by the relatives of the deceased, all stretched prone upon their beds. This howling was echoed by the community gathered outside.

To the wild mourning, seven selected men issued from the house carrying a small pot of ground corn made into paste. Four of them scattered pinches of this to the Four Winds; that is, in the direction of the four World Quarters, while the other three ate the remainder, symbolic of its being eaten by the dead, in the meantime invoking the Sun on behalf of the dead.

These seven men then re-entered the house accompanied by the assembled community. The mourners now arranged themselves in a line and began a march about the hearth Fire, various members of the procession from time to time presenting the aged priest who was directing the ritual with sacrificial gifts of tobacco and corn meal to be tossed into the Flame. During his procession the chiefs kept their seats, as was customary for them at all times.

The sacrificial ritual concluded, the funeral guests next made presents to the bereaved family, the men offering ar-rows, knives, and other masculine items; while the women donated food, clothing, and handsome skins. To this com-munity gift, heaped upon the proffered skins, the family added the personal possessions of the dead. The skins were then wrapped and made fast, and rewrapped in reed mats — a great and valuable bundle.

Throughout the presentation ceremony, says Espinosa, it was customary for an old man and a young one to keep up a mournful chant, accompanied by the monotonous rhythm of a calabash rattle and a *tom-tom*.

Of the three men who had eaten the meal at the opening of the funeral service, one now took up the bundle of gifts, a second lighted a torch at the hearth, and a third provided himself with a ceremonial packet of dried grass and kind-ling material. The community mourners again formed in line, the three specially designated performers in the lead, and proceeded to the waiting pyre.

Arrived beside the pyramid of wood, the first laid his bundle upon the pyre, the second arranged his kindling stuffs, and the third, amid a loud outcry, applied the torch.

Presumably the torch was then quenched in cold water, since, according to Adair, this was customary among the Louisiana peoples, the death torch and the war torch being the only forms of Fire that could be so treated without danger of bringing down disaster on the worshipers of Flame.

The funeral ceremony being now complete, Espinosa assures us the community at once indulged in a great feast with much hilarity, since it was assumed that sufficient honor had been done to the departed one that his spirit would be gratified when it looked upon the Earth.

SYMPATHY FOR THE STRANGER

Joutel confirms the many times repeated statement of the extreme kindliness of these people with the story of one of La Salle's soldiers buried beneath their Red Land soil.

Feeling that the French had not done justice to the situation by the simple reading of the Catholic ritual, a distressed Indian woman made daily pilgrimages to the stranger's grave to place upon it food and water, that the spirit of the paleface might not suffer in its long journey to the After World.

AFTER LIFE NOT AN IDLE LIFE

Of the beliefs of the *Tejas* concerning after life, C. E. Castañeda, in his translations from the Spanish Fathers, gives us the following discussion: It was thought that the spirits of those who died went to a large house where they were to wait until every one in the world died, at which time all would start together from this house to a new world.

In the meantime they were not to stand about idly waiting, but were to work, and work hard. However, it seems that the older residents in the house of death did not have to apply themselves as strenuously as the newcomers, but had leisure to watch for arrivals, crying as soon as each appeared: "Here he comes, make him work hard till all have assembled!"

The last act of the officating priest at a *Tejas* funeral, according to Castañeda's findings, was to whisper an admonition of industry to the departing spirit in order that he might deport himself well in the life to come.

THE DEATH OF THE MIGHTY

According to the CASANAS MANUSCRIPT and in accord with Louisiana authorities on the same subject, the death of a Great Cheiftain among the *Tejas* was a matter for unlimited awe and almost unlimited ritual.

Contrary to the usual custom of immediate burial among the *Asinai,* the body of the grand ruler of the confederated peoples was held until all the nine Nations could assemble for the ceremonies.

In front of the door of the deceased two poles were erected, one bearing a globe made of grass (a Sun symbol) and the other a Moon made of sticks. Before these images the nine united Nations danced fourteen days and nights, and then went home again.

We may be sure that these dances were all matters of magical import, fraught with a thousand meanings unintelligible to the good Spanish missionary whose sole idea was to substitute Christian baptism for the heathen rite of purification by sacred Flame; and it is a great hindrance to further knowledge of these ancient peoples that he failed even to describe the ceremonies.

The records of De Soto's expedition show that in Louisiana the death of a great provincial ruler, the Sun, looked on as the living human counterpart of the Life Giver, was considered a disaster almost equal in magnitude to the destruction of that Orb. At such a time, in order to propitiate

163

the angry Powers; that is, to offset the Bad Medicine through which the calamity must, perforce, have occurred, many babes were sacrificed.

Intimates of the dead ruler, including his wives and servants, were strangled — so that his mighty spirit should go properly attended to the Other World. Strangulation, the official form of execution, avoided spilt blood and therefore did not subject the executioner to the Blood Right.

ANCESTOR WORSHIP

According to the reports of the earliest Spanish and French explorers, bones of dead rulers were placed in the Temples, those of the most recently dead occupying the position of honor behind the Fire in front of the altar.

When the next ruler died, so say these old reports, the bones of the predecessor were put into the altar, presumably behind the curtains of painted skins described in Chapter Five.

Lafitau tells us that among the *Natchez* it was the custom of the reigning chieftain to go into the Temple each day to exalt the spirits of his ancestors with ceremonies peculiar to them and to the Sun.

Thus do we have, in the southern garden lands of North America, if all that we are told by the ancient historians be true, a system of ancestor worship very like that practiced among the Incas in their vast Peruvian Empire.

FOOTNOTES

[1] Compare this description with the totally unsympathetic but graphic description of the TONKAWA funeral in Chapter XX.

In MY SEVERAL WORLDS Pearl Buck mentions hearing Chinese women run into the street calling their dying children — hoping to stay the soul from leaving the body.

XVII
The Fighting Fringe

"The fields of the border country were over-run by buffalo."
Nuttal.

THE BUFFER STATE

Beyond the edge of the Southern Forests, skirting the Buffalo Range, was a "buffer state" composed of five Tribes including the *Wichita,* the *Waco,* the *Ionie,* the *Anadarko,* and the *Tewakana* — the fighting fringe of the civilized Nations.

These Tribes, closely allied with each other, and with the *Caddo* and the *Asinai,* were perforce, peoples whose culture was intermediate between that of the settled villagers to the east and the nomadic Buffalo Hunters to the west.

The *Wichita* believed their ancestors came out of the *Wichita* Mountains, and both they and their ancestral ranges were sometimes referred to as the *Towyash* from the term *toyavist,* which, Josiah Gregg tells us, was the *Comanche* word for "mountain."

One division of the *Wichita* is said to have drifted southwestward, away from the old alliance, to join up with the *Apaches* — presumably the *Lipan-Apaches.* The Spanish found these people gardening in the valleys of the Rio

Grande, and in the Texas Cross Timbers. They knew them as the *Jumana*, but referred to them familiarly as *Las Pintadas* — the "Painted People." Anglo pioneers shortened this to *Pintos*.

The French referred to the five allied tribes as *Pani-Piques* or "Prick Faces." The Anglos revised this into *Pawnee Picts* — an Indian-Scotch linguistic mixture.

All descriptions go into detail with respect to their extreme practice of tattooing — an art indicative of a kinship with Pacific Islanders.

These peoples had permanent houses of wickerwork like the gardening Indians, but were possessed, also, of movable skin tents like the Plains Indians. Every Tribe had given peculiarities in the construction of skin tepees. For instance, the *Comanches* let the lodge poles stick out through the Smoke openings at the top, while the *Wichita* brought theirs just even with the circular edge of the skins round the Smoke hole, thus giving their nomadic dwellings the form of truncated cones, very like their permanent houses.

The intermediate Tribes on the prairie outlasted the gardening Indians in the Timber Lands. Says Marcy, who explored the Red River country in 1852: "The village of the *Wichita* has forty-two lodges, each containing two families of about ten persons. These lodges are made by erecting a framework of poles placed in a circle in the ground, with the tops united in an oval form and bound together with wattles . . . a very commodious and comfortable domicile. The interior arrangements are such that every person has a bunk, forming a couch which is far from uncomfortable.

"When seated around their Fires in the center of the lodges, they (the Wichita) have an air of domestic happiness which I did not expect to find."

"The *Wacos* live about a mile above the *Wichita,* in a village constructed precisely like the other."

"The lodges are about twenty-five feet in diameter at

the base, twenty feet high, and have very much the appearance of a group of haystacks."

Each of the five Tribes planted garden patches, but, as we are informed by a traveller of more than two centuries ago, their fields were frequently overrun by the buffalo and their corn stamped down; nevertheless they continued to plant tobacco and maize, putting the old women out to shoo away the lumberly beasts that threatened the crops.

As a protection against marauders, they buried their stores of shelled grain in the Earth whenever they took up their skin tents and set forth on a buffalo hunt. As a protection against the surprise attacks beloved of the Plainsmen, they set lookouts in the lofts on the tops of their houses to spy out the enemy while still afar off.

The religion of these Tribes differed somewhat from that of their more easterly neighbors in that they had no sustained Fire of any variety, since they were frequently away from home for long intervals; but their devotion to the Sun was as fixed and faithful as that of their allies in the gardening regions, or of their enemies on the Plains.

APPEARANCE OF THE PAWNEE PICTS

The *Wichita* are said to have been a comely people, a statement evidenced by photographs in the Texas Archives. The dress of both sexes was the same as that of the East Texas Nations. It is interesting to note that the *Wichita* women permitted their hair to flow long and loose, in direct contrast to the *Tonkawa* women of Central Texas, who, while otherwise attiring themselves in the same fashion as the women of the *Wichita* and the *Asinai,* bobbed their manes like the *Comanche* matrons.

The position of women in Indian society seems to have been invariably indicated by the method of handling the hair, and bobbed hair was ever a symbol of subjection.

From Josiah Gregg we glean the following description of the five intermediate tribes: "The *Wacos, Wichita* and

167

their kindred tribes are . . . chiefly remarkable for their profuse tattooing whereby they have sometimes acquired the title of 'Pawnee Picts'; the females particularly make a perfect calico of the whole under jaw, breast and arms, and the mammae are fancifully ornamented with rings and rays. The tattoo, in fact, seems to constitute the chief female ornament of these Tribes; for their only gown consists of about a yard and a half of . . . (cloth) or else a small dressed skin, suspended from the waist."

THE GHOST THAT WALKS ON TEWAKANA HILL

The *Wacos* had their principal village site where the city of Waco now stands, while the *Tewakana* were situated on the solitary eminence in Limestone County, which stands today, a silent monument to their tribal name. It is thought that this hill may be that which was known and revered as *La Tortuga* (the Turtle) by the *Tonkawa* long before it became the stronghold of the *Tewakana*.

Less than a century ago extermination came to the Tribe domiciled on this hill in a terrible battle with the *Cherokee* who had been pushed from the older southern states into Texas by encroaching pioneers.

A feud arose between the two peoples which led to war. The *Cherokee,* having been repulsed from the height, sat down in council on the prairie to figure out a means of dealing with the situation. They were at a distinct disadvantage, having no protection from the barrage of arrows descending whenever they attempted to charge the eminence. The *Tewakana* were in a seemingly impregnable position, having crowned the elevation with stone piles overspread by tough hides, in lieu of battlements. Shots from behind these ramparts took deadly toll of the attacking party.

But the *Cherokee* formulated a plan. The hill was covered with tall dry grass. Whizzing arrows, carrying lighted flares, ignited this powder-dry growth at the very edge of the barricade.

Then, indeed, did consternation reign on Tewakana Hill. The dwellers there, forced from their defenses by Smoke and Flame, were cut down almost to a man. A scant handful, only, is reputed to have slipped away under cover of the confusion, bearing the infant son of their slain chief.

Thus has arisen the legend that sometimes at Dawn and sometimes at Sunset the figure of a silent Indian may be seen standing alone on this, the highest point of the Texas prairies, gazing afar out over the rolling lands where once his father reigned — ruler of men! Master of the wild herds on the broad acres sweeping from the foot of Tewakana Hill!

He has never been seen to come. He has never been seen to go. Perhaps it is only a reader of old tales, blessed with an active fancy, who discovers him there — but from time to time rumors drift through Texas that the Spirit of the Last Chieftain has been seen again, mantled in the Indian Summer haze wrapped about Tewakana Hill.

TALL TALES TO MATCH A TALL NEW COUNTRY

However, the legends that arise now concerning the ghosts of the dead past are nothing to the "tall tales" that arose to entertain an awe-struck and expectant public during the exploration of the wide Southwest: A monk set down in his diary, in all seriousness, the statement that: "Here are large thick trees with big sharp thorns on them. If a horse falls on one (cascading down the steep bank of an arroyo, perhaps) both horse and horseman remain transfixed!" No doubt the Spanish dagger plant was a terrifying prospect to a timidly seated rider on an unruly mustang; nevertheless, its pointed qualities appear to have been a trifle over-estimated by the good monk.

BULL-DOGGING THE COMANCHES

With the story of the "Spanish dagger" and its possibilities for an introduction, we arrive at a still "taller" tale set down by a Spanish engineer, one José María Sanchez. Says he: "The *Comanches* are now at peace with Bexar (San Antonio) and occupying themselves with fighting the *Huasos* (Wacos), their chief enemies on the frontier. This Tribe is doubtless very powerful, and still refuses to become an ally of the *Comanches*. The quickness of the *Huasos* is marvelous, for it is a proven fact that when the *Comanches* flee in battle, the *Huasos* pursue them on foot, overtake them, and with one leap, spear them through the back — or, catching the horse by the tail, they throw it down and put their adversaries to death!"

This tale must have had wide credence in the early annals of Texas, for another account dealing with the same subject tells us that the *Comanches* kept their horses' tails sheared for fear of the Nation of terrible "track men" who could overtake mounted fugitives, and, with one twist of the wrist wound in the tail hairs of the horse, break the neck of both rider and steed!

The underlying idea probably had its origin in the mourning conventions of the *Comanches* which caused them to shear the tails of their ponies when returning from an unsuccessful raiding expedition.

FISHERS ON HORSEBACK

As a matter of truth, the five frontier tribes, though probably always expert runners, took to the horse nearly as readily as the *Comanches* when the Spanish colonial policy made that hitherto unknown animal available throughout the Southwest; and we are told that these corn-planting buffalo hunters even fished on horseback, riding down the clear streams and stabbing their quarry with long-handled spears.

THE INVETERATE ENEMY — THE APACHE

Certainly it behooved the "boundary patrol" of the civilized Indians to keep well abreast of the times in matters of warfare, for we are informed by Los Rios, who traversed

"New Spain" in 1691, that "the *Apaches* come to the head-waters of the Guadalupe and sometimes to the very borders of the *Tejas* country. They come to kill buffalos and carry away the skins, because in their own country there are no buffalo. When it gets cold they return to their own territory."

Since we have already been informed that the Buffalo Range was something like a hundred miles from the *Tejas* border, we can but assume that the hides the *Apaches* carried away from the adjacent region were plundered from parties of returning gardeners, through methods described in THE PEACE PIPE and in THE PRODUCTS OF THE CHASE.

There can be little doubt that the eternal vendetta between the citizens of the *Apacheria* and those of the *Tejas* country would have wiped out the straw settlements of the latter before the thatching was on, had it not been for the five patrolling Tribes acting as a powerful courageous "fighting fringe," for the garden lands.

THE GOLDEN DOMES OF THE QUIVIRA

Actually, the straw thatching of *Wichita* domed houses glinting in the Sun were the "golden domes" of Coronado's *Quivira*, which place was first revealed to him by that home-sick *Caddo* captive furnished as a guide out onto the Buffalo Range by the Cacique of the Pecos — the captive familiar to historians of the Spanish Southwest, from the shape of his hair-do, as "the Turk."

XVIII
Ashes of the Fires

"Never did a North American Indian acknowledge that he recognized in the white man a master; nor was there ever an emotion of inferiority to the white man experienced by the Indians."

Cushman.

LEGALLY DRAWN AND QUARTERED

After Columbus brought the "new" world into international limelight, the "powers that were" in Europe put their diplomatic heads together and came to an agreement concerning the parceling out of the hitherto unsuspected territory.

By the terms of this agreement, the European Power that first sent explorers up any given stream was to have jurisdiction over the watershed of that stream from its mouth to its source, without regard to "savages" already occupying the area. In case representatives of two Powers should explore a stream simultaneously, the watershed was to be divided between them.

Thus it happened that France claimed the Mississippi from its source down and Spain from its mouth up — while, in Texas, the French flag floated as far west as Nacogdoches, due to La Salle's venture into Matagorda Bay, and the

Spanish flag as far east as San Antonio, due to Coronado's jaunt across the Staked Plains, — which, incidentally, were not "staked" until he pegged them down.

THE BLOOD RED BANNER

Over the vast space between the Bourbon Lilies and the Battlements of Aragon and Castile, a new national emblem appeared before many years — one never officially included among the "flags that waved over Texas" — for the *Comanche*, mounted, carried his blood red banner ever southward, down the Brazos and the Colorado, till it flashed to the Gulf.

ASHES TO ASHES

When Texas was opened to Anglo-American colonization — authorized on the part of the new and harassed Mexican government so as to establish a buffer between itself and the spreading *Comancheria* — the Temple Fires were cold beyond the Trinity. Few, indeed, of the *Tejas* remained to offer hospitality to the pioneer drifting inexorably through the timbers behind his ox teams, as his predecessors, behind their oxcarts, drifted inexorably through Europe, down to the Mediterranean, a thosuand years before.

"How can man die better than in facing fearful odds for the ashes of his fathers and the temples of his gods" may be sung of the southern Indians as appropriately as of those other southern peoples for whom poets have lamented through the ages. For, ere the Sacred Fires were extinguished forever, men and women fought side by side against the European invasion of the garden lands; and, when the battle was lost, flung themselves into the fiery furnace of their blazing city, there to be consumed by the element they worshiped, rather than capitulate to the men in iron.

INDIANS OF THE SOUTHWEST

BETWEEN THE UPPER AND NETHER MILLSTONES

To the Nations spared by bayonets, a less glorious, though no less certain end came through fraternizing with white traders, exchanging pelts for beads and for "fire water." Moreover, European diseases, particularly smallpox and measles, when they reached the gardeners for the first time, mowed them down by families and by towns till whole peoples perished of plagues that were only aggravated by the old remedies of sweating and cold baths. Dying too fast for interment by convention, the bodies were left upon the bosom of the Earth where they were consumed by the "slow Fires of decay."

Continuously crowding from the north, British colonies blocked escape in that direction, forcing the natives they were supplanting down upon the last outposts of Indian civilization — the *Tejas*.

SIFTING THE ASHES

Despoiled by the Spaniard, cheated by the French, exterminated by the Anglo-American, the southern Indian has been denied even a place in history save bloody references to the tomahawk with which he strove to hold his ancestral acres from intrusion, his Temples from profanation, his very body from the sword. His single existing monuments are the mounds he raised through the slow labor of basket brigades, carrying ton after ton of Earth, to form the bases for his altars and the covers for his sepulchres.

Concealed in this consecrated Earth is his story, to be liberated only by the archaeologist who shall sift the tons by handfuls, as patiently and as reverently as they were placed there. Until this task be done, we have for consideration the earliest written chronicles of those Tribes and Nations whose past is a part of the as yet ungarnered history of Texas and the Southwest.

THE LITTORAL TRIBES

Karankawa, in Texas pioneer history, ordinarily refers to a semiaquatic Tribe occupying the coastal lagoons — a Tribe poisoned against the white man by the pirate activities of Lafitte and his henchmen, and by the military ardor of James Long, before Austin's settlers arrived at San-Felipe-on-the-Brazos.

The *Karankawa* having nothing else to steal, Lafitte's men stole a woman; and when the Indians attempted to avenge the act, Dr. Long, with true racial loyalty, trained a cannon on them from Bolivar Point. With such an introduction, it is small wonder they failed to appreciate the advantages of white contact.

Anthropologically speaking, the term *Karankawa* covers a number of Tribes adjacent to the coast — Tribes melting indistinguishably into the *Coahuilteca* and the *Tonkawa* to form a great racial bloc.

By many, the *Attakapa,* or Man Eaters, of Louisiana are held to be culturally one with the Texas *Karankawa.* The dividing line between these historically separate, even if culturally same people appears to have been to the north of Galveston Island. Their "separation" seems attributable to the *Attakapa* appearing in French documentation and the *Karankawa* in Spanish and Anglo documentation, which is not a true ethnic distinction!

A COMANCHE HOME

XIX
The Cannibal of the Coast

"The Karankawa were the 'longbows' of Texas."
Smithwick.

CRONKS

The cannibal of the coast in Texas was the *Karankawa,* nicknamed "Cronk" by the settlers. Although he paused occasionally for a few days, or even weeks, and pitched his windbreaks, hardly to be dignified by the name of "tepees," in some good crabbing spot, he was a wandering soul, forever afloat on the brackish lagoons at the Gulf edge.

Noah Smithwick, blacksmith, reaching San Felipe when Austin's colony was the center of Anglo-Americanism in the Texas wilds, says: "The Karankawa Indians . . . lived mostly on fish and alligators, with a man for fete days when they could catch one. . . .Many . . . (men) were six feet in height with bows and arrows in proportion. Their . . . faces were rendered hideous by the alligator grease and dirt with which they were besmeared from head to foot as a defense against mosquitos."

Miss Alice W. Oliver whose father settled directly on the *Karankawa* coast, gives a more favorable picture: "The men were very tall, magnificently formed, with very slender hands and feet. They were not very dark, and many of them had very delicate features, and, without exception, splendid teeth." But she describes the women as short, fat, and work-bowed.

Gatschet, who collected all available notes on the *Karankawa* and published them in PAPERS OF THE PEABODY MUSEUM, Volume I, says the name *Karankawa,* meaning "dog-lovers," originally applied only to the houseboating people of the coast. Now it has been extended to contiguous and related Tribes reaching far inland and shading off into the *Coahuilteca* and *Tonkawa.*

NEIGHBORS

Beyond the *Karankawa* country, which reached no farther north and east than Galveston Island, the lagoons and sand bars were given over to the *Attacapa,* or "man-eaters," another semiaquatic and cannibalistic people who ranged far beyond the Sabine's mouth.

Inland from the lower range of the *Attacapa* was a small tribe, often alluded to, though not important in Texas history, the *Bidais.* References to this — one is almost tempted to say "ghostly" people, so lightly do they flit through the pages of old records — tell us little of their life and customs; but a note gleaned from General Teran's diary by the drafts-man, Sanchez, says: "The *Vidais* who comprize about forty families, the oldest natives of Texas, consider themselves the owners of all this land. It is a tradition among them that the *Comanches, Lipanes, Taehucanes,* and many other Tribes all come from the north. They are peaceful and very poor. They live between the Trinity and the Neches."

Bidais, says Gatschet, meant "shrub" or "brush"; hence, these were the Brushwood People.

Still farther in than the *Bidais,* but also on the border of the civilized Nations, were the *Keechies,* another small group appearing now and then in old histories, sometimes seeming to be settled, then again moving about with make-shift tents. From these two Tribes westward, the *Tonkawa* folk reached to the territory of the *Lipan-Apaches* who, in turn, extended far across the Rio Grande.

MORE VANITIES

De Solis, who visited the *Karankawa* and the kindred *Coupanes, Guapites,* and *Coxanes,* at the San Rosario Mission, near Goliad, tells us "These tribes are distinguished from one another by the stripes they paint on themselves in one manner or another; also in the cut of the hair. They adorn thmselves; that is, they paint themselves with vermilion, and on some occasions with black, the eyes arched and reddened.

"They paint themselves in stripes all over, different figures being formed with the stripes, now of animals, now of birds, now of flowers. These are the married and the corrupt ones; but the maidens have only a small stripe, from their foreheads as far as the chin, which crosses through the point of the nose and through the middle of the lips.

"They make holes in the wings of their noses and the tips of their ears in order to hang beads in them, also little shells, small conch shells from the sea, and small stones of various colors.

"In the woods and on the coast, the men go entirely naked, but the women are always decently clad. From the time they (the women) are born, they put on a *pabigo,* or breechclout of Spanish moss which covers the body decently, and which they keep on until they die, renewing it when necessary."

Gatschet and Miss Oliver give us further notes on personal appearance. "The peculiar distinctive marks of the tribe were: a small circle of blue tattooed over either cheekbone, one horizontal line extending from the outer angle of the eye toward the ear and three perpendicular parallel lines, about one-fourth of an inch apart, on the chin from the middle of the lower lip downward, and two others under each corner of the mouth.

179

"The custom of head-flattening . . . was much in favor. . . . The babies of both sexes had to undergo the process and the *foreheads* only were flattened. A piece of cloth was first applied, then a thin board, then a cloth inlaid with moss . . . to make a wad." This affair was bandaged to the head and allowed to remain for about one year. The baby was carried on the mother's back wrapped like a cocoon.

The long black hair of the men, sometimes sunburned to a reddish tinge, was worn in a single braid often terminating in a Rattlesnake's rattle which "made a faint ringing sound as the wearer walked." Both sexes went bareheaded and barefooted, and the children entirely naked.

ALL HIS WORLDLY GOODS

Of the Tribes about San Rosario, De Solis says: "They exchange or barter their wives. If one of them likes the wife of another better, he gives him his and something of value besides. They lend them to their friends; they sell them for a horse, for beads, or for any other thing they esteem." He adds: "Though the men behave in this manner, the women are very decent."

The *Karankawa* on the coast, Gatschet tells us, had but one wife — presumably he could afford no more, for his worldly wealth was small. His supreme possession was his boat which Miss Oliver describes: "One side of the log was hewed flat and the log was then dug out, the ends bluntly pointed, leaving a triangular place or deck at each end." Two families always traveled together, using separate boats, but erecting only one shelter when a landing was made, at a spot where both water and firewood were obtainable.

The lodge poles for these rude shelters, called *ba-aks*, were sharpened at each end and driven into the sand like wagon bows, crossing at the top, resulting in a structure shaped like half an orange. Over the framework were thrown such loose skins as the companion families owned — never enough to make a complete cover, so that they had to be

180

moved during the day as the Sun or the Wind changed position.

When taken from the shallow "hold" and spread out on the sand inside the *ba-ak,* the domestic equipment comprised a few pots, decorated with black and red paint and made with conical bottoms to be set in scooped out hollows of sand; rude wooden spoons; needles of fishbone made with nicely smoothed eyes; threads of fine deer sinew; a few soft, beautifully dressed skins used for beds and seats; and the precious Fire sticks, always kept in a skin-wrapped, watertight bundle. The children occasionally had wooden blocks with roughly carved features for dolls.

Burdens, especially fagots, were carried into camp strapped on the shoulders.

THE MENU

Cabeza de Vaca, America's most noted "shipwrecked mariner," and the first European to fall afoul of the "longbows" of Texas, states that during his sojourn among them, they were so lacking in digestible foodstuffs that children were nursed until their twelfth year — a probable exaggeration. The *Karankawa* did, however, have a most unappetizing *menu* consisting of fish, which he seems to have preferred in a decayed state; alligators; carrion; snails; worms; crabs; conchs; water birds; the *tuna,* or fruit of the prickly pear, when it was in season; and the roots of marsh plants, which, according to the settlers, he was accustomed to pound up for breadstuff. Gatschet's notes inform us that bread was baked in thin layers, or *tortillas,* on stone slabs propped before the Fire.[1]

For seasoning, *chile* was preferred to salt.

Occasionally the *Karankawa* paddled his hollow log up a river and shot a deer, or traded for corn with the interior Tribes, but for the most part he kept to the brackish shallows.

Like his immediate neighbors, he had winter sanctuaries

in the thornbrush or in bamboo thickets, where rattling screens of cane or curtains of Spanish moss offered protection from wintry onslaughts. These same sanctuaries, as soon as the Spanish livestock "went native," became similar refuges for the longhorn, the mustang, and the razorback, allowing them to breed by the thousand — a new and bountiful meat supply for the coast Indians.

De Solis, who knew these tribes only after the infusion of imported animal life took place, says: "In the woods they live on horses; mules; deer, since there are many; bison, which abound; bear; wild boars *(javelinas);* rabbits; hares; dormice; and other quadrupeds; with snakes; vipers; wild turkeys; geese; ducks; prairie hens; partridge; cranes; quail; and other birds that are on the beach or on the banks and margins of rivers; with all kinds of fish which abound.

"They delight in the odor of the polecat which they also eat, as well as decayed meat, which smells horrible."

From this discourse, it would appear that this racial bloc differed widely, both from the gardening Nations, and from the Plains Tribes, in religious beliefs concerning the spiritual values of food; since, unlike the former, they devoured Snakes, and, unlike the latter, they risked the intake of many creatures forbidden at the table set by the "keeper of the hearth."

They ate, Gatschet says, with their fingers, although Miss Oliver mentions the possession of wooden spoons.

THE LONGBOWS

Fish were shot with the bow and arrow, not from the boat, ordinarily, but while the hunters were wading in the shallows — the name given the *Karankawa* by the *Lipan-Apache*s being "those-who-walk-in-the-water."

They were expert marksmen, fond of archery tournaments, where they shot straight into the air to see whose shaft went highest, or at targets, being able to hit the mark with precision at a distance of a hundred yards.

Of other sports, wrestling was the supreme diversion; so much so, that their name among the *Tonkawa* was "the wrestlers." They threw hatchets with great skill, often using knives to settle their differences. They had ballplay, but, unlike most Indians, no betting or gambling is reported amongst them.

The Gatschet PAPERS give considerable detail concerning the longbows which came at least to a man's chin, were made of red cedar, were about two inches wide and an inch and a half thick at the middle, and were always kept well oiled and polished.

"The bowstring was formed of twisted deer sinew of many fine strands, aggregating one-fourth of an inch in diameter, making a very strong line, perfectly smooth and hard. Great pains were taken to keep the line smooth and in repair, any slight tendency toward fraying being at once mended.

"The arrows were about a yard long, the shaft something over half an inch in diameter with a sharp thin steel head about three inches long, the shank of which was set in a cleft in the shaft, which was wound with sinew. The arrows were feathered with wild geese wing feathers, three being set equidistant around the shaft, in slots or clefts and then wound. The feathers were about six inches long and showed about one half inch from the shaft.

"The bow was held in the left hand in the firm grasp of the palm and fingers, so that the thumb was free to move; the shaft of the arrow thus rested on the first thumb joint, so allowing one of the two lower feathers to pass on each side of the thumb and also clear of the bow, and permitting accurate aim. The bowstring was drawn to the *left* cheek by the first two fingers of the right hand hooked over the string, one above and the other below the arrow shaft."

"Around the left wrist was a small strip or braclet of undressed deerskin worn by women as well as by men — probably a guard against the twang of the bowstring."

Regardless of how low the *Karankawa* may have been

in the scale of civilization, it will be noted that he readily took up the use of steel or iron, since he was using metal arrow points by the time the settlers arrived.

As aids to the chase, and as domestic companions, these Indians had numbers of dogs, which, say the early Spaniards, were voiceless — whether artificially muted or a special breed without barking facilities, remains unknown. They huddled in the "hold" with the other members of the family when the *Karankawa* were afloat, and had their place beside the hearth Fire when on land.[2]

The Sign Language and the Smoke Signals

Of manners and customs, other than those already set down, little is known concerning the coast Tribes. Gatschet says they counted on their fingers up to ten, beginning with the little finger and going to the thumb, which was called "the father," and that, in designating quantities, they used about the same devices as those listed for the *Tejas* in THE MAGIC ART.

In ordinary intercourse, they attracted each other's attention with shrill whistles; but when wishing to catch the attention of those without the tribe, especially with regard to requests, they indulged in ceremonial weeping for half an hour or more. A possible explanation of these wails is that given to French missionaries by "weepers" farther north, who explained that strangers always reminded them of their dead who had gone into other worlds, thereby becoming strangers to them.[3]

That the *Karankawa* was versed in the American Esperanto is evidenced by this statement from De Solis: "All the tribes have one thing in common — the sign language, with which they talk, not only for hours, but for entire days. Those who are newly come to these lands immediately take up the signs in order to understand and make themselves understood by all the Indians of the many diverse Nations."

He then takes up the matter of native telegraphy: "They are very sagacious and cautious; and they send messages by Smoke signals, some signals calling them together, others warning them to flee, others giving notice of anything new. The proper Smoke for each being given, as soon as one gets the message he passes it to another; and he, in turn, gives it to those who follow; and, in a very short time, whatever news there is has been made known and forewarned against in the province."

Gatschet adds to this discussion: "On clear days, generally at noon, they signalled news by columns of Smoke from their camp Fires which were started from small pits in the ground, every Indian having a Fire in front of his lodge. The column of Smoke was made to ascend in more than twenty different ways, sometimes diverging or curling in spirals, sometimes rising up in parallel lines. Some looked like the letters V and Y others resembled spiral lines, or two parallel zigzag lines moving upward, or twin columns standing close to each other."

"At night," says Miss Oliver, referring to the camp hearths, "the horizon was often dotted in various directions with these little Fires."

Bartlett tells us: "The well-known Indian signal of a puff of Smoke suddenly rising from Earth . . . is produced by making a Fire in a hole and then smothering it with leaves. The hole is suddenly opened, when the Smoke rushes forth in a dense body and rises high in the air in a perpendicular column."

THE MITOTES AND THE TORTURES

Supreme in religious ritual were the *mitotes* and the Tortures. Like other Southwestern Indians, the *Karankawa* looked to the Sun as the all-powerful element of Nature. He employed the Smoke ritual, but not with the Pipe. He smoked like the Mexicans; that is, wrapper fashion, blowing the Smoke to the seven sacred directions from his nostrils.

His Witch Doctors used the sucking device described in THE MAGIC ART; and, as set forth in ORIGIN AND IMMORTALITY, he was accustomed to pay his devotions to the spectacle of the Setting Sun.

De Vaca, when the storm waves deposited him, presumably on Galveston Island, was mistaken for a Sun God because of his blondness and his arrival from the direction of the Dawn. His hosts, insisting that he perform miracles through his supposed magical powers, created a perilous situation from which he escaped by resorting to "the laying on of hands" — and so great was the faith of his clientele that apparent cures resulted from his impromptu ministrations.

De Solis gives the following description of social and ceremonial dancing seen in South Texas: "They are very much given to the dances they call *mitotes*. Some of these are festive and happy, others funereal and sad, being distinguished from one another by the instruments played for them. For the festive ones they play a tambourine that is made of a tortoise shell, or a half gourd, or with a pot; and a whistle of reeds; and an *avacasele*. For the sad ones they play a certain instrument called the *cayman*. This is very harsh and melancholy; and to its discordant notes they add . . . cries accompanied by gestures, grimaces, and . . . contortions and movements of the body, jumping and leaping in a circle.

"For the *mitote* they light a big Fire and dance around it, circling without ceasing for three days and nights. The women never join in the dance but stand at a distance, with their hair over their faces, helping by the utterance of melancholy cries.

"They have several (spirits) to whom they dedicate their *mitotes;* one is the god *Pichini*, another . . . *Mel*. To these they pray with their dances, either for liberty and for triumph over their enemies; or good success in their campaigns; or abundant harvests in their plantings; or plenty of deer, buffalo, or bear. They have their priests and call

186

them *Conas,* and their captains and chiefs and call them *Tamas.* To this office (presumably the chieftainship) there are many pretenders, and they administer tests for admission, such as scarifying the candidates from the back of their heads to the soles of their feet with something like combs made from the spines of sea-fish, causing them to shed much blood. They are also taken off to canebrakes and kept fasting for many days, whence they come out emaciated and almost dead.[4]

Miss Oliver also describes the *mitote.* "Once in a while they held a solemn ceremonial, always celebrated at the Full Moon and after a very successful hunt or fishing expedition. A number of Indians assembled in a tent which had been enlarged for the purpose, in the middle of which was a small Fire upon which boiled a very strong and black concoction made from the leaves of the yaupon tree (*Illex casseene*). From time to time this was stirred with a sort of whisk, till the top was covered thickly with a yellowish froth. This "tea" contained in a clay vessel was handed round occasionally and all the Indians drank freely, seated in a circle round the outside of the tents and looking very grave.

"One tall Indian . . . stood within the circle and passed round and round the fire, chanting in a monotonous tone. He . . . was wrapped up to his head in skins and his face concealed. His long, black hair streamed over his back, and he bent nearly double as he moved about, seldom raising himself to an erect posture.

"The chant rose and fell in a melancholy sort of cadence, and occasionally all the Indians joined in the chorus which was *Há-i-yah, Há-i-yah; hái, hái-yah, hái-yah, hái-yah.* The first two words were shouted slowly, then a loud *hái,* then a sucession of ascending and descending tones, ending in an abrupt *hái!!,* very loud and far-reaching.

"There were three instruments of music, upon which the Indians accompanied the chant. One, a large gourd filled with stones . . . was frequently shaken, another was a fluted

187

piece of wood, which was held upon the knees of the player and over which a stick was quickly drawn producing a droning noise; the third was a kind of rude flute, upon which no air was played, but which was softly blown in time to the chant.

"This . . . was always kept up all night, and as the chorus went on, the chanting became louder. . . . The Fire, allowed to burn up furiously, illuminated the Earth and sky."

Adair describes an instrument which was probably the *cayman*, saying he chanced to see, in the summer of 1746, some Indians playing on one of their old sacred musical instruments "which pretty much resembled the Negro-Banger in shape but far exceeded it in dimensions;" being about five feet long, and a foot wide at the head part of the board, with eight strings made out of the sinew of a large buffalo. The Prophet, who held the instrument between his feet and alongside his chin, took one end of the bow, whilst a lusty fellow held the other; and they, by sweating labor, scraped out such jarring sounds as might have been reasonably expected "to drive out the Devil if he lay hid anywhere in the house."

The name *cayman* is a West Indian word, meaning alligator — the bellowing tone of the instrument resembling the bellow, or roar, of that mighty saurian.

De Solis gives a considerable dissertation on South Texas Tortures: "When one Tribe makes war with another, the one that conquers puts all the old women to the knife and carries off the little children for food to eat on the way. The other children are sold. The vagabonds, grown women, and young girls, are carried off to serve their captors, with the exception of those withheld to sacrifice in the dance before the gods and spirits.

"This is done in the following manner: they set a stake in the ground at the place where they are to dance the *mitote* and light a big Fire, meanwhile tying the victim to the stake. All assemble together, and when the harsh instru-

188

ment, the *cayman,* begins to play, they begin to dance and leap, with well-sharpened knives in their hands, making gestures and fierce grimaces, accompanied by funereal and discordant cries. As they jump around, they approach the victim and cut pieces of flesh from his body, which, in his sight, they roast in the fire and eat with great relish; and so they go on, cutting off pieces, and quartering him, until he expires.

"They scalp him and put the scalp on a pole in order to bring it to the dance as a trophy. They do not throw the bones away, but distribute them; and each one whose turn it is to get one, walks along sucking it until it is finished. They do the same by the missionary priests and Spaniards if they catch any.

"They hang other victims by the feet, put Fire underneath them, and so go on roasting them and eat them up. For still others, they make and light long, inch-thick poles of resinous pine, which is plentiful. After torturing a victim with these, they set fire to him, half roast him and eat him up. Sometimes they do not use a knife to hack their victims in pieces, but tear them apart with their teeth and eat them raw."[5]

Oblivion

So much for the *Karankawa,* cannibal of the coast. He was a poor creature at best; yet the story of the mimic war by which he was driven from his ancient haunts is silvered with that thread of pathos marking all accounts of conflict between the Indian and his exterminators — if the tale be fairly told.

Perhaps the oldest inhabitant of Texas soil, he was the first to be driven from it by the merciless settler. Tradition says after the final defeat a single surviving "war canoe" put out to sea to be swallowed by the foam-crested waves of the Gulf; while the remaining tribal remnant, a mere handful of old men, women, and children, were last seen "begging their way into Mexico and oblivion."

189

INDIANS OF THE SOUTHWEST

FOOTNOTES

[1] *Tortilla* is a Spanish word for "omelet." In South American countries it still refers to an omelet. In the interpenetration of cultures in the Southwest it was used to refer to a specific type of Indian bread — the wafer-like bread made on the *comal* or hot baking stone.

[2] Pictures brought recently from the Orinoco region in South America by Dudley South of Houston show the longbow in constant use today. These pictures also show tattooed women whose facial structure looks identical with that of women photographed around Fort Sill, Oklahoma when southwestern Indians first were herded into that area by federal agents. They show boats similar to the *Karankawa* boats except that the Orinoco boats have bamboo archings for shade which have not been described by observers of the *Karankawa*.

South describes a current use of fish poisons like the method described under FISH STORIES in Chapter XI; and he describes in detail the use of the blowgun, a weapon known to southern and southwestern Indians only as a child's toy. The reason for not using it as a hunting weapon in these areas is simple. Geographers tell us that the slightest air current will deflect the dart, and that only few places in the world afford an opportunity for its use in any purposeful fashion. In the deep, still jungles of the Orinoco country, South says, the Head Hunters use their longbows for deer, but they use the blowgun for birds. In a delightful talk to the writer's anthropology class, he gave this description:

The hunter's hammock, his only bed, is always with him. (We find no reference to the use of hammocks among North American Indians.) When he has stalked a flock of bright macaws to their roost tree, he slings the hammock in a neighbor tree, giving himself a perch higher than the roost. He goes to sleep in midafternoon before the birds come home.

190

THE CANNIBAL OF THE COAST

At Dawn, as they begin to rouse, he is a wide awake. One by one, as they start to preen, he sifts down the noiseless darts, tipped with *curare;* and the birds sink, paralyzed, to Earth. If he wishes to take them alive, he doses them with salt water, to counteract the *curare.* Otherwise they go on the menu after their bright feathers have been plucked to make headdresses — coronets more delicate and graceful than the Eagle Feather diadems of more northerly Indians.

If the hunter should prick himself with a dart, he applies salt water to the wound and so suffers no ill effects.

[3] The *Caddo,* particularly, were "weepers."

[4] Compare this scarifying test with that which is described by Payne in Chapter IX.

[5] Use of the cross was universal among primitive peoples. The American Ku Klux Klan adapted their Fiery Cross from ancient pagan practices of the Scotch Highlanders. Placement on the cross was not intended to punish a captured enemy but to provide an ordeal for determining the power of his Medicine (his magical potency) and of his gods as to whether he could withstand death; or at least in what manner, and how long. The cross was used for this ordeal — that is, as a magimeter — because the death that ensued thereon did not entail the shedding of blood and so laid no one liable to the universal law of *Lex Talonis* described in Chapters XIV and XXIV as THE BLOOD RIGHT and in Chapter XV as THE SATIATION OF THE BLOOD LUST.

EPITAPH

Adapted from a speech of Tecumseh by General Sam Houston in a speech to the United States Senate:

As a race they have withered from the land. Their arrows are broken and their springs are dried up. Their cabins are in dust. Their Council Fires have long since gone out on the shores and their war cry is fast dying away to the untrodden West!

Slowly and sadly they climb the mountains and read their doom in the setting Sun! They are shrinking before the mighty tide which is pressing them away. They must soon hear the roar of the last wave that will settle over them forever.

Ages hence, the inquisitive white man, as he stands by some growing city, will ponder on the structure of their disturbed remains and wonder to what manner of person they belonged. They will live only in the songs and chronicles of their exterminators. *Let these be faithful to their rude virtues as men, and pay tribute to their unhappy fate as a people!*

THE REMNANTS

Indian Death Chant:
Oh Sun, we must die, but you live forever!
Oh Earth, we must die, but you live forever!

Indian Death Chant

THE ALIBAMA-COOSHATTE

Tecumseh's lament blends with the war cry of Mirabeau
Buonaparte Lamar: *Let the sword do its work!* meaning its
"work on the Indians." Considering that Sam Houston was
an adopted *Cherokee* tribesman, the husband of the prin-
cess, Tiana, who died in youth wearing the tattooed star of
her rank (a blue dot the size of one's little fingertip) on
her forehead, it is small wonder he and Lamar were forever
at loggerheads as to the policies of the Texas government.
One human memorial remains from the frantic drift of the
Southern Nations westward into Texas, seeking to escape
the Anglo sword. This is the *Alibama-Cooshatte* Reservation (*Creek*, or *Muscoghe* remnants) near Livingston in the
Texas Big Thicket.

The story of these people who reached Texas in 1809,
of their contract with the Spanish and Mexican governments,
the Texas Republic and the State of Texas, is graphically
told by P. V. Malone whose research will soon be available
among doctoral theses at Texas Southern University, Houston. Of all Indians, they alone, even though they were almost the last to cross into Texas, have retained their organized identity there. Let it be understood, in this respect,
that plenty of Indian blood flows in Texas veins from the

Panhandle to the Gulf, and from the Sabine to the Rio Grande; and equally clearly understood that the Articles of Annexation whereby the Texas Republic was affiliated with the Republic of the North (The United States) after securing independence from the Republic of the South (Mexico) made only *tribal Indians* (those not "christianized and settled on the land") the wards of the federal government. As such, they were to be removed from Texas, across the Red River into what is now the State of Oklahoma — the "Home of the Red Man." The *Alibama-Cooshatte* remain because they did have, as village-building, corn-planting Indians, a specific contract for land.

THE CHEROKEE

Like the *Alibama-Cooshatte,* a remnant of the *Cherokee* also had a contract with the Mexican government for land in East Texas; and were also exempt from the Annexation edict. The last of these *Cherokee,* with other Indians escorted by the local Indian agent, Major Neighbors, fled, as he said "out of the land of the Philistines" into Oklahoma to escape massacre at the hands of Anglo settlers coming in from "the States" just prior to the Civil War. Major Neighbors was assassinated by the would-be massacrers as he returned to the Piney Woods. In this Hate Period of southwestern history, when the world above the Texas Hill Line and west of the Mississippi is described by travellers as "one vast scalping party," with the pioneer hatchet as quick as the tomahawk to "lift the hair," the *Alibama-Cooshatte* stood their ground. Their story, as told by Malone, is a historical vignette within the matrix of the History of Texas.

THE MAN OF TWO COUNTRIES

This vignette compares with the as-yet-unwritten story of the Kickapoo remnant that crossed over Texas into Mexico during the Civil War. All Southern Indian Nations, as aboriginal progenitors of the southern plantation system, had adopted the institution of African slavery in lieu of

194

their own labor system. Unwitting that the independence of Mexico from Spain was predicated on a war to insure the "equality of peoples," the Kickapoo migrated to Mexico with their slaves, expecting to re-establish their plantations in Coahuila. Instead, they were relegated to a reservation north of Musquiz and their slaves were placed on a similar reservation, the two together forming the settlement of Nacimiento. Both groups now enjoy the dual protection of Mexico and the United States.

THE SEMINOLE SCOUTS

Scattered along the road from Bracketville, Texas into Coahuila is a smattering of *Seminole* Scouts, employed at times as guides to expeditionary forces of the federal government. The *Seminole* proper are a "new people" in that they have derived in historic time from an ethnic and cultural intermixture of the ancient *Creek,* or *Muscoghe,* with the African slave. Their major settlement is in Florida.

THE WESTERN BAD MAN

The tremendous and still living story of the *Athapascan* peoples, or *Apaches* in general, far exceeds the capacity of this book. Among Anglo frontiersmen, the *Apaches* encountered on the Buffalo Range, particularly the *Kiowa,* do not lack for champions to proclaim them, in opposition to the *Comanches,* as the finest riders, the bravest warriors, the truest treaty makers of all Indians. *Geronimo!* the name of their last great war chief echoes now as the warcry of American legionnaires.

It must suffice for the purposes of our story here to give the historic spread of these Indians on the map of the Southwest; and to consider that, once they had obtained the horse by running off mustangs from the Spanish ranches in northern Mexico and New Mexico, their activities on the Buffalo Range were very like those of the *Comanches* whom the Spanish knew as *Los Ciboleros* — the "Buffalo Hunters."

The Spanish gave many names to the various tribal segments of the *Apache*. In the desert country of northern Mexico, particularly the stony wilderness of the *Bolson de Mapimi*, the *Tobosos*, or *Yaqui*, were wont to appear out of nowhere, frightening the mild-tempered *Coahuilteca* quite literally into their graves. Across the Rio Grande, into Texas' Big Bend, the *Jicarillo* and the *Mescalero Apaches* trailed the vanguard of *Lipan-Apaches* southward.

REFORMED BAD MAN — THE APACHE CONVERT

Hardly to be classified with national and tribal "remnants," yet not elsewhere classifiable for purposes of this book, is today's folk-spread of Spanish-speaking descendents of the *Yaqui*, the *Jicarillo*, the *Mescalero,* and the *Lipan,* many of whose ancestors became, like the *Coahuilteca* and some of the *Tonkawa*, the "mission Indians" of Spanish time; and who, as such, intermarried with families of Spanish stockmen and miners. Because they were baptized by Franciscan missionaries and taught the Spanish language by their inlaws, they were not scraped off the earth like the *Tonkawa* and shipped to Oklahoma in Texas' great rejection of Indian peoples.

THE MESCAL PITS

One use for the "cased skins" described in THE PRODUCTS OF THE CHASE and in the CARNIVORAN was to store the fermenting juices of the *agave,* or *maguey* plant: the *pulque,* the *mescal* and the *tequila.* Bartlett tells the method of manufacturing these beverages. "A hole is dug some ten or twelve feet in diameter, and about three feet deep, and lined with stones, and on this are piled the bulbs of the maguey, which vary in size from one's hand to a half bushel measure, resembling huge onions. These are again covered with a thick layer of grass; and the whole is allowed to remain until they are thoroughly baked. They are then removed to large leathernbags, and water is poured on them to produce fermentation. At the end of a week the bags

196

are emptied of the *maguey* and its liquor, which, after undergoing the process of distillation, is ready for use."

The Texas Hill Country abounds with "ring mounds" — circles of heat cracked stones the use of which is no longer remembered by any local inhabitant; but in the Big Bend area and in northern Mexico and the rest of the Border Country, descendents of the *Jicarillos* and the *Mescaleros* still know their business. In 1926, on the Cinco de Mayo, "barbecued *maguey* hearts," looking like giant roasted pineapples, were peeled off for sale as a sweetmeat in San Antonio's Haymarket Square. "They are like tobacco, and like candy," the vender cried scooping off a sample with his fingers for a lady, "and so good for the health! Two weeks ago I was thin, like a shadow, and now behold me!" and he spread his hands to cup his fat rotundity. Even so, the Indian trader in the ancient festivals of the *Apacheria* and the *Comancheria* must have hawked his wares. But this was before the stuff fermented. Far down in Mexico, the *Toltecas,* or Wise Ones, had a saying: "The *pulque* gods are rabbit gods, because rabbits have less sense than other animals."

THE BASKET MAKERS

Whether the *Mescaleros* and the *Jicarillos* were one with the sandal-shod Basket Makers that anciently inhabited the caves of deep West Texas is a question yet to be answered. The fact remains that the Athapascans were weaver Indians, and that the woven straw sandal and the skin moccasin met and overlapped in this area, just as the beehive oven and the flat stone metate met and overlapped. Recovered artifacts show an interpenetration of cultures from the Timber Lands, the Plains and the Desert. Spanish records tell of an historical struggle for domination. But so far, burials bundled in reed mats with woven straw sandals accompanying the skeletons hold the oldest place with respect to geological recordings.

Downfall of the Horse

The horse, symbol of military superiority throughout the Barbaric Age of human achievement, meant less to some Indians than to others. Now that we are past the Barbaric or Horse Age into the Atomic Age, the horse has lost its significance; and so, except for tradition, has that great *Apache* who rose to power with the *Comanche,* on horseback, the *Kiowa.* As ranking stealers of horses from the Mexican ranches, they became the ranking Indians of our barbaric yesterday.

The Navajo — Philosopher and Friend

The seizure of sheep and goats from the same ranches applies, by the same token, to the rise of the *Navajo* as the ranking *Apache* of today. *Navajo* acculturation based in large part on the arts of sand painting and weaving, plus a psychic ability to withstand Euro-American cultural contact in the formulation of vital concepts, has brought about a kind of cultural miracle in the overall acculturation of the American Southwest — a crystalization of a Neolithic culture in the midst of modern time! This "miracle" has occurred because linguistic isolation and the desert have served as barriers to create a culture cradle for the evolution of a distinctive *Navajo* folk genius. But, however they may be related to the Plains folk, the *Navajo* must be classified as a people of the Great American Desert and not as a people of the Great Plains.

The *Navajo* could not have withstood the cultural crucifixion of "white contact" at the hands of a federal bureacracy, and have come out with their tribal philosophy alive and vital, had they not previously adapted their culture traits to accommodate pastoralism — the backbone of Spanish colonialism throughout the Americas. Their acceptance of pastoral pursuits, inclusive of herding and weaving, has held them to the slow pace of Neolithic Time in this, our Modern Age of bluster, hurry, tension and stomach ulcers.

As Neo-Neolithics, they offer what is becoming more

and more a retreat for the world-weary denizen of the skycrapers; and their Medicine Men afford a Healing Art unknown to the psychiatrist in his multi-story eyrie above the cement sidewalks. The *Navajo* is trained through his philosophy to believe in constant change — but a change controlled by a maturity of folk wisdom garnered through tribal experience. As each day's Sun goes down on his ancestral sand paintings symbolizing his greatest concepts, he erases the picture. When Morning comes, he paints anew; but the fresh design is always governed by the old. In this manner he meets the challenge of life; and, fortified by the past, is able to take Eternity in his stride!

Like the *Comanche* to the Era of the Horse, so is the *Navajo* to the rising tide of American respect for its aboriginal past — but, instead of *the enemy*, the Navajo is a cultural guide, philosopher, and friend in our present era of frenzied modernity.

At this point we turn a circle from the present-day history of Indian Tribal and national remnants to resume the story of their early contact with the Euro-American — a point in time exemplified by the sight and sound of an Indian seated outside a frontier trading post lustily beating a tribal rhythm from the resounding depths of a five-gallon lard can!

THE HILL TRIBES

How widespread were the *Tonkawa* in time and space we cannot know till archaeological exploration of the Southwest is complete. Suffice it to say, now, that they and their kindred roamed from the mouth of the Rio Grande to the Trinity, from the Gulf to the Staked Plains; that they fought sometimes with and sometimes against the *Tejas;* that, for the most part, they were readily amalgamated with incoming Europeans. The "cannibal ally" of Texas history refers only to one outstanding group of *Tonkawa* people — a group that, despite its alliances, retained its ancient racial customs to its last independent gasp and then was removed to Oklahoma.

Testimonials to Anglo comradeship with the *Tonkawa* are many, but the sole official record of any award for the aid they must have rendered Texas during that six weeks of destiny between the Declaration of Independence on the 2nd of March, 1836, and the decisive Battle of San Jacinto on the 21st of April is a statement that they were called to the Town of Houston, then the capital of the Republic, and each "paid off" by General Houston, first president of the Republic, with ten pounds of warpaint.

The service they rendered is unnamed. One can but conjecture that the *Comanche* warwhoop was unheard in the Runaway Scrape by which women and children of South Texas, together with the official families of Coahuila, made their escape to the Piney Woods (the sister states of Texas and Coahuila were joined in the rebellion) only because the manpower of the *Tonkawa* was massed on the hill line between them and the *Comancheria.*

THE TRAVOIS

XX

The Child of Fortune

Any day you'd find him "a-sunning" in the Sun!

THE HEART OF THE HILLS

In the Hill Country of central Texas once lived a simple-hearted Indian who danced and sang through the days, hunted the deer through the evergreen shadows of the cedars, and followed the hill streams down into the prairies seeking mesquite beans to grind for bread. This was the *Tonkawa*. South of him lived his kindred, the *Coahuilteca*.

His only sorrow lay in death when some fierce *Apache* struck the tribe a mortal blow, or, later, some *Comanche* raiding party left destruction in its wake.

Though he preferred peace, the *Tonkawa*, when cornered, fought like any other man. If he got the best of the scrap, he ate the flesh of his opponents in order to absorb their martial spirit and thereby be the better equipped to maintain possession of his game-filled, flower-tapestried hunting ground.

His was the Balcones Fault Scarp, that strange Earth Crack, cutting away for mile on mile where the Edwards Plateau rises in purple ridges on the west, and on the east, the black prairies slant to the sea. His were the hundreds of ice-cold springs gushing from the broken strata along this mighty cleft, his the rock-lined caves dripping with wild honey, and his the groves of black walnut and pecan bordering the streambeds.

THE PRAIRIE LANDS

On the sloping stretches of the Prairie Lands, Nature's necromancy laid a sky-blue covering each pleasant, rainy spring. The great shedding herds of the *cibolo,* maned like lions, cast their winter coats, as they cropped the blossoming lupine; and, so the white settlers said, marked the Earth with "wallows" as they rolled, bellowing in the damp air.

Fortunately for their peace of mind, neither the buffalo, feasting on the perfumed flowers, nor the *Tonkawa* hunters, creeping through the Dawn with the hope of feasting on the buffalo, had anything in their philosophy to hint that the lupines were prophetically shaped — that where they raised their myriad blooms would one day rise the calico-bonneted heads of stranger-women — that the flower beloved of the buffalo would come to bear a name and a significance totally alien: the Texas state flower, or "bluebonnet," first called "buffalo clover" by the pioneer.

Yet they might have been forewarned, for there are botanists who believe that the heavenly blue flower marks the old road of the Spanish army and colonials as they moved through Texas, out of the Mexican desert into the Indian corn lands across the Trinity. The same flower, they say, brightens the pastures in Spain whence came the hay horses and oxen consumed while crossing the Black Land prairies.

However the flower came, the name of the animal is both Spanish and Indian — another evidence of the centuries-old blending of cultures in the Southwest. *Cibolo* is the Spanish version of the Indian word of which the English form is "buffalo." It is a favorite name with Anglo-American pioneer families in Texas who spell and pronounce it "sea-willow."

Through untold centuries before the iron axes of the settlers rang through his wooded paradise, or the bronze bells of the Spanish missions donged across the Prairie Lands,

the *Tonkawa* danced his *mitotes* undisturbed, offering sacrifices to the spirits of Nature, among them, perhaps, the En-
chanted Rock, a mighty granite boulder spread, like an upset mixing bowl, over six hundred and forty acres of land
in what is now Gillespie County.

The central and south Texas tribes, more particularly
the *Coahuilteca,* were destined to become the "mission Indians" of history. Being tractable folk, they were eventually
absorbed into the populace of both Texas and Mexico,
losing identity entirely as aborigines.

The *Tonkawa* proper received less from the benefits of
baptism than other denizens of the area; and, for his sins,
perhaps, or at least for his omission to embrace the Christian faith with a due amount of fervor, was cut to pieces
by the *Comanches* when the white invader of Texas left
his cannibal ally to shift for himself during the Civil War.
The old feud between *Tonkawa* and *Comanche,* breaking
out afresh, ended with almost complete annihilation of the
minor people. Such *Tonkawa* remnants as remained when
the federal reservations were formed still exist as a racial
fragment in Oklahoma.

It is not possible to draw an ethnic line between the
Texas *Tonkawa* and the *Coahuilteca.* Either the *Tonkawa*
was the eastward moving front of a vast *Coahuiltecan* expan-
sion, or the tribal bands were so closely allied that their
culture traits overlap indistinguishably, due to generations
of neighborliness in the same habitat. Suffice it to say, for
the nonce, that Coronado found "dog drivers," the *Tonkawa* with their dog *travois* that preceded the pony *travois,*
arriving on the Buffalo Range and setting up their tepees
for the Summer Hunt as his expedition came eastward out
of the Rocky Mountains.

The Jacal and the Dugout

The earliest Spanish expeditions into Texas found large
villages of thatched straw huts or birdcage-like *jacals* (ha-
cals) at all the artesian springs along the Balcones Fault

Scarp, or Texas Hill Line. Largest was the *Yanaguana* Village at San Pedro Springs, now well within the corporate limits of San Antonio. It is interesting to see how modern cities follow this Indian village pattern through northern Mexico and Texas — because of living water.

The rectangular post-and-lintel brush house, with its simple gable roof, if found in these first villages, is still in use on both sides of the Rio Grande, and far down in Mexico. Its alternate is the "dug-out" where the desert does not furnish sufficient growth for an above-earth shelter. Where the desert dweller is dependent on the tough sotol stalk rather than on corn as his staff of life, he uses such dried stuff as there is to build a peaked top for the pit he digs himself to live in, and forgets about the "four walls" of houses in less arid territory.

THE WOLF DANCE

While he was in his heyday, the *Tonkawa*, like the other southern Indians, celebrated innumerable festivals, among them the Wolf Dance by which he perpetuated the story of his tribal origin.

Each year, in preparation for this ceremony, says Parker, the *Tonkawa* braves erected a great brush arbor, after the fashion of shelters used for "camp meetings" in the same territory today. Under this arbor, where the air was rich with the pungency of bruised cedar boughs, the men of the clan gathered, each cloaked completely in the skin of a timber wolf — monarch of the Texas hills.

As night came on the gathering "wolves" sat on their haunches around the lodge and bayed the Moon. Then they rose, flourishing their plumed tails, and circled the walls, sniffing, scratching, shying away from one another, snapping, snarling, playing after the fashion of their kind, yet preserving a rhythm to their movements — a rhythm set by the monotony of the *tom-tom*.

Round they went, and round, till it became obvious that

there was purpose in their search — something they were smelling out — something interred, that, dog-like, as their paws flew faster and faster in the Earth at the center of the lodge, they were digging up.

Finally, rousing from the disturbed soil, dazed, blinking, flinging the dirt from his shoulders with a tremendous shrug, came a live *Tonkawa,* symbolic Adam of his tribe.

His ceremonial interment was managed, perhaps, by means of a reed through which he breathed while underground; and was, in all probability, part of his initiation into the warrior group.

The countenance of the resurrected *Tonkawa,* as it became less and less bewildered, grew more and more downcast. At last he said to the wolves with a puzzled and desperate air: "You have brought me into the world, and I do not know what to do; it would have been better to let me remain as I was. I shall starve in *this* world!"

After much putting of their heads together, and tongue and tail wagging, accompanied by snarls and growls, several of the larger wolves retired into a dark corner, whither they returned with a bow and arrow which they solemnly presented to the newfound man, saying: "Go now; fight as we do; take what you need and kill what you will, for you are armed."

Then the man rose and threw off his lethargy. He danced in thanksgiving for the bow and arrow; and the wolves threw off their skins, became men and danced with him — for they were the *Tonkawa!*

The first Spaniard to come on the peoples of the Southwest was Cabeza de Vaca who traveled on foot, after shipwreck, from Galveston Island, up through the Texas Hills, around past the Pueblos, and down to Mexico City. Held slave by the *Karankawa* for seven years, he, with four companions, one the black man, Estevanico of Azamor, escaped in the *tuna* season while the big Get-Together of the *Karankawa* was in full swing.

He reports of the Indians in the Hills, who must almost

206

certainly have been *Tonkawa*: "When they are in a part
of the country where their enemies may attack them, they
place their houses on the skirt of a wood, the thickest and
most tangled they can find, and near it make a ditch in
which they sleep. The warriors are covered by small pieces
of stick through which are loopholes; these hide them and
present so false an appearance that if any come upon them,
they are not discovered. They open a very narrow way, entering into the midst of the wood where a spot is prepared
on which the women and children sleep. When night comes
they kindle Fires in their lodges, that, should spies be about,
they may think to find them there; and before Daylight
they again light these Fires.

"If the enemy comes to assault these houses, they who
are in the ditch make a sally; and from their trenches do
much injury without these who are outside seeing or being
able to find them. When there is no wood in which they
can take shelter in this way, and make their ambuscades,
they settle on open ground at a place they select, which
they invest with trenches covered with broken sticks, having
apertures whence to discharge arrows. These arrangements
are made for the night."

This is the earliest historical account of the Prairie and
Hill Tribes.

FORTUNE'S CHILD

The Spanish, searching in every direction for gold, ran-
sacking every Indian province, looked on the *Tonkawa* as
miserable and degenerate because of their lack of accumulated wealth with which to laden the invaders' pack mules,
and because of their scanty attire. As a matter of fact, the
Tonkawa, in his breechclout and moccasins, was much
more comfortably equipped for slipping through the torrid
cedar brakes after the keen-eared deer than were the *Conquistadores,* rattling along, as some humorist has said, "like
so many crates of tomato cans." How their super-heated

207

armor must have winked and blinked in the Texas sun, against the white glare of the chalk lands, startling the game for miles!

Tonkawa, Gatschet tells us, was a Waco word meaning "they-all-stay-together" — evidence that it was their custom to live in communities, like the *Tejas;* though their temporary "lean-tos" bore no resemblance to the impressive straw domes of East Texas.

Says Gatschet: "The lodges of the *Tonkawa* . . . are cane or willow-stick lodges, flat on the top, open on one or two sides, and covered with brushwood." Skins and wattle were also used on the closed sides. The *Tonkawa* word for "lodge" was *yetsoxan,* translated by Gatschet as "interwoven," meaning "brush lodge."

Near the campsites of all the Texas Indians, says Roemer, were deep stacks of scraped deer hair, which, of course, formed the eternal harborage for fleas.

The narrator who visited the "Cronks" in the Mission San Rosario has given us this picture of the "Tonks" seen near Austin: "The camp of the Tonkawa was situated in the center of a thick grove. Their huts were small, conical in shape, made of light branches, and covered with the same material, plus an occasional buffalo skin. In the center of each was the fireplace.

THE PRAIRIE WARDROBE

"The men lie about while at home, but the women are in constant motion, either curing meat of the game, tanning the skins, preparing the food, or making clothing. The elder women work the hardest.

"The men wear earrings and other ornaments on their necks and hair, made of bone, shell, and showy feathers; while the women wear only black stripes on their mouths, noses, necks, and breasts. On the breast the stripes are painted in concentric circles from the nipple to the base of each breast. They wear nothing but a piece of deerskin

208

around their waists, leaving the rest of their bodies naked;
and they wear their hair short."

A generation later, Sallie Reynolds Matthews paints a
picture reflecting a pioneer woman's view of the Tonkawa
encampment: "Among the people who came to (Fort Griffin) for protection against the Comanche was a small tribe
of . . . Tonkawa. They were a kindly people, never molest-
ing anybody or taking anything that did not belong to them.
They did beautiful beadwork and were very painstaking
with any handiwork they undertook. Their sewing on the
buckskin moccasins and bootees was exceptionally neat.
They wore few clothes. The women's dress consisted of a
piece of cloth pulled tightly around the waist, coming below the knees, and added to that was a garment of one width
of calico with a slit through which they slipped the head.
This extended below the waist in front and trailed to the
ground in the back and when the wind blew . . . it stood
out like a sail. (They) were partial to materials with large
figures in bright colors. Red and yellow calico we called
'Indian calico' because of their predilection for these
colors."

(The writer's mother, Josephine Butler Jourdan, used
also to describe visits from the *Tonkawa,* made to the Sneed
Plantation near Austin in pre-Civil War days. The grown-
up young ladies in the family would bestow dresses on the
Indian women, each of whom would depart with all the
dresses she had received put on one over the other, the
longest first and the last and shortest on top, so that each
dress — sometimes four or five — was distinctly visible.
This, one may well liken to Veblen's definition of "conspicuous wealth"!)

"These Indians were socially inclined," Mrs. Matthews
continues: "they liked to come into our houses and visit.
One day (one) came to our house with her papoose swung
in a blanket on her back, she holding the ends over her
shoulder, that being the usual way of carrying their
babies."

INDIANS OF THE SOUTHWEST

Whenever a statement is made concerning Indian clothing, it is well to keep in mind the fact that all Indians, even to the tiniest child ordinarily seen naked, had their festive attire, which was, quite naturally, reserved for fete days.

THE OREJONES

Hodge mentions the *Orejones* or "big ears," a *Coahuiltecan* tribe, so-named by the Spanish because of their tremendous auditory appendages — which were, of course, artificially enlarged by the method Adair describes in VANITIES OF THE VILLAGERS. According to the Abbe Domenech, it seems to have been the custom of these Indians to add to their collections of trinkets and earbobs the religious medals received at the missions, stalking away well-pleased with the Blessed Virgin or a saint or two wedged between a boar's tusk and a bear's claw.

BUFFALO BY-PRODUCTS

De Mézieres, a French officer in Spanish service, says, speaking of the importance of buffalo to the *Tonkawa*: "Besides their meat, it furnishes them liberally what they desire for conveniences. The brains are used to soften the skins, the horns for spoons and drinking cups, the shoulder blades to dig up and clear off the ground, the tendons for thread and bowstrings, the hoofs to glue the arrow feathering. From the tail hair, they make ropes and girths; from the wool, belts and various ornaments. The hide furnishes saddle and bridle, tether ropes, shields, tents, shirts, footwear, and blankets to protect them from the cold."

It would seem from this account that the *Tonkawa* kept well up "with the Jones" among Indians having everything that he could need in the way of native equipment.

THE PEDERNALES OR FLINT MINES

Along the broken strata of the Fault Scarp, he had access

to an inexhaustible horde of the most perfect flint which he mined, not only for his own use, but in all probability, as an article of commerce, exchanging beautifully manufactured knives, awls, and skin scrapers for luxuries and necessities produced by the neighboring Nations.

Beside his flint mines, he had a superb deer range, one of the best in the western hemisphere, where it was possible for him to slip silently over the chalk hills, between the low-growing cedars, until he could almost touch the unsuspecting quarry, before he loosed his arrow. How skillful he was in the chase is evidenced by the statement of an American trader who told Sibley he had sometimes obtained from the *Tonkawa* as many as five thousand deerskins in a single season. Before the ox-wagons of the pioneers started on their southward trek, however, the main market for Tonkawa goods was with the East Texas Nations, as described in THE PEACE PIPE.

HOSPITALITY

Among *Tonkawa* conventions of hospitality, soldiers, traders, and Indian agents comment on the reception of all guests with honor, and on the provision of maidens for the amusement of visiting gentlemen unaccompanied by their wives — even though the sojourners were the insolent *Comanche* "lords" who made their desires known with imperious and "high-handed" gestures whenever they arrived at the hill camps.

THE WEATHER SIGN

For all of its delights, the Hill Country did have its drawbacks. One was the "flash floods" that, with the sun shining bright in a clear blue sky would roll soundlessly down the canyons of the creeks and rivers, as high as a man's head, and deadly with the weight of their swift-rolling waters. They caught the Spanish and the Anglo unawares, but not the Tonkawa. "Listen," he told these wilderness-un-

211

sophisticated neighbors, "Listen! When of a sudden the crickets cease to sing, when suddenly it is so still you *hear the silence* — get your cattle and goods out of the lowlands, the *water is coming down.*"[1]

TONKAWA RELIGIOUS MYSTERIES

A note from Gatschet furnishes us this information concerning the *Tonkawa's* religious, or magical beliefs: They "will give to their children *Comanche* and English names besides those from their own language, which they are unwilling to communicate to others. . . . They believe that when somebody calls an individual by his or her name after death, the spirit of the deceased may hear it and be prompted to take revenge upon those who disturbed his rest; but if called in another language this would have no effect on the spirit."[2]

Different tribes had different methods for "laying" the spirits of the dead, and for disguising and protecting the living from the untoward designs of dissatisfied or vengeful ghosts — fear of the dead being a psychological factor in all primitive religious patterns.

While the Plains Tribes had their *peyote,* and the gardening Nations their Yaupon Tea, the Indian of Central Texas had the *frixolillo,* the vivid orange-red bean of the local "mountain laurel," that could addle his head and bring him dreams and visions with the best, when he was in religious mood. Moreover, these beans, if their flint-like cores were drilled with stone awls, made necklaces so ornamental that a string two yards long was worth a pony — after the ponies became currency.[3]

The *Tonkawa,* like the *Karankawa,* had a very bad reputation for undue indulgence in human flesh. Certainly the excuse cannot be made that his was a scanty food supply. He gave the matter a semblance of etiquette, however, by claiming it was "ceremonial" and "symbolic" — a magic rite performed to endow himself with the superior courage, cunning, and strength of the enemy — thus setting forth his orgies as a compliment to the shock troops of the *Apacheria* and the *Comancheria* — neither receiving the pleasantry with the slightest grace.

That these repasts actually did have a ritual aspect, though it may have been secondary, is set forth by the quotation from Noah Smithwick given in this chapter, and by historical descriptions of the Battle of Plum Creek where the victorious Texans looked on while their *Tonkawa* allies stripped and devoured flesh from the arms, hands, and feet of the *Comanche* dead, those being the portions of the anatomy thought to contain the desired spiritual elements. From still another quarter, we hear that expectant mothers were accustomed to nibble the fingers and toes of dead warriors that their children might be fleet of foot and strong of arm — no more a "superstition" than ideas among women of our own day who believe the unborn child may be affected by what the mother sees, hears, or feels.

THE COMANCHE REACTION

Nothing on Earth so infuriated a *Comanche* as to find that a low and beastly *Tonkawa* had actually got the spirit of a *Comanche* on his inside. The kind of temper tantrum he indulged in on discovering the gnawed remains of one of his compatriots is amply demonstrated by Herman Lehmann, of Fredericksburg, Texas, who, captured by the *Apaches* as a child and adopted into their Tribe, later became, also by adoption, a full-fledged *Comanche* warrior.

Says he: "The *Comanches* and *Tonkeways* had been at war a long time, and the *Tonkeways* had been nearly exterminated. The hatred the *Tonkeways* had for the *Comanche* was fierce, for they blamed the *Comanche* for all of their misfortunes, and eventually made a treaty with the white people and combined with them to exterminate the *Comanche*, acting as scouts and trailers and warriors for the whites.

213

"When we found those *Tonkeways* in camp (evidently the *Comanches* were on a specific trail) our chief gave a war whoop and we all joined in one continual yell as we charged that camp.

"They fled at the onslaught and several of them were killed. We took possession of the camp, and what do you suppose we found on that fire roasting? One of the legs of a *Comanche!* A warrior of our tribe!

"Our chief gave the cry for vengeance and we all joined in the chorus. We immediately gave chase. One look at those stern faces and drawn muscles would have shown that (we) meant utterly to annihilate (our) enemy."

THE DUEL

"The *Tonkeways* had collected in a ravine and were prepared to receive our charge with a deadly fire, which for a moment checked our onrush; down would come a horse, over would tumble the rider, but on, on, we came in our frenzy.

"At first I was terrified and it seemed like I could not face death that way, but I was in the front rank and my comrades in the rear pressed me onward. Then I caught the spirit of vengeance. I became enraged, spurred on my steed and fought courageously.

"One of the *Tonkeways* rode out of the ravine to challenge a single combat. A *Comanche* made a dash at him, but fell mortally wounded. Another went and received a death blow. It seemed like human blood had made the *Tonkeway* bold, and somehow our shields would not ward off his bullets, but the third warrior to advance got him.

"At this single combat, by seemingly general consent, a cessation took place and at this recess every warrior loaded his gun and prepared for eventualities. The combat between the two warriors was of but short duration, and when the *Tonkeway* brave fell there went up a yell from both sides, exultant from us, a yell of rage from the *Tonkeways*, and in a very few seconds we were in a hand-to-hand conflict with the *Tonkeways* and they were soon vanquished.

"Those cannibals fought bravely, and eight of our men lay dying on the battlefield, while forty or fifty were more or less desperately wounded. But our work was not finished.

"We scalped . . . (the dying enemy) amputated their arms, cut off their legs, cut out their tongues, and threw their mangled bodies and limbs on their own campfire, put on more brushwood and piled the living, dying, and dead *Tonkeways* on the fire.

"Some were able to flinch and work as a worm, and some were able to speak and plead for mercy. We piled them up, put on more wood, and danced around in great glee as we saw the grease and blood run from their bodies, and were delighted to see them swell and hear their hides pop as it would burst in the fire."

Thus did the infuriated *Comanches*, losing all sense of discretion and throwing aside their customary caution, mete out punishment to the enemy that had dared to devour a *Comanche* warrior.

INDIAN HUMOR

Mrs. Matthews also cites an incident that puts one in mind of the recent Lumbee uprising anent Ku Klux Klan activities in North Carolina.[4] "A Tonkawa came to father one day with a story that was most amusing to himself. It seems he had been out hunting . . . when riding over a hill he saw down in the valley at quite a distance some Indians of his own tribe skinning a buffalo they had just killed. In order to frighten them, he emitted some blood-curdling yells, typical of Indians on the warpath. They took him to be a Comanche, and, to use his own words, 'they lunned, and they lunned, and they lunned,'[5] so this wiley fellow went down and helped himself to the buffalo. He told the story with great gusto and could hardly talk for laughing, now and then bending double with laughter."

INDIANS OF THE SOUTHWEST

Feast of the Ghouls on Webber's Prairie

Noah Smithwick, in telling his experiences among the Texas Tribes, gives us the details of a cannibal feast witnessed on Webber's Prairie. After killing and scalping a *Comanche*, the *Tonkawa*, on the vengeance trail with a company of recently despoiled Texans, their allies, refused to pursue the chase farther "saying they must return home to celebrate the event, which they accordingly did by a feast and scalp dance. Having slashed off the flesh of the dead *Comanche* they borrowed a big kettle from Puss Webber, into which they put the *Comanche* meat, together with a lot of corn and potatoes. When the stew was sufficiently cooked and cooled to allow of its being ladled out with the hands the whole tribe gathered round, dipping it up with their hands and eating it greedily. Having gorged themselves . . . they lay down and slept till night, when the entertainment was concluded with the scalp dance.

"Gotten up in . . . war paint and best breechclouts, the warriors gathered round in a ring, each one armed with some . . . (musical) instrument which they operated in unison with a drum of dried deerskin stretched tightly over a hoop, at the same time keeping up a monotonous (chant of) *Ha, ah, ha!* raising and lowering their bodies . . . (in perfect rhythm) every muscle seeming to twitch in harmony."

Meanwhile some old woman would present to each dancer "in turn an arm or leg of the dead foe, which they would bite at viciously, catching it in their teeth and shaking it like savage dogs.

"And high over all waved from the point of the lance the scalp, dressed and painted, held aloft by a patriotic squaw. The orgies were kept up till the performers were forced to desist from sheer exhaustion."[6]

Tonkawa Friendship

In the life story of Elizabeth Owens we find this para-

216

graph: "The Carancahuas bore Mrs. De Leon ill will. They had planned to make an attack on her and her family and invited the Tancahuas to join them. The two tribes met and made preparations for the war dance over the dead bodies of their intended victims. But the Tancahuas, being friends to Mrs. De Leon, deceived the Carancahuas. They cut their bowstrings, killed thirteen of the tribe and took their scalps to Mrs. De Leon, dancing around her home with the scalps stuck upon their spears, as evidence of friendship and protection."

A TONKAWA FUNERAL

Smithwick tells of a *Tonkawa* funeral held at practically the same spot as the cannibal feast, prefacing his description with the remark that "an Indian funeral is very suggestive of the demonstrations made by cattle over the blood of their kind."

The tribe, he says, after the death of one of its members, made "the darkness hideous for two nights . . . with shrieks and yells" then buried the departed brave and immediately pulled up stakes and moved away.

"Just before the burial took place, while the dead warrior lay in state wrapped in his best buffalo robe," a young woman entered the tepee "with a pair of . . . new beaded moccasins, with which she was in the act of clothing the feet of the corpse," when an old woman who stood near "snatched them from her and with a dexterity which would have done credit to a professional juggler, slipped them under her shawl substituting an old pair and wrapping the feet up in the robe.

"When time for the funeral arrived, the white men present were requested to retire which they did for the space of half an hour, when they returned to find every vestige of the camp gone, nor could the most diligent search discover the place of interment; there was not a clod of new earth to designate the spot, not a blade of grass had seemingly been disturbed, so careful were the Indians to obliterate every trace" — supposedly by resetting the turf in exact position over the grave.[7]

THE CANNIBAL ALLY

The time has come, in less than the span of a single memory, when that same turf, trod for generations by the feet of the *Tonkawa*, bears not one mark of their ancient occupancy, save a dropped flint here and there, and an occasional refuse heap, or kitchen midden. However, beneath the turf, lies an archaeological story so old it has just been hinted at — how old the scientist dares not whisper, even in his dreams, till further proofs appear. History gives us only the final chapter of that story; but the chapter history does give, tells of the day when the cannibal ally, in very truth, kept the wolf from the white settler's door.

FOOTNOTES

[1] These sudden, soundless floods result from heavy rains far up on the Plains.

[2] See statement by Julia Lee Sinks, UNIVERSAL BELIEF IN IMMORTALITY, pp. 159-60.

[3] The *Peyote* Cult, based on the schizophrenic effects of chewing *peyote* "buttons" — the seed of a pincushion-shaped cactus the size of a man's hand — is not to be confused with the drinking of *pulque, mescal* and tequila which are alcoholic beverages obtained from the *agave, maguey,* or century plant. The latter grows in a basket-shape, sometimes as large as a small room, and runs its flower-shoot, after years of time, twenty feet into the air. It is cultivated commercially to supply the "pulque joints" of Mexico and the southwestern United States with a goodly part of their stock in trade.

Peyote originally was condemned under the United States Narcotics Laws but the Oklahoma Indians persisted in gathering the crop from the *Peyote* Hills below Eagle Pass-Piedras Negras on the Texas-Coahuila border, and in contending for their ancient ritual in the American courts until they succeeded in legalizing the *Peyote* Cult as a "native American church." This cult, as described by Ruth Underhill in her book THE NAVAJOS, bears no relation to the activities of an opium den, or of a pulque joint.

4 The *Lumbee* are a modern Indian organization, said to number some 30,000 persons of *Cherokee* descent, on the Lumber River in North Carolina. In January of 1958, led by their own ex-servicemen, they simulated an "uprising" that is said to have "raised the hair," although it took no scalps, with respect to a Ku Klux Klan rally directed against their free intermingling with other ethnic groups of the community.

5 The sing-song speech of an Indian untutored in the use of a language with an intonation entirely different from his own is very like the same speech of an untutored Chinese. Both change the "R" in English or Spanish to an "L" — like the Chinese laundryman heard in Mexico crying: *"La lopa! La lopa!"* (The Spanish word for clothes or "laundry" is ropa.)

6 According to White Parker, son of Quanah, "squaw" is a white man's word. It is derogatory and was never employed by Indians.

7 Compare UNIVERSAL BELIEF IN IMMORTALITY, Chapter XVI.

THE PLAINS AND DESERT TRIBES

The *Comanches,* a branch of the vast *Shoshonean* stock (from over the Bering Strait), came out of the Rocky Mountains to form three tribal divisions on the Great Plains — the Northern, Middle, and Southern *Comanches.* The latter, maintaining the *Comancheria* in Texas, Oklahoma, and the Arkansas Ozarks, became, after they acquired the horse, and allied themselves with the *Kiowa* in New Mexico, the most powerful of all Plains peoples.

The *Apaches,* of *Athapascan* stock, dominated an equally enormous territory extending through Old Mexico, New Mexico, and Arizona, and, eventually, parts of Texas. Their strongholds were in the Mexican Mountains. The barbaric organization they built, based on the horse, was much like that of the *Comanches.*

The *Kiowa,* the third great people of the Indian "horse era," enter formal history in blood pact with the *Comanches,* though they were *Apaches* by ethnic affiliation. So vast was the spread of the *Apacheria* that the *Mescalero Apache,* named for cult rituals based on the schizophrenic effect of fermented cactus juice, Mescal; and the *Lipan-Apache,* are thought of in southwestern history, like the *Kiowa,* as distinctive peoples. The *Mescaleros* and the *Lipans* both moved in onto *Pintada* and *Tonkawa* territory in the Texas Big Bend and in South Texas as soon as possession of the mustang gave them an advantage over older occupants of the soil. Their real advantage lay in their adjacency to the Spanish ranches of northern Mexico where they could seize mustangs instead of having to trade for them.

THE "SWOOP"

To pick up an injured man or a dead body, the rider on the left would swing to the other side of his horse so that the two men, reaching down between the horses, (ponies, and therefore low to the ground) could seize and lift the victim, swinging his body over the neck of the horse previously agreed on.

XXI

The Rider of the Plains

"This is the Indian that fills our ideal of true savage life — the Arab of the Prairie — the model of the fabled Thessalian 'Centaur,' half horse, half man, so closely joined and so dexterously managed that it appears but one animal, fleet and furious. The *Comanches* are considered the best horseman in the world!"

Thrall.

UP FROM SAVAGERY

The average person, thinking of a Texas Indian, calls to mind a whooping and befeathered Redskin, in full gallop — on a foam-flecked, walleyed horse — brandishing a bloody scalp!

In other words, the average person, in thinking of a Texas Indian, thinks always of a "horse" Indian, and always in terms of the forty years' war that raged between the Plains hunter and the Anglo-American settler for control of the southern Buffalo Range.

To think thus is to ignore the eons before the conquest of Mexico. To think thus is to fail to evaluate the three centuries between the conquest of Mexico and the opening of Texas to immigration from the "States" — three centuries in which the *Comanche* rose from a savage hunter on foot to a barbaric herdsman on horseback, dominating Texas — the "Lord of the Plains."

The Spanish Charger

Biology tells us that before the arrival of the *Conquistadores* on their caparisoned mounts, no Indian ever saw a horse; and tradition tells us that before the arrival of Cortes with his blond beard and pale cheeks all Indians looked to the East, the Land of the Rising Sun, for the coming of the Sun God — the "Fair One."

History tells us that the first Indians to gaze upon a knight in armor were stricken dumb with amazement, falling on their knees in religious awe, prostrate before a long awaited vision! Certain at last of the realization of an ancient dream!

Alas, history does not stop at this point. It continues to tell us that at the terrifying sight of man and horse dividing, as the rider clankingly swung himself to Earth, the Indians fled in horror — discovering they had embraced, not the fulfillment of tradition, but a travesty. Their god from the Dawn Lands was a monster — Death, clad in iron!

The Mustang

But though the Conqueror shackled the *Montezumas* and set the cross on the pyramids of the Sun in the Mexican garden lands, his activities resulted in a burst of glory for the Plains Tribes. A meteoric rise to power beyond their wildest imaginings! The colonial livestock loosed in Mexico made its way into South Texas, into the uninhabited Brush Country, there to thrive, unmolested, until thousands of wild horses. mantled only in their flowing manes — lineal descendants, nevertheless, of the velvet-hung chargers of the Conquest — galloped forward to meet the *Comanche* on the *mesas* and in the canyons of the Staked Plains.

223

INDIANS OF THE SOUTHWEST

THE SOCIAL REVOLUTION

The *Comanche,* ever seeking the "buffalo holes," let fly a lariat and made the mesteña his own, thus becoming, mounted, master of the Buffalo Range — master of the mustang herds as well, measuring his wealth in ponies, trading livestock, supplying his age-old enemies, the *Kiowa* and *Apache,* with horses till the whole Southwest was alive with mounted barbarians — circling Mexico — bounding the "States!" A sweeping, whirling, nomadic civilization of the semiarid wastes, rivaled in history only by the Tartar and the Arab!

THE BUFFALO MYTH

As for the "buffalo holes," Dodge tells us all the Indians of the Plains believed the buffalo to be recreated each year to the southward — recreated by the hands of the Great Spirit, under the Earth — whence they issued in spring from two great holes, in two great moiling streams — numbering uncountable myriads of shaggy brutes with sharp little crescent horns and iron forelegs — following the greening grass northward, till the whole buffalo country, from the Gulf to the Saskatchewan, teemed with humped herds. Tradition, says Dodge, located these miraculous holes in Texas, between the Canadian and the Pecos — just where the *Comanche* was headed when he met the galloping mustang.

THE FOOT TRAILS

What the *Comanche* was like before he had the horse, we can only surmise. He kept no records of his history beyond the tattoo marks on his person that perished with his individual passing, and we have no intimate knowledge of his ways and customs until the westward flowing tide of Anglo-American civilization reached the Mississippi — when it became necessary for the American government to set outposts on the Great Plains. By the time these forts were built the *Comanche* had been long in the saddle.

For the pre-historic or pre-horse period of his development, suffice it to say that for him the buffalo was Nature's
storehouse, furnishing him with food, clothing, and shelter;
that his religion was one of the many prevailing forms of
Sun worship, with magical divination as its principal element; and that his ancestors were the *Shoshones* whose home
was in the Rockies, whence the *Comanche* straggled out
onto the Plains at the heels of the buffalo herds.

Culturally speaking, the status of the *Comanche* was
raised from savagery to barbarism by the acquisition of the
horse. The sudden elevation went to his head. No longer
a fierce beggar at Nature's gate, dependent on her capri-
cious bounty, he became a despot, a nomadic tyrant —
levying tribute by raiding other men's painfully constructed
strongholds, exalting himself through the careless dispen-
sation of other men's hard-earned goods!

THREE-CORNERED WAR IN TEXAS

The *Comanche,* the *Kiowa,* and the *Apache* struggled for
control of the Buffalo Range while still on foot. Eventually
peace, sealed with a pact of blood brotherhood, was concluded between the *Kiowa* and the *Comanche* — a peace
which only added to the uneasiness of the Spanish garrison
in San Antonio and the *Tonkawa* Tribes in the central hills,
each knowing full well the *Comanche* was minded to do
away with both and have a clear path to the Gulf when he
and the *Apache* should settle their long-standing feud. Thus
three-cornered war raged in Texas decades before the never-
resting "settler" brought his hungry plow and plunged into
the middle of the fray. And thus the *Comanche,* years before
the Empires to the south had burst their Spanish bonds, became the scourge of Mexico.

THE MEXICAN MOON

Somewhere in the course of the three important centuries between 1519 and 1820 we are told that the *Comanche* calendar changed its ancient terminology, September becoming the "Mexican Moon"; while the trail to Chihuahua was cut deep in alkali by the flying hoofs of ponies speeding southward to raid the ranches of the *Dons.* In September the *tunas* were ripe, offering sustenance to man through the dry lands, while the *Comanche,* mounted, was able to maneuver the buffalo so as to have a herd waiting for him on the homeward trail.[1]

Bareback and unencumbered he whirled into Mexico! More slowly he returned, driving the flocks of the pillaged *haciendas,* leading horses loaded with laces and silks and golden altar vessels — himself bearing on his silver-mounted saddle bow the daughter of a *Don.* In fact, according to the Oklahoma *Chronicles,* it was now that the name of *Comanche* was bestowed upon him — as an abbreviation of the Spanish phrase: *El Camino Ancho,* the Broad Road, or Wide Open Road, into Mexico.

LORD OF THE PLAINS

Small wonder the Spanish and later the Mexican garrisons slept but fitfully in San Antonio. Small wonder the Anglo-American found he had bitten off more than he bargained to chew, when, flushed with the success of San Jacinto, he sought to strike his greedy plowshares into the unrived Prairie Lands. The *Comanche,* watching unseen in the hills, waiting to learn whether he should fight Mexican or Texican, was to remain master of the Buffalo Range for another forty years.

FOOTNOTES

[1] *Tuna* is the common name in Mexican markets today for the fruit of the prickly pear, or *nopal.* In both the Spanish language and Maori, as in English, this word applies to specific seafoods. Cf. *aceituna,* the Spanish word for olive.

XXII
Children of the Sun

"In their devotions, they appeal directly to the Sun and to the Earth, saying that one is the great cause of life and the other the receptacle and producer of all that sustains life."

Parker.

THE PLAINS PANTHEON

In attempting to interpret any man's history, we must first attempt to ascertain what he believed, his religion being the key to his psychology. The *Comanche*, viewed in the light of Indian theosophy, is much more understandable than the *Comanche* viewed through the bloody haze of human conflict.

Colonel Richard Irving Dodge, stationed among the Plains Indians for thirty-five years, made a general analysis of their beliefs — special references to the *Comanche* arising from discussions between himself and Major Neighbors, Indian agent for the Texas Tribes.

According to this analysis, all Indians of the Plains believed in the Good and Bad Gods, hitherto described under THE INDIAN PANTHEON; in the eternal conflict between the two; and in the division of the spirits of Nature into good and evil forces. This division, Dodge says, formed "the stumbling block of the missionaries" who attempted to convince their flocks that good and evil, alike, proceed from the will of a single deity; at the same time, proclaiming the fatherhood of God to man. The unhappy thought of a father who, though all-powerful, permitted ills and sorrows to afflict his children, was forever irreconcilable with Indian philosophy.

So strongly did the *Comanche* feel on the subject of the Bad God, says Dodge, that he held it practically taboo in conversation. This reticence, unshared by other Plainsmen, gave rise to the supposition, as stated by Schoolcraft, that he did not believe in the negative element of THE INDIAN PANTHEON.

From Dodge's analysis, we also learn that, contrary to the views of the southern agricultural Indians, the Plains Tribes looked on the West as the home of the Bad God, locating their Happy Hunting Ground in the eastern skies. The gardeners, it will be remembered, thought to arrive at "the other house" by following the Sunset Path westward to the Under World.

The *Comanche,* perhaps, more than any other Indian, believed himself truly the "child of the Sun," product of its golden rays, continually reborn of the Earth Mother, but born each time only after an extended excursion in celestial pastures.

According to Roemer, *Tehas* in the *Comanche* language meant the Happy Hunting Ground. They held this view of Texas for the beauty of its prairie game preserves and because they could look down from the hills each spring on a bluebonnet-carpeted Earth that was like a reflection of the sky. This phantasy fits in with the *Comanche* concept of immortality that closes this chapter.

THE "OPEN, SESAME!" TO HEAVEN

Of Mysteries in his religious pattern, the greatest was the paramount importance attaching to the scalp. This, apparently, was his "Open, Sesame!" to the Happy Hunting

Ground — the seat of his immortality. Was not the crown of the head, where the hair rayed out, a divine and sacred symbol of the Sun?

Once this favored bit of skin was lifted, according to innumerable testimonials, the *Comanche* looked on life as annihilated — put out like a blown candle — yet only if the scalp were taken after death. A scalp removed before death, whether by accident or design, affected immortality not a whit![1]

The moment death occurred, then, the value of the scalp was supreme, and to preserve it on a fellow tribesman of infinitely more consequence than to have preserved his life; while, by the same token, scalping a foe was of much more merit than simply sending his spirit out of this world into the next, whither it would eventually return — to plague the *Comancheria* anew.

As for rewards and punishments in the Indian's future life, to the best understanding of his beliefs, but one human characteristic was deemed worthy the notice of divine eyes — courage. The woman who died in childbirth, the warrior who died in the fray — these, and these alone, were expected to receive special consideration in the world to come. This belief was, perhaps, the basis for every warrior's preparing his "death song." Desiring to enter the After World with due credit and dignity, he fortified himself against the possibility of the Tortures by having ready this means of preserving his composure under all odds; it being the object of his torturers to break down his composure and send him, disgraced and shamed, into eternal ridicule.

SCALPING VS. HEAD HUNTING

Taking of the scalp appears to have been a short-cut or stream-lined form of the head hunting which was customary to Indians in timbered areas. Plains fighting did not allow for a careful preparation of the "head" such as Dudley South describes as still customary along the Orinoco. According to him, the full "head" (known to museums as a *tsanta*) is actually only a dried skin prepared by running a knife around the neck of a dead enemy and up the back of the scalp, which is then peeled off with the face intact.

The triumphant hunter sews up the slit in the back of the scalp, the lips and the eyes, and, meanwhile, has built himself a slow fire beside which he has banked a mound of sand. Turning the skin sack with its dangling hair right side out, he fills it with the heated sand and hangs it in the smoke from the smothered coals. He empties and refills the "head," whenever the sand cools, for several days — until shrinkage and hardening of the skin is complete. His trophy is then ready to display on the wall of his bamboo hut.[2]

On the open Plain, we are told, the scalp was seized in a matter of seconds. The scalper ran his knife around the top of the head, seized the hair in his hand, braced himself with a foot on the dead body, and gave a yank that resulted in "lifting the hair" with a resounding POP! forever unforgetable in the ears of pioneer observers. The scalp was later stretched and dried on a buffalo chip, and the hair oiled and groomed, whereafter it was worn at the taker's belt, on his shield, or on his horse's halter.

LIMITATIONS ON IMMORTALITY

To the zealot of the Plains, Dodge says, limitations on immortality, other than the loss of the scalp, were three — strangulation, death in the dark, and mutilation.

Fear of strangulation arose out of the belief that life, the "soul thing," issued from the mouth at the moment of dissolution. Thus, if death occurred through choking, the passageway was closed, and the soul, unable to free itself from the mortal coil, remained forever cabined in the burial ground.

Next to fear of strangulation came fear of death in the dark, for the soul that left the body in the dark was bound to wander in the dark, forever and forever more.

As to the effect of disabilities and mutilations, the soul, which never really lost its human shape, went forth to the After World burdened with whatever handicaps it had been accustomed to endure in this. One who was blind remained forever blind. One who was without a thumb became a thumbless ghost. Especially sad, says Cushman, was the fate of the woman who perished with her babe unborn. It could never be born in the After World and must be carried without surcease through eternity — or, at the least, for a hundred years.

Such indignities as the body suffered *after* death, provided the scalp were not removed, also permanently affected its shade. Thus, if the feet were cut from the body, the unhappy spirit was forced to dispense with them from that time on.

Mortal wounds, however, or sudden mortal illnesses, were discounted; it being assumed that their effects vanished at the moment of dissolution.

Burial Customs

Concurring in the general Indian belief that all inanimate objects had their shades and shadows to be liberated whenever destruction overtook their natural forms, the Plains Indians, like the gardening Indians, filled the graves of their dead with every known necessity. Sometimes they, too, executed wives in order to lay them beside their husbands, and it was common practice to slaughter ponies on the burial ground.

Dodge and Neighbors tell us the death place of an important personage was always abandoned, since such a spot was looked on as particularly under the influence of the Bad God. In many instances, not only did abandonment occur, but the afflicted tribe completely wrecked the camp site in a general hysteria of fear and grief.

If death transpired where there was opportunity for proper observance of ceremony, great care was exercised

231

with the body which was bathed, the face overlaid with vermilion, and the eyes sealed with red clay. The best apparel obtainable was used for the funeral garb, the bereaved family sometimes actually bankrupting itself in an effort to secure what was looked on as a proper and suitable "shroud."

The skin of a man's Totem Animal, constituting his family coat of arms, and all the scalps he had taken, were fastened to his shield, says Dodge, and his bonnet of Eagle feathers, if he were entitled to one, set on his head. He was then placed in his grave, in what is frequently described as a "sitting position," with the lariat of his favorite pony in his hand. When the shallow soil was filled in, or a cairn of stones built over his body, the pony, together with other members of the herd, was dispatched on top of the burial, so that their spirits might accompany the spirit of their master to the Happy Hunting Ground.

Of horses left alive which had belonged to the deceased, all had their tails shaved as a symbol of mourning, the bereaved wives shaving, also, their own already "docked" heads.

Throughout the burial ceremony the air was split with the wails of the widows, it being the duty of the harem to hold a howling match. Though as many women as desired might join this chorus, it was the special privilege of the new-made widows, and of them, alone, to gash their bodies with freshly whetted knives until they were in a bloody welter — some, without any coercion in the matter, actually succumbing to the excess of their wounds.

"When a young warrior dies," says Parker, "they mourn a long time, but when an old person dies, they mourn but little, saying that they cannot live forever, and it was time they should go."[3]

He tells us also that *Comanche* burials were made with the face to the East, at the highest point of the highest available hill, a site appropriate to those worshipping the Sun.

Texas archaeologists find that the "sitting position," mentioned by many "old timers," often applies to what is technically known as a "flexed burial"; that is, the arrangement of the body on its side with its knees drawn up under the breast. A study of primitive beliefs shows this form of burial to be used by peoples looking on the Earth as the "great mother" — peoples expecting to be born again — for it is the position of a child in the womb. The expectation of rebirth, according to Captain James Hobbs, an Indian citizen by adoption, was a part of *Comanche* theosophy, and is, perhaps, explanatory of their use of the flexed burial. However, after acquiring horses, it is possible that they also employed an actual seated burial to facilitate the spirit in its ride to the Upper World.

A PLACE IN THE SUN

And now, if we may believe as Hobbs says the *Comanche* did, the spirit of the departed warrior mounted the spirit of his slain pony — his ghostly quiver of ghostly arrows at his back, the wraith of his lance in his hand, the shadow of his shield on his arm — to gallop skyward, followed by his phantom herd loaded with phantom possessions heaped by his friends in and about his grave. Straight into the eye of the Sun he sped, passing through its Fire, into the phantom pastures of the Happy Hunting Ground, there to remain for a hundred years.

At the end of the century following death, so the ancient men told Hobbs, each spirit must return to Earth that the tribal numbers might remain forever "as many as are the leaves upon the trees."

FOOTNOTES

[1] The much publicized "scalping of Wilbarger" at Pecan Springs, now a suburb of Austin, Texas, undoubtedly occurred while the victim was unconscious, and so, was

233

thought to be dead; and some *Comanche* warrior must have suffered considerable embarrassment if ever it became known in his social circle that Wilbarger lived for twelve years after the surprise attack that cost him his hair.

Pioneer descriptions of women, particularly those with long blond hair, left dead with the scalp on, can be accounted for by this chapter plus "Captive Ghosts" in Chapter XXV.

[2] For further details on the *tsanta*, see H. S. Dickery, M.D., *The Misadventures of a Tropical Medico*, pp. 286-298.

[3] Compare mourning customs in Chapters XVI and XX.

— Cunningham Collection

OLD WOMAN HICKS — PAWNEE INDIAN

XXIII
The Medicine Bag

"Meda was an Indian word meaning 'mystery.' "
Cushman.

EVERY MAN HIS OWN PROPHET

The principal religious practice of the *Comanche* was magical divination, concerned with the content of his Medicine Bag — the spiritual essence binding him to his personal and individual guardian in the supernatural world.

In arriving at a consideration of the Plains Indians we come to something of a reversal of values in Indian theology — the reversal arising from natural differences between nomadic and settled social life.

Among the gardening Indians, the palladium, the Sacred Fire, the national Medicine, was the supreme object of awe and veneration, while a member of the priestcraft was unfailingly at hand to direct every form of religious activity.

With nomadic peoples, "community religion," so to speak, cannot exist in intensified form, and community ceremonials are necessarily rare; consequently, in the widely scattered population of the Plains, every man had to be, in large part, his own priest and his own prophet — individual interpreter of the wills and ways of his gods. Hence the overweening importance of the Medicine Bag on the Buffalo

Range. From Cushman's discussion of the matter, the Medicine Bag of the gardening Indians seems to have been identical in every respect with that of the Plains Tribes.

SELECTION OF THE SUPERNATURAL GUARDIAN

The selection of his Medicine was the most tremendous and sacred event of a man's career, coming to him at puberty, while he was lost in the religious trance through which it was customary for Indian youth to seek communion with the Good God.

That the American Indian believed any form of mental aberration to be an intensified spiritual condition is indicated in three definite ways; first, whether priest or layman, he sought to induce such a condition whenever he desired a divine revelation; second, he looked on dreams as supernatural phenomena; third, he mistook the insane for individuals under the direct influence of unseen powers — fearing them, it is true, but treating them, also, with respectful attention.

The pubertal trance, an Indian initiatory rite to manhood, was brought about at the discretion of the local priests by putting the candidate under the influence of some native narcotic such as the *peyote,* the *frixolillo,* or the button snakeroot, and sending him forth in this condition to a retired place — the top of a mountain, or the fastness of a canebrake — where he remained hours, and even days, engaged in fasting, meditation, and prayer.[1]

The vigil was broken by the Good God's vouchsafing a vision or a dream calculated to make known to the candidate his own peculiar magic medium, the mysterious bond between him and that supernatural power which henceforth would act as the watchdog of his destiny.

A wind rustling through the grass, a mustang galloping across the prairie, a whirlwind overhead, a dog barking, a leaf fluttering from a tree — any one of these simple occurrences was sufficient to end the vigil and send the candidate home to offer sacrifices to his new-found Medicine.

FOREWARNED IS FOREARMED

Every few days from the time of his entry into manhood the *Comanche* "made Medicine" — an act amounting on his part to consultation of his private oracle. Into a container reserved especially for the purpose, he stirred the ingredients of the Tribal Medicine, which was known to all adult men of the Tribe but kept secret from women and strangers. To this mixture he added his private element — a handful of dried grass, a few horse hairs, a pinch of dust from the lodge floor, a splash of dog blood, or a powdered leaf. The manner of the combinations of these items, their consistency, form, or color, told him whether he might look for good fortune or bad in the immediate future.

"Should the Medicine be good," Dodge tells us, "a small quantity is put up in tiny bags of dressed deerskin and tied in the hair of the warrior, in the tail of his war horse, and on the necks of his women and children. Should any be left over, it is carefully burned in the lodge Fire. Should the process develop bad Medicine, the mixture is carried outside the camp and carefully buried in the ground, no one touching it."

Particularly did a man turn to his Medicine if he had a new project in view, such as setting forth on the warpath or attempting a trading expedition in enemy territory.

Much confusion exists among the old scribes on the subject of the physical construction of the Medicine Bag. Many observers believed that since the Bag was often made of the whole skin of a bird or an animal that the guardian spirit was the bird or animal thus represented. This idea is unquestionably erroneous, since Cushman and others who knew the Indians well, state emphatically that the identification of the guardian spirit was a life and death secret. Once any person other than the man concerned be came aware of this identity, the guardianship ceased, and a new one could be set up only by capturing the Medicine Bag of an enemy slain on the battlefield. Meanwhile, to be without a proper, personal oracle was to be left uncomfortably at the mercy of evil forces in the Spirit World.

Because the Medicine Bag was pre-eminent among religious features of the Plains, it is not to be supposed that the Plains people were utterly lacking in professional Medicine Men, or that they had no palladiums such as were in vogue among the agricultural peoples. It is true, however, that they had no permanent Temples save those landmarks which they invested with supernatural powers and worshiped as spirit-endowed — including among these, mountains, lakes and streams.

NEW FIRE IN THE COMANCHERIA

A reference to New Fire among the *Comanches* is given in the MEMOIRS OF ELLIS P. BEAN. "Once a year they meet with their head chief on the Salt Fork of the Colorado River, where he causes all the Fire to be extinguished, and then makes New Fire for the new year; and the bands also severally change their hunting grounds. This meeting takes place in the New Moon in June. At the place where they meet are lakes of salt water, so covered with salt that they can break up any quantity they want."

Also, in an old article called TRIBES OF THE THIRTY-FIFTH PARALLEL we are told: "They have yearly gatherings to light the Sacred Fires; they build numerous huts, (evidently the sweat lodges) and sit huddled about them, taking Medicine for purification and fasting for seven days. Those who can endure to keep the fast unbroken become sacred in the eyes of the others. While the ceremony proceeds perfect silence reigns — not a word is spoken. But . . . (at times) they arise and dance until they are exhausted; then resume their seats on the ground."

From the above statement, accredited to Jesse Chisholm, it would appear that the *Comanches* had in their ritual a close approximation of the Green Corn Dance without using corn as an element in their culture.

Dodge tells us that on the Plains the leading Medicine Chief and the Civil Chief were frequently one and the same person, and that the shaman, or Witch Doctor, who ranked far below the Medicine Chief, or Prophet, in general esteem, was the idol of the womenfolk.

It was the particular business of the Medicine Chief to establish the Tribal Medicine, to consult it, to make sacrifices to it on behalf of community interests, and to change the magic formula if its beneficent powers seemed to grow weak. Unlike the shaman, he could not resort to jugglery and tricks to hold office, but must have genuine faith in his own ability to commune with the Great Spirit, allowing himself no material aids save fasting and narcotics. Thus, he must be a man capable, in all sincerity, of "seeing visions" and of "dreaming dreams."

In a description Dodge gives as to what was seen by one of his lieutenants, who accidentally came on such a ceremony, we find certain details concerning the making of auguries on the Plains. "Everything of furniture, bedding cooking-utensils, etc., had been removed from the lodge, which had evidently also undergone a thorough cleaning. . . . Around the circumference of the lodge, in a solemn circle, sat the old men and warriors. In the centre two forked sticks had been planted in the ground, about six feet apart, and from a pole, laid across, was suspended an iron pot, filled with food. Under the pot was a Fire, and at the base of each of the forks was another smaller Fire. From one fork to the other, on the side fartherest from the door of the lodge, was a wide semicircle of buffalo chips which had been plentifully sprinkled with powdered charcoal. Inside this semicircle was a rectangle of about twenty by thirty inches of fine white sand, divided into two equal rectangles by a strip of black charcoal, two inches wide. In one of these rectangles was the figure of a horse in black, in the other a similar figure in red. Between the outer sides of the rectangles and the inner side of the semicircle of buffalo chips, was another small Fire.

"The ceremonies, which had been suspended on the entrance of the lieutenant, were now continued. The Medicine Man took from a pouch a small quantity of dried leaves and sprinkled a pinch on each fire, causing a pungent aromatic odor, stronger than incense.

"The Medicine Pipe was then filled and lighted by the Medicine Man, who, holding it in both hands, and pointing it now up, now down, ejected puff after puff upward, downward, laterally, over the fires, over the pot, over the images of horses and in every direction, as if to envelop everything within its potent influence.

"The chief then took the Pipe and went through a similar performance. He then informed the lieutenant that they were worshiping the Good God, and trying to find out from him whether they were going to have plenty of ponies this year — and so dismissed him. This is the only instance within my knowledge of a white man's being permitted to have even a peep at these sacred Mysteries."

Dodge attempts no interpretation of his lieutenant's observations, though he hazards the guess that the method of divination employed might be similar to that usually employed in the consultation of the personal Medicine, or oracle.

Fire and Smoke being the only variable elements in the scene, it may be safely assumed that the answer of the gods devolved on one or the the other of these, especially as we know that all Indians looked on Smoke as a divine messenger. Since black was the color of death — or dearth — and red a symbol of vitality, it is, perhaps, not far-fetched to assume that these were the meanings ascribed to the figures of the ponies. Hence, it follows that either the flare of the Fires or the settling of the Smoke wreaths, in regard to these pictorial representations, must have been the method of determining the augury.

240

THE RAIN MAKER AT WORK

Concerning the activities of the Rain Maker, who, though he commanded less respect than the Prophets, in Dodge's opinion, was rated somewhat higher than the Witch Doctor, we have a description from Eastman, said to have been an *Apache* captive for a number of years. His description begins after three men had already sacrificed their prestige in attempting to break a drouth, for to fail was to face everlasting disgrace.

Wak-a-dah-me took the stand the fourth morning on top of the Medicine Lodge. He was much more gaily attired than any of his predecessors. In addition to a shield ornamented with "red chains of lightning," he carried in his left hand a bow and a single arrow. The concourse was as great as on any previous day. Striking an attitude, he tossed up a feather to ascertain the course of the Wind, then, turning to the mob below, he began a lengthy harangue:

"*Apaches!* Children of the Sun! — You behold me here a sacrifice. I shall this day relieve you of your distress and bring joy to your lodges, or I shall live among the dogs and old women for the remainder of my days. My friends, you saw which way my feather flew. I shall hold my shield in that direction, and the lightning will draw a great cloud, and this arrow, which is feathered with the quill of the white swan, will make a hole in it.

"Warriors! This opening in the lodge at my feet shows me the Medicine Men. They are seated in a circle and are crying to the Great Spirit above who commands the Sun and clouds. Three days they have sat there. Have they done aught to relieve your distress? Ompah tried and failed because on his head was the raven. It flies *above* the storm. Warrahpa is the beaver and he lives *under* the *water*. How could he succeed? My friends, I see you are in great distress, and nothing has yet been done. This shield belonged to my father, the Mad Bull. It was taken from a black cloud, which will come over us today. I am the son of my father, and will surely bring you relief. I have done."

241

Thus flourished Wak-a-dah-me, alternately addressing the clouds and the people.

It so chanced that as he was speaking, a small cloud appeared on the horizon; and as it approached grew larger, until the heavens were overcast. Then, drawing his bow to its utmost tension, he let fly the arrow, which sped up into the gathering blackness, and was lost to view. Presently the sky was illumined with a vivid flash, and peal upon peal of Thunder followed in rapid succession. The crowd dispersed, running to their lodges in the greatest confusion; but the warrior who had brought about this happy state of things remained at his post strutting around the apex of the lodge in all the might and majesty of his new-made glory. Even Rain could not drive him from the scene of his triumph. There he stood, the moist cynosure of all eyes.

After this all was joy and gladness. Wak-a-dah-me was loaded down with honors, and every chief in the Tribe was anxious to have him select one of his daughters for a wife. He accommodated six of them. "From this time forth he was an honored and puissant warrior, chief, and Mystery Man."

Having seen how a Medicine Man of the magician order might be made, we come to the healing art as practiced in the *Comancheria* and adjacent territories.

The Healing Art

Among the Plains Indians, as among the gardeners, the "healing" ceremony consisted of attempting to rout the evil spirits from possession of the body by means of noise. Attempted exorcism began with the howling rites of the shaman or Witch Doctor, assisted by the women, the shaman howling at the bedside, the women forming a chorus without. If the howling was not of sufficient force to drive away either demon or patient, says Dodge, a *tom-tom* was suspended over the sufferer's head and beaten full force till death or a cure took place.

242

Wounds were considered differently from sickness, being perfectly understandable as to cause. These were, in many instances, treated with such efficacious remedies as herb poultices, crude surgery, and sucking to remove poisons. In this kind of case, noise was made use of merely as a preventive — to keep the evil spirits of sickness — fevers, for example — from entering into the patient's body through the opening of the wounds.

Of the steam bath in the *Comancheria,* Marcy tells us: "In every Comanche village may be seen small structures consisting of a framework of slight poles, bent into a semispherical form and covered with buffalo hides. These are called *medicine lodges,* and are used as vapor baths. The patient is seated within the lodge beside several heated stones upon which water is thrown producing a dense hot vapor which brings on a profuse perspiration, while at the same time the shaman or Medicine Men are performing incantations accompanied by music on the outside.

"Such means are resorted to for healing all diseases and I am also informed that their young men are obliged to undergo a regular course of steam bathing before they are considered worthy of assuming responsible duties of warriors."

When an epidemic occurred, according to the statements of adopted captives, the sick were sometimes gathered together and steamed for hours in the vapor baths, after which they were removed from their beds and flung into an icy stream, if one were handy. If they survived the plunge, they were rolled in buffalo robes and put to bed again, sometimes being given a rubdown with fresh killed meat into the bargain.

The method was always effective, for those who did not die, recovered; and the Indians, having no thought, either of succumbing or recovering, but only of winning or losing in a struggle against a malignant spirit, were satisfied.

In relation to mosquito-borne diseases, Charles A. R. Campbell tells of the Indian welcome to the dragonfly, or "snake doctor" in the coastal regions of the Southwest. Each year when the migration flew in, it was welcomed with a tremendous demonstration because the Indians thought this Winged One "drove the sickness away." Actually the dragon-flies ate the mosquitos; and the sickness, particularly malaria, died down temporarily.

Also along the Gulf Coast, Indians thought the Wind from the North — *El Norte* — was the harbinger of health; and for the same reason: this strong wind blew the mosquitos out of range.

Some diseases were more powerful than the Medicine Man thought he could cope with; when this happened, just as a house might be burned down after a death had taken place, so the victim became taboo to all other persons. Travelers describe coming on sick Indians in the Southwest left to die alone while the Tribe moved swiftly away, pausing only to build prickly pear barricades across the trail to prevent the Sickness from following after them. This was particularly true of unfamiliar epidemics brought by the Euro-American, such as smallpox and measles.

Among charms and amulets, objects presumed to prevent the occurrence of evils by their own innate magic power, Dodge speaks particularly of feathers from the roadrunner, the *Paisano* — known to the Plains Tribes as the Medicine Bird. No man would start on any enterprise without at least one of these precious quills on his person, while whole skins were hung over the lodge doors to keep out henchmen of the Bad God.

The Indian Sacrament

The position of the Smoke Spirit in the Indian Pantheon and the significance attaching to the Pipe have both been previously discussed, the first in THE SACRED FIRES and the second in THE PEACE PIPE.

With many Indians, especially those of the far south where the tobacco plant had its origin, smoking was habit-

244

ual. As has been said, the Indian of the tropics generally used the "soothing weed" in "wrapper" form; that is, as a cigar or cigarette, but most of the North American Indians employed a pipe almost invariably, even social smoking being of a ceremonial nature. The line of demarcation between the forms of smoking appears to be in Texas and Oklahoma, for the *Lipan-Apache,* who was really a Mexican Indian, but who also infested the eastern side of the Rio Grande, "rolled his own" in the husk of the sotol stalk, and smoked incessantly, says Herman Lehmann; while the *Comanche,* according to other historians, invariably employed a Pipe. He would have learned the practice from trading with the *Caddo* League, of which the *Pawnee* were a part, and from the *Asinai.*

Among the *Comanches,* as among the gardeners, there were common Pipes for social use, Council Pipes for state occasions, a specially dedicated Peace Pipe, and a most sacred Medicine Pipe for solemn religious ritual. Etiquette forbade the use of the Peace Pipe and the Council Pipe for any ordinary purpose, but to touch the consecrated Medicine Pipe to profane lips would have amounted to sacrilege so profound as to bring on a general catastrophe.

The *Comanche,* who found it somewhat difficult to secure a plentiful supply of tobacco by trading, substituted *killikinick,* a mixture of tobacco and singed sumac, or, running short of the former, used the latter pure.

Says Parker, anent this practice: "Whilst in camp one evening during our march, I observed two Indians ride up and dismount. One of them stooped down, pulled something from under his horse's feet, and walking to the camp Fire, held it over the Flame. Prompted by curiosity, I went over and found him preparing sumac for this *evening's smoke.* He had pulled a bunch of the green branches of the plant, and now held them in the flame just far enough and long enough to singe and curl them; he then rubbed them in his hands, filled his Pipe, lit it, and mounting, was gone, the whole process not detaining him five minutes."

On "lighting up" even for social purposes, Noah Smithwick assures us the *Comanche* invariably employed the Smoke ritual described under THE PEACE PIPE; that is, blowing the Smoke to the seven world divisions in reverential salute to the Sun. Dodge adds that no Plains Indian ever smoked alone — or on horseback — which seems not quite in accord with the statement just made by Parker. However, the *Comanche* was a flexible individual, subject to changing his ways and customs almost at a moment's notice — if a new practice pleased him. Thus, two chroniclers, varying a decade in their observations, could scarcely be expected to agree in all points concerning his mannerisms.

On trail, a group of hunters, desiring to smoke, perhaps for purposes of divination, says Dodge, would dismount and squat in a circle. The ritual of smoking was ever the same — the first puff upward, the second down, and so on; then the Pipe was passed back the opposite way, untouched by lips, until it reached the first smoker, who started the ritual over again. It will be noted that the Pipe was passed round the circle in the same direction as was taken by men dancing in a circle among the gardening Indians.

To refuse to smoke in a properly situated group was a mortal offense, equivalent in insult to the gesture of the "civilized" gentleman who slapped the cheek of a contemporary with the gauntlet of his glove.

Perhaps it may be necessary to modify the statement that the Medicine Bag occupied the supreme position in the religious practices of the Plains, since smoking undeniably held, here, as elsewhere, the position of a sacrament, engendering definite conventions, or rules of smoking deportment.

CONVENTIONS OF THE PIPE

Tobacco from both groups was mingled and shaped into a miniature pyramid on a satin-white deerskin.

Women ordinarily did not smoke with men; children and teenagers never did.[2]

246

Smoke from the Pipe was Man's breath, ascending to God and carrying to him Man's Word; hence the absolute truth must be spoken.

It was blasphemy to touch the sacred Medicine Pipe.

It was disrespectful to the gods to pass in front of the Peace Pipe, every decoration on it having magical import.

It was equally disrespectful for an unqualified person to smoke the Peace Pipe or the Council Pipe.

The Peace Pipe was respected as a passport in all Indian territory.

White predominated in the decoration of the Peace Pipe and red in the decoration of the War Pipe.

The War Pipe was smoked as a definite ultimatum of hostilities.

It was an insult to refuse to smoke with any given Indian group.

Smoking ordinarily occurred with the smokers seated in a circle.

The Pipe was passed round the circle to the left with the course of the Sun. No Indian would smoke a Pipe received from the opposite direction. Special respect was paid to Pipe ashes which were ordinarily deposited in some specific place.

Warriors anointed themselves with Smoke from the War Pipe. Compare with experiences of French missionaries who found Indians rubbing themselves with "the Medicine of the Cross," by first passing their hands over the crucifix and then over their bodies.

The author has never seen in print the actual ritual of smoking the Pipe, in either Spanish, French or English narratives. It was described in confidential conversation by a Pawnee Indian who said: "We do not wish it ever to be printed in exact detail, for if it were, it might be carelessly imitated; and we look on it as a sacred ceremonial." Out of respect to this attitude, the exact ritual is omitted from this book.

HOLY PILGRIMAGE TO THE PIPESTONE QUARRY

Abbe Domenech, in his SEVEN YEARS RESIDENCE AMONG THE INDIANS tells us of the Pipestone Quarry in Minnesota: "The old Indians assert that the discovery of this quarry is owing to the annual migrations of the buffalo, and that the hunters, in following the track traced out by these animals, were led to the Fountain of the Pipes (the Indian name for the quarry). Whatever be the cause, the pathway formed by the migration of the buffalo is still visible."

He cites from Catlin's fifty-fourth letter on the Indian this legend: "Many centuries ago there occurred a deluge, which destroyed all the nations of the Earth. The tribes of the Red Men assembled on the *Coteau des Prairies* to escape from the inundation; but the waters, continuing to increase, soon covered the entire mass of Indians, and their flesh became changed into red stone." He gives a second legend, the complement of the first, but without a reference, in which he says that the Great Spirit once seated himself on this stone, called all the Indians together about him, shaped a piece of stone into a Pipe with his hands, and developed for them the Smoke ritual. He then assumed the shape of an Eagle and vanished upward in a cloud of Smoke from his own Pipe. It was then that the stone became red and smooth and melted into a mass thirty to forty-five feet high which covers much of a three-mile-long valley. His instruction was that the rock was the flesh of the Indians, and where the Smoke from one of the stone Pipes ascended, peace between Indians was to be forever the rule. Says Domenech: "Whenever (they) went to the Fountain of the Pipes, they became sacred and inviolable even in the eyes of their greatest enemies, and were lodged and fed in every village through which they had to pass. Arrived at the quarry, they fasted and abstained during three days, and offered sacrifices to the Spirit of the Fountain of the Pipes before they began their excavations."

FOOTNOTES

[1] See Chapter XX, Footnote 3, on the *Peyote* Cult.

[2] The first time women were included in the Ritual of the Pipe in Texas history honored the return of Angelina of the Tejas, after years of residence at the missions in Coahuila, to act as interpreter for Captain Ramon in 1716. Eventually, she became the "uncrowned queen" of the Red Lands, acting for both the Spanish and the Indians in public affairs.

See Chapters VII and IX for further references to the Pipe.

CASPARIS SHIELD AND COVER

XXIV
The Sign of the Snake

"They never travel twice on the same trail."

Parker.

THE NOM DE PLUME

Despite the fact that the *Comanche* looked on himself as a child of the Sun, superior to all other Indians, and infinitely superior to the white man, he called himself a Snake — his gesture in the sign language indicating himself being that of a snake wriggling backward. The right hand, forefinger extended, was clinched to a fist at the left breast, then rapidly withdrawn, with a wavering motion, across the body — the epitome of stealth.

THE HORSE TAIL THIEF

His supreme ambition was not vested in war. A truly great warrior must be an even greater horse thief, he argued, else what would he ride in battle? Even more to the point, what would he ride on raids?

So perfect were the *Comanche* Indians in their chosen art, freebooting, that the pioneers believed them able to throw a spell over animals, holding the best watchdogs dumb and the most vicious horses docile while emptying the stock pens. Even roosters, it is said, did not crow while *Comanches* were in the neighborhood.

Soldiers and Rangers who knew the *Comanche* well, tell us he wore three kinds of insignia on his shield: bear teeth indicating he was a great hunter, scalps indicating he was a mighty warrior and horse and mule tails indicating he was an accomplished raider — the highest distinction of the three.

Says Parker: "The estimation in which a successful robber is held is illustrated by an anecdote of an old chief, who said he had four sons who were a great comfort to him in his declining years, as they could steal more horses than any other young men in the tribe."

The Master Craftsman of Trail and Sign

In order to be successful in his line, it was necessary for the *Comanche* to be a master of trailcraft; that is, in the art of spying out and interpreting any disarrangement of Nature. Two words of utmost importance in his vocabulary, therefore, were "trail" and "sign."

According to the definition offered by Colonel Dodge, "sign" was the evidence that some person, animal, or thing had touched Earth at some particular spot, while "trail" was a series of "sign," one mark following another in related order. The art of trailing, then, consisted of evolving "trail" from "sign."

An Indian had to know all the landmarks of the country, all the water holes and common routes of travel, and the habits of all the animals and tribes likely to cross the area under his observation. So expert were many of them in reading and in eradicating "sign," that their ability in this direction, like their ability in spiriting away livestock, seemed little short of uncanny to the less sophisticated "whites."

Not only did an Indian know every landmark for hundreds of miles, but he was able to draw maps so accurately that another Indian who had never seen the territory in question could follow directions without difficulty. For draftsmen's implements, say Lawson and others, these natural topographers used a stick and the Earth, or the ashes of the camp Fire.

KINDS OF SIGN

"Sign" may be considered in two great divisions: formal communications and informal evidence. Under formal communications come all deliberate disarrangements of Nature, among them paintings, or "picture writing," and special groupings of stones or bones — communications comparable to the oft-sung "gypsy patteran."

Examples of informal, or incidental sign include dropped articles, footprints, and old camp Fires. Some tribes built their Fires with the sticks radiating from and burning at the center, while others laid the sticks parallel and burned them at one end. Marcy tells us the abandoned camps of the *Kiowa* and the *Comanche* might be distinguished by the fact that the former made their Fire pits about two feet in diameter while the latter made them only about fifteen inches. Every tribe had its own moccasin pattern, some making pointed and some square toes, some making seamed and some unseamed soles.

Gregg tells of the differences between a war party and a family party: "The lodge poles are often neatly prepared and in conveying them one end of each frequently drags on the ground; whereby the trail is known to be that of a band with families, as war parties never carry lodge poles." Parker adds that a tenderfoot of his acquaintance, on seeing such a trail for the first time, exclaimed: "We must soon overtake them, for here is the track of the chief's traveling carriage!"

Various frontiersmen describe the finding of bone patterns left at abandoned camp sites, indicating the number of and direction taken by recent campers, while Gregg says bleached buffalo skulls were set up as trail markers.

ROCK SIGN

Little is known of picture-writing save that devices among certain Tribes indicated numbers, direction, defeat, victory, and other fundamental ideas — the same ideas Cremony describes in "Rock Sign."

Says he: "Signalizing by stones is . . . difficult to comprehend. Perhaps the most skillful detector of such notices (among Anglo-Americans) was 'Kit Carson'. . . . No man in the United States has had greater experience, and no man possessed a keener instinct to detect Indian signs. I must confess my inability to do this . . . subject full justice, but will give the result of my observations. The traveler is often surprized to notice a number of stones on one side of the road, lying apparently without any set arrangement, when he can observe no others within reach of his eye. A careful observation will convince him that they never *grew* in that region but were brought from some considerable distance. . . . A closer examination will show that these stones are regularly arranged, and that the majority point to some special point of the compass, while the number of those who planted them is designated by some concerted placement of each stone. . . . In . . . countries . . . where deluges of Rain pour down during the rainy season, the heaviest side of a stone will, in course of time, find itself underneath, and when this order is reversed, especially under the circumstances above cited, there is good reason to believe that it has been purposely done. This belief becomes certainty on seeing that each one of the group, or parcel, is precisely the same way. Besides, a stone which has been long lying on one particular side, soon contracts a quantity of clay or soil on its nether surface, while its upper one has been washed clean. If it be turned over, or partly over, the difference becomes easily discoverable. If one stone be placed on end so as to rest against another, it means that the party so placing it require assistance. If turned completely over it indicates disaster during some raid; and if only partly turned, that the expedition has been a failure. Success is noted by the stones being left in a natural position, heaviest side down, but so arranged as to be nearly in line."

Adair tells us it was the custom of the gardening Indians always to break, but not detach a twig on a conspicious branch, setting the twig in the new direction taken whenever a turn was made, so as to indicate to the party following the route taken by the preceding one.

A Man Is Known by the Trail He Leaves

Again we refer to Cremony for one of the most explicit discussions of "trail" and "sign" to be found in old writings. Says he: "If a mounted party has been on the road, their numbers, quality and time of passage are determined with exactitude, as well as the precise sex and species of the animals ridden. The moment such a trail is fallen in with they (the Indians) follow it eagerly . . . until they find some of the dung, which is immediately broken open, and from its moisture and other properties, the date of travel is arrived at nearly to a certainty, while the constituents almost invariably declare the region from which the party came. This last point depends upon whether the dung is composed of grama grass, barley and grass, corn, bunch grass, buffalo grass, sacaton, or any of the well known grasses of the country for as they are chiefly produced in different districts, the fact of their presence in the dung shows precisely from what district the animal last came. When barley is discovered the *Apaches* have reason to believe that Americans have been over the route, and when maize is found they feel confident that the travelers were either Mexicans or people from that country. These remarks apply only to unshod horses, for iron prints speak for themselves. The difference in sexes is easily told by the attitude each assumes while urinating — the male stretching himself and ejecting his urine forward of his hind feet, while the female ejects to the rear of the hind prints."

MORE CAMOUFLAGE

The reverse side of being able to discover and identify "sign" was to be able to eradicate it, and for this the Plainsman had his methods of camouflage. His first act, on stealing horses from Spanish or Anglo-American settlements, was to remove their shoes, thus making their tracks similar to the tracks of ownerless mustangs.

At other times, wishing to throw his enemies off his trail, he notched the hoofs of his own horses to make their tracks like those of buffalo.

A favorite stunt of Plains Indians was to hide themselves in the prairie grass beside their contentedly grazing ponies, and thus draw small parties of unsuspecting enemies into bowshot by tempting them with the promise of securing loose stock — it being but the matter of a second for the Indians to spring aboard their ponies, bareback, ready for the chase. And instead of holding their ponies back by their weight, they seemed literally to "lift them from the ground."

It was a customary ruse of *Comanche* war parties to separate, all members taking a different way to the goal; a maneuver closely comparable to that of the gardening Indians as described in THE WARRIOR'S AWARD. It was also a common method of extinguishing "sign" to fire a large portion of the prairie, galloping through and ahead of the Flame, so that the tracks of the party left the charred area each by a separate route.

Of the ability of the Plainsman to assimilate himself in the landscape, Cremony says, speaking of the *Apache* in particular: "He can conceal his swart body amidst the green grass, behind brown shrubs, or gray rocks, with so much address and judgment, that any but the experienced would pass him by without detection at the distance of three or four yards. Sometimes they will envelop themselves in a gray blanket, and by an artistic sprinkling of Earth, will so resemble a granite boulder as to be passed within near range without suspicion. At others, they will cover their persons with freshly gathered grass, and lying prostrate, appear as a natural portion of the field. Again, they will plant themselves among the yuccas, and so closely imitate the appearance of that tree as to pass for one of its species."

The *Apache* hunter lay concealed for hours, watching every motion of the Mexican *pastore,* till he had learned all the arts of the *Mesta* — the Spanish Stock Industry, part Gothic, part Moorish, part native Iberian — that had just been transported to the "new" world. When he was sure he could himself handle the herds by means of the *pastore's* long whip[1] and his own familiar lariat, the *Apache* devised a special means of getting the sheep and goats to his private territory.

Surrounding a flock of these "small cattle," *Apache* warriors set woven hobbles on enough pairs of animals to form a hollow square. Into this square they drove the rest of the flock. This animal formation was then herded northward, grazing as it went, penned by its own flesh.

FORMAL SIGNALS

Besides his ability to read and to camouflage "sign," the Plains Indian had several methods of telegraphy. First among these were Smoke signals by day and Fire signals by night — comparable to the gossip of the drums in Africa — which were used all over North America. This form of signaling has already been discussed to some extent in THE CANNIBAL OF THE COAST.

Cremony, however, offers an interesting discussion of the subject, applying directly to the Plains. Says he: "Smokes are of various kinds, each one significant of a particular object. A sudden puff, rising into a graceful column from the mountain heights, and almost as suddenly losing its identity by dissolving into the rarified atmosphere of those heights, simply indicates the presence of a strange party upon the plains below; but if those columns are rapidly multiplied and repeated, they serve as a warning to show that the travelers are well armed and numerous. If a steady Smoke is maintained for some time, the object is to collect the scattered bands of savages at some designated point, with hostile intention, should it be practicable. These signals are made at night, in the same order, by the use of Fires, which being kindled, are either alternately exposed and shrouded from view, or suffered to burn steadily as occasion may require." He also discusses signaling by means of torches carried through mountain areas by swift runners, comparable to the "fiery crosses" once used in Scottish hills.

EXTENSION OF THE SIGN LANGUAGE

In ordinary speech, Dodge tells us, the Plains Tribes had each its special language or dialect, and it was not customary for an Indian of one Tribe to learn the spoken language of another, even though they might live in adjacent lodges. On the other hand they all understood the gesture language — the Esperanto of America — and a person really proficient in its use — an expert story teller, for instance — might entertain a whole village for hours without the use of a spoken word.

Of this matter Marcy says: "Their language is both verbal and pantomimic; the former consists of a very limited number of words, some of which are common to all Prairie Tribes; but the latter, which is exceedingly graceful and expressive, is the court language of the Plains."

An extension of this sign language into much larger and more sweeping gestures, gestures that completely cleared the body, and often included the horse, became the second form of Plains telegraphy — the form out of which grew, eventually, the signal system of the United States Army and Navy, and, perhaps, the semaphore system of modern traffic guidance.

INDIANS OF THE SOUTHWEST

An example of such signals in use among the Plains Indians is the danger signal. A *Comanche* scout, posted on rising ground, sighting a group of hostiles somewhere below, would suddenly dash round and round in galloping circles, thus indicating to the scout next in line the necessity for getting the warriors into military formation.

It will be seen in THE AEGIS BEARER that to circle the foe was the *Comanche's* favorite war tactic — thus this signal was utterly expressive of the idea it was intended to convey. A scout sitting serenely on his pony lost in apparent appreciation of the landscape gave the indication opposite to the danger signal. The Smith boys, onetime captives, tell us the Indians had a specific signal identifying themselves, as members of their race, to one another — a signal never apprehended by Rangers or by federal troops on the frontier. This signal was given between two individual Indians, or between groups of Indians so far away from each other as to be able to distinguish nothing save human presence. In case of a group, a lone horseman would advance a short distance. He would then ride about thirty steps to the right, then about sixty to the left, then back to his starting place. Should the signal be answered in kind, Indian knew he was meeting Indian; should it be ignored he knew he was approaching white men. The individual Indian simply started weaving from right to left, and watched to see what the stranger would do.

Army officers have left behind them the oft-repeated statement that an Indian could see and interpret with the naked eye that which appeared to be a mere animated black speck to a "civilized" man using high-powered binoculars. Possibly the preceding paragraph explains this phenomenal vision.

Astonishing descriptions are also given of the ability of Indian military commanders to control their troops by "heliograph," putting them through all manner of maneuvers by the use of Sun reflections from a clear quartz crystal, a bit of tin, or a chip of mirror glass.

OUR LOST HERITAGE

It is, in all truth, a matter to lament that the Indians of the Plains, like the Indians of the garden lands, had no method of record keeping — nothing save their uncertain memory spans, and the heraldry tattooed into their own perishable flesh, with which to preserve their hero tales and traditions. Given a literature to crystallize the products of their poetic imaginations, their grandiose oratorical style, and their astonishing mode of civilization, they must have handed down an argosy of tales worthy of a high place in classical lore.

FOOTNOTES

[1] The long "snaking" whip still appears on Mexican streets as the *pastores* of that country bring their mixed "herds" to market — a few turkies, two or three goats, half a dozen hogs. It appears far back in African cave paintings for the same purpose, drawn as an extension of the human hand.

LOOPED QUILL AND SINEW STITCH

XXV

The Aegis Bearer

Two Spanish officers in Texas in 1808:
"They look like the armies of the Moors on a feast day in our own country."

A SOUL TO SAVE — EDUCATION FOR SALVATION

The *Comanche* warrior with his Sun shield on his arm was more than a mere fighting man — a taker of scalps. He had an immortal soul to guard. He fought, not at close range with a tomahawk where the odds were equal, but at long range, with whizzing arrows twanged from his short, powerful bois d'arc bow. It was his first duty, to himself and to his tribe, not to jeopardize his immortality. The youth of the *Comancheria,* expertly trained in the military art, was trained to a method peculiarly adapted, not only to the environment, but to the philosophy of his people.

The first thing any Plains child learned was to ride. He started in a pack on his mother's back. Next he was strapped to her saddle. By the time he was four he was expected to manage a pony of his own.

His first toy, after he passed the teething stage, was a bow and a quiver of arrows adjusted to his size. In company with other lads, he roamed the territory about the camp, shooting at birds and small animals, at any mark whatsoever that offered a chance to practice his aim.

Almost before he was knee-high to a grasshopper, he went to pasture with his father's horses, acting as herdsman, practicing with the lariat, roping and riding each animal in turn, bringing to perfection the skill he would require as an adult whose very existence depended on horsemanship. When the *Comanche* took over the mustang, he took neither saddle nor bridle. He invented his own equestrian technique. The lariat, noosed, served to lasso the horse, and then was given a twist about its lower jaw forming a hackamore to guide it.[1]

By the time he was old enough to ride herd, the boy was old enough to begin training in the actual tactics of war — the use of the shield, the use of the loop, the circle formation, and the removal of the dead from the battlefield.

TACTICS OF WAR

The shield was used after the Greek and Roman fashion to fend off arrows, and, if in close quarters, lances. The *Comanche*, however, preferred to keep his lance for hunting. The boy in training, according to Hobbs, was given a shield while mounted on his pony. He was then subjected to a hail of blunt-tipped arrows, which, however, raised knots of no mean proportions on his head if he failed to parry with the shield.

In conflict, a warrior had to keep his shield in motion in order to "glance" the missiles of his opponents. A shield held rigid against the body was liable to be penetrated. In retreat it was flung over the left shoulder to cover the back. Two warriors retreating double-mounted held their shields, one to the left and one to the right side, thus semienclosing themselves.

The use of the loop was looked on by white men as the most remarkable of all the seemingly miraculous feats of *Comanche* horsemanship. A braid of rawhide, of just sufficient length to drop under the horse's chest, was brought round the animal's neck and held in position by inter-braiding with his mane.

The rider could then throw himself parallel to his horse's body on the side away from the enemy by dropping his shoulder-pit into the loop, maintaining his balance by means of a heel gripped over the ridge of the horse's backbone. He was thus completely protected from bowshot by his mount, save for the exposed heel. Not only did this heel serve to clamp him to the horse, but it was the muscular spring by which, with a skillful motion, he flung himself astride when danger was passed.

The Circle and Charge

The approved military procedure for a Plains attack was the "circle and charge." Where two or three travelers, or a dozen, were spied, the vastly out-numbering *Comanches* would form two lines. These twin columns would then descend in a grand rush, enveloping their prey with two oppositely revolving dust rings, a thunder of hoofs, and the war-whoop that is accredited with being the most blood-curdling sound ever issued from a human throat.

Dropping into the loops under their ponies' necks on the side away from the foe, the upside-down bowmen would send a barrage of arrows against the enemy. If their opponents were pioneers, dependent on guns and powder, the circling Indians would turn in on them the moment the guns were empty, cutting down whom they could during the reloading process. This was the *charge*. The moment the guns were up again, the riders were back in the circle, milling furiously round and round, protecting themselves by the bodies of their horses.

The actual purpose of this maneuver was to hold the victims at bay till their ammunition, whether bullets or arrows, was expended, when it would be simple enough to rush in and make captives of the lot. Although soldiers and settlers often escaped the succeeding Tortures by committing suicide, Dodge says such was not the practice among Indians.

REMOVAL OF THE DEAD — THE SWOOP

The loop was concerned not only with the circle and charge but also with the removal of the dead from the field of conflict. In practice, one man was appointed to play corpse. Two warriors in training then raced their horses neck and neck, dividing so as to pass, one on either side of his prostrate form. Dropping into their loops, the novices essayed to pick up the body from the ground and fling it over the neck of the pony, in front of the rider previously agreed upon. But this was a man's task. Boys were trained, singly to pick up strips of buckskin from the ground, then shields; the objects growing gradually heavier, until, by the time they were budding warriors, two youths could manage the weight of a full-grown man.

The drill for this swooping act was repeated over and over till recruits were perfect in the maneuver which was of extreme religious significance, its invention a direct result of belief in the scalp as the seat of immortality. Incidentally, it accounts for the empty battlefields that so annoyed the frontier soldier and mystified the pioneer.

THE SURPRISE PARTY

In war the Comanche's chief objective was plunder. He would take captives if he could. The women wanted them. The warrior himself enjoyed foreign wives. He would take scalps only if he could manage it without risk, for what would horses and saddles and silver buckles, or even a string of scalps, profit a man who, by the loss of his own crowning glory, was precipitated into oblivion?

Thus the surprise attack, the sudden rout of the enemy, the appropriation of enemy goods, and an immediate backtrack on the home trail, was the invariable program of a *Comanche* raid.

Offensive attacks were never undertaken save when *Comanche* numbers were overwhelming, and even then not at night. Though a man's comrades might make ever so valiant a rescue of his body, death in the dark meant an eternity in the dark, and the cautious *Comanche* had no more intention of risking everlasting banishment from the realms of the Sun than of risking the total loss of his immortality.

BOW AND ARROW *vs.* FIREARMS

As to the relative values of Indian and white armament before the invention of the revolver, and, much later, the high power rifle, we have many testimonials affirming the superiority of the former. Says Cremony: "The bow and arrow in the hands of skillful warriors, proves very deadly; it makes no noise, and for night attacks (Cremony dealt principally with the *Apaches* who differed from the *Comanches*, somewhat, in religious conceptions) or for the taking off of sentinels, is far superior to the gun. . . . It is the best weapon that can be used on the chase, or, more properly, on the hunt, as half a dozen animals may be slain in a herd before their comrades are aware of the fact . . . They are so light that they can be worn without the slightest encumbrance . . . They can always be relied on, at close quarters, when other weapons fail, or when ammunition, . . . [with which the Indian is never well supplied] gives out."

Gregg says: "There is hardly any more effective weapon than the bow and arrow in the hands of an expert archer. While the musketeer will load and fire once, the bowsman will discharge a dozen arrows, and that, at a distance under fifty yards, with an accuracy nearly equal to the rifle. In a charge they are eminently serviceable; for the Indian seems to discharge his arrows with about as much certainty when running at full speed as when standing."

Bows were kept unstrung until needed, but an Indian could string his bow much more quickly than a white man could load his musket.

BEATING THE BUSH

The "circle and charge" was a military operation for the open plain. The *Comanche,* by the time he was firmly ensconced in Texas, was partly in the woods. Particularly was this true where he held his great home encampments — about the headwaters of the Brazos and the Colorado. Gradually he followed these rivers down into the thicker timber growth until his domain extended from the Arkansas to the San Saba. He therefore developed a maneuver for exterminating those of his enemies who took refuge in the brush.

Once an opponent disappeared in a thicket, the attacking warriors would stake half their ponies and double up on the rest. They would then begin a single circle about the crucial spot. One or two of the double-mounted warriors would slip off — if possible, unnoticed by the prey, whose attention was distracted by the others. While their comrades continued to distract the quarry, these braves, acting in very truth, the part of their namesakes, the snakes, would silently and sinuously wriggle themselves through the undergrowth till able to aim a mortal blow.

SNAKING THE CORPSE

If the bush fight went against the *Comanches,* and some of the warriors who attempted to slip into the covert were picked off by the concealed enemy, it was imperative, of course, to remove their bodies, and to do so by some means other than the "swoop," which, like the "circle and charge," was a maneuver for open ground.

In the new situation, the bodies were rescued by means of the lariat. If it could be wielded from an adjacent cover, well and good, the bodies were simply lassoed and "snaked" into the next bit of brush where they might be handled with safety. If there was no cover near enough from which to send the circling noose, several lariats were tied together, and a warrior, holding his shield upright in front of him, crept forward on hands and knees to tie the elongated rope about the anatomy of the dead. The body was then "snaked" away as in the first instance.

No Respect for the Scalped Dead

The *Comanche* had no intention of abandoning the bodies of his dead, no matter what the circumstances, unless the scalps were gone. In that case, though afforded all the opportunity in the world, he would not touch them, not even to secrete them from the vultures and the wolves.

Eternal Vengeance

Frequently confused, in the white mind, with torture practiced on the battlefield, was a form of vengeance based on the belief that bodily mutilations affected the future of the dead.

The *Comanche*, if sufficiently infuriated in the fight, might fracture his dead opponents' bones, tear out their vitals, and otherwise maltreat their persons, but spare their scalps, in order to send them into the next world, a troop of despicable wrecks. One *Comanche* Band whose chief's daughter had been slain by white men, says Herman Lehmann, vowed to disembowel eighteen white maidens — one for each year of her life.

Captive Ghosts

Also, according to *Comanche* beliefs, it was possible for a warrior to take dead captives as well as live ones. This he accomplished by leaving the slain unscalped, their ghosts being forced, thereby, to enter the spirit world beholden to him, and to await the coming of his spirit at the entrance-way, in order to join its train of shadowy servitors. Only the bravest and most admirable of foes were treated to this attention, however, since the distinction of a scalp in hand was not easily outweighed by expectations of future glory.

The fortunes of war, when the battle waxed hot, could

affect the *Comanche's* immortal standing in an even more material way than those already mentioned. They could curtail his ghostly property rights.

Under ordinary circumstances, as has been said in CHILDREN OF THE SUN, it was not only the custom, but the duty, of his family and friends to send him into the celestial pastures as fully panoplied as possible. Death on the battlefield often allowed for none of this pomp and circumstance. If the bodies of the dead were many and the way home far, the survivors rolled their comrades into the nearest waterhole, thus preserving them from scalp hunters and scavengers, and, incidentally, fouling the water for many a day to come.

TREE BURIAL

If there were only one or two dead, and the homeward trail long, and no pursuit behind, the war party might stop, if a large tree came handy, and borrow the *Cheyenne* practice of tree burial. Both Sowell and Hobbs describe such incidents. The bodies, wrapped in buffalo robes, were each set astride a limb, braced erect by ropes from the shoulders to boughs above and from the feet to boughs below. Bows, arrows, lances, and shields were all hung beside the dead, and as many ponies as could be spared from the retreat were shot beneath the tree. Other ponies in the party had their tails shaved — symbol of chagrin and ill-fortune.

APACHE BURIALS

If an engagement with *Apaches* took place, the latter followed the practice of stuffing their dead in rock crevices, first wrapping them in woven mats if any were obtainable. Such a burial, reconstructed, is on exhibit in the Anthropology Museum of The University of Texas.

BAD MEDICINE

Of taboos or negative conventions regarding his conduct,

267

the *Comanche* warrior had two in particular not yet mentioned: he would never retrieve an arrow which had taken a human life, though he was careful to collect all others that were salvageable, either in hunting or in warfare, and he refused under any circumstance to be numerically counted.

With the Plains Indian, before pressure from behind became so great as to force him into a struggle for survival of the fittest — that is, before the Anglo-American pushed the displaced forest Indians across the Mississippi — war seems to have been the great gamble — a supreme game of chance. The first blood drawn in battle indicated which side the Fates — or, rather, the Spirits — had it in for on that particular day, and hostilities were likely to cease with the initiatory casualty.

In Indian life, as elsewhere, it is said that the bloodiest conflicts were engaged in by the youngest men. On the Plains this circumstance arose out of the necessity for a youngster to prove himself before he could be admitted to warrior rank; none being admitted, says Parker, till "he has stolen stock and taken scalps."

Actual war, as set forth in THE ROBE OF STATE, was a matter to be declared by the Council; in which case, Gregg tells us, the councilors, seated in a circle, smoked the War Pipe; and the military, gathering round them, caught the Smoke in handfuls to anoint their bodies.

The *Comanche* military was organized in squads, says Sanchez, each with its leader. When war was under way, these groups gathered round a great Fire, leaving an opening toward the enemy country. They took turns in boasting of their deeds and prowess, until the War Chief, mounted, dashed through the opening to check his steed just at the Fire's edge. Presumably it was now his turn to harangue the crowd.

If there was necessity for an infantry, special details were made, it being considered much more hazardous to operate on foot than on horseback.

268

THE SPIRIT OF YOUTH

A war leader might get up a raid at any time by the simple expedient of soliciting volunteers. This was done in picturesque fashion. All *Comanche* towns were laid out in squares like city blocks with comfortably wide thorough-fares between. A chief, wishing to organize an expedition, mounted his horse, equipped himself with a long lance from which floated a red flag tipped with Eagles' feathers, and, holding this banner aloft paraded the streets singing his war song. All who so desired fell in behind him, thus signi-fying their desire to follow on the trail.   ,

Thereafter, during the day, the shields belonging to these aspirants for fame hung on shield-racks before the doorways to absorb the all-powerful Medicine of the Sun. The racks, as shown by Catlin, were tripods of three lances tied together at the top with a thong.

Parading took place every twenty-four hours till the party was sufficiently strong to set out for the goal. In the evenings, young girls serenaded the lodges of popular warriors, urging them to join the expedition.

Each warrior provided his own horse and equipment. The war pony, like the hunting pony described in THE BIG PARADE, was a specially trained animal, used for no other purpose. If obtainable, a white or cream-colored horse was chosen and painted blood-red from nose to tail as a part of the customary martial Medicine.

Roemer gives a graphic description of military pageantry in the *Comancheria*. "In the twilight . . . in festive . . . at-tire . . . their faces were painted red and the majority of them wore (a) . . . headdress made of buffalo skin with the horns of (the) buffalo attached. . . . In one hand (each) car-ried (a) long lance painted red, in the other a round shield made of tanned buffalo hide, painted in (bright) colors and decorated with a circle of feathers which fluttered in the breeze whenever the shields waved to and fro.

"The horses . . . were mostly light in color, their heads

269

and tails . . . painted a carmine red.

"The troop paraded several times before us in a slow gallop and finally disappeared in the darkness.

"This was a . . . party of young warriors preparing for a raiding expedition into Mexico."

A raiding party might be gone as long as two years without exciting comment.

Such a party, returning from Mexico or elsewhere, on arriving in sight of the homefolk, would halt and send forth a signalman to ascertain the status of affairs within camp. This he did by means of a circular blanket wave. A reply in kind indicated "All's well!" in the community, and no strangers present. The signalman would then announce that scalps were in hand, and captives; and the command would march forward to be met by the women with the Scalp Pole.

WOMEN'S RIGHTS

To bear this Pole was an incomparable privilege, ordinarily accorded to a woman both old and honored, who led the procession of her sisters, all leaping and shouting and behaving with a joy and abandon expressive of intense emotion. Scalps! Magic rings, flaunting streamers of human hair! Certain evidence that the Good God was on the right side and the Bad God with the enemy.

The captives were at once turned over to these vivacious matrons whose right it was to determine which should be adopted into the Tribe, which enslaved, and which reserved for the Tortures. Captive women, however, were usually retained as booty by the warriors who seized them.

Two gala events were now in order — the Scalp Dance and the Tortures.

THE RELIGIOUS ECSTASY

If smoking — a method of casting lots, a seal of contract, an oath, and a form of divine communion — was the sacrament in Sun worship, so the Scalp Dance, at least with the *Comanche,* was the supreme expression of religious ecstasy.

It was, however, not so much an act in admiration of his gods, as of himself. What he did in the Scalp Dance, so far as can be ascertained from existing partial descriptions, was to tell the gods what a great man he was; and he is not reputed to have been a modest person!

Courage being the single divine characteristic inherent in humanity, the *Comanche* who had taken an enemy scalp was exalted to the core of his being. There could be no other thrill equivalent to calling the attention of the Great Spirit to his *coup!*

Lest the supreme Being fail to appreciate the extent of his valor, the exultant warrior, Dodge states, spent hours dramatizing the incidents of the fight in which the *coup* occurred. Once under the great brush arbor, or Dance Lodge, with the Scalp Dance in full swing, he gave himself up to heroic pantomime, going through his act again and again, till there could be no doubt left in the mind of any onlooker, either mundane or celestial, as to what took place on the battlefield.

Only established warriors took part in this Dance, those who participated in the recent battle leading off. But merely to watch and listen to the shrieking, pantomiming performers — merely to gaze upward at the supreme, mystic substance of the scalps — was enough to throw the veriest dotard into a fever of religious excitement. Once in progress, the celebration lasted until exhaustion brought it to an end, by which time the whole population of the camp, including women and children, had reached a pitch of excitement amounting to hysterical frenzy.

The orgy over, says Dodge, the scalps were returned to their owners. However, if no fresh ones were taken for a long time, they might be called forth to do duty again when the need was felt for a real rousing revival of the Indian variety.

INDIANS OF THE SOUTHWEST

LAYING THE GHOST

A proper division of glory while engaged in combat was a matter governed by martial etiquette. The man who dealt the mortal wound took the scalp. Where there was doubt, the matter was settled by testimony and arbitration. Where there was indiscriminate slaughter, the first man to touch a body with a lethal weapon might claim the trophy. Some Plains Tribes used wands called *"coup* sticks" instead of weapons for counting *coup.* Possibly this was the purpose of the little sticks, topped with fox tails, often seen among the *Kiowa.*

The cleansing and mounting of scalps was a ceremony in itself. Only persons who actually participated in the fight took part in this ritual, says Dodge. With the utmost care they fleshed and stretched their prizes, hastening the drying process, according to HODGE'S HANDBOOK, by spreading the scalps on buffalo chips. Lastly, each was mounted on a flexible wooden hoop and the streaming hair combed and oiled.

Among the *Apaches,* who were forever at war with the *Comanches,* Cremony tells us it was a necessary purification of the region where a battle occurred for each man engaged in the conflict to burn a few hairs from the head of a dispatched enemy. By this means they drove the souls of those who died from the place of carnage. Failing to secure a scalp after making a killing in the *Commancheria,* they were never willing thereafter to venture into the immediate territory watched over by outraged *Comanche* ghosts.

The Comanche took every precaution, save one, in protecting himself against magical evils thought to result from tinkering with human hair. Though the scalp was of supreme importance on the Plains, all hair had value in establishing control of the spirit. Hence all body hair, including eyebrows and eye lashes, was dispensed with, and the head hair, in many tribes, reduced to a scalp lock. The *Comanche* and the *Apache,* though otherwise subscribing to

272

the conventions, retained a full suit of head hair, wearing it in single or in double braids, or flowing loose. Thus, either one, if captured, furnished a scalp that could be divided into several military tokens. And it may be appropriate to note at this point that a white man's body was sometimes almost literally skinned for the sake of its hirsute adornment.

THE LATEST SHOW

Second only to the Scalp Dance in emotional appeal were the Tortures. These, says Dodge, were looked upon as entertainment of the first water — a delightful sort of practical joking to be borne by a person of pride with as little notice of the proceedings as it was humanly possible to take. Nor were the women behind the men in thinking up novelties in this direction.

The Plains Indian, we are told, showed the effect of a very considerable amount of research in human anatomy, having figured out just how many bones could be broken or split, just how many inches of skin toasted, and just how much amputation occur before his victim would expire and end the sport. Even children were encouraged to experiment in this direction, using frogs, birds, and other small animals.

However, in the light of information such as that concerning the existence of the "blood principle" cited in THE MAGIC ART, it would seem that Tortures on the Plains, as elsewhere, had an underlying religious symbolism.

Burning at the stake, the preferred method of the Torture in the gardening area, was not a general Plains custom; nevertheless the local manner of pegging the victim down and kindling smaller fires about his person to crisp his skin with slow heat was not a more kindly alternative.

Nor does the average modern mind appreciate the humor involved in tying the victim to a tree, cutting out his umbilicus, fastening it to a pony, and then stampeding the pony.

White Superstition

Indians, on the other hand, felt entirely conscience-free in such matters — so much so, that a sage once justified it to an Anglo-American with irrefutable logic, arguing from the white man's own premises.

"You believe in one god and no more — is it not true?" he asked.

Then, on being assured of the affirmative: "You believe he is an all-powerful god?"

"Yes," said the white man again.

"Well," concluded the Indian, "you believe in just one god, and that he is an all-powerful god, and that he is a *good* god. Yet he lets you get hungry and starve to death. He makes sicknesses that cause you great pain. In other words, he uses Tortures; yet you say he is a *good* god — then the Tortures must be good, too!"

Not only is this an instance of the Indian's ability in oratory, an ability more fully set forth in THE ROBE OF STATE; but it substantiates Dodge's thesis, quoted in CHILDREN OF THE SUN, concerning "the missionaries' stumbling block" and definitely proves that the thinking Indian looked on the white man as "a superstitious fool."

Fine Feathers on Foul Birds

Putting aside the thought of the Scalp Dance and the Tortures, and considering only military drill in the *Comancheria*, we find that to watch the mustering of warriors on the open Plain, according to old accounts, was a sight sufficiently dazzling to make the head swim.

Every Indian, in martial practice, removed his cumbrous wooden saddle and rode on painted skins, which, if he had sufficient vanity, hung to the ground, covering the body of his horse like the trappings of the Spanish knights. From the loop of the hackamore beneath his pony's chin he might drop a hooped scalp. If he had risen to sufficient rank, he merited either a "warbonnet" of plumes or, if he were a prophet, a headdress of buffalo horns with the tail of the animal depended therefrom — such a headdress as was worn by other sons of Mars in classic times — the curve of the horns symbolizing the moon. Of clothing, he retained only his leggins which came to his thighs, his breech-clout, and his moccasins. Behind his left shoulder was slung his decorated quiver of feathered arrows. On his left arm hung his shield — a great Sun symbol in itself with a loosely set ruffle of feathers circling its rim to fluff and fall, fluff and fall, with a motion that mazed the human eye. His left arm was bound with buckskin to save it from the bruising twang of the bowstring. By his right side hung an always oozing buffalo paunch — his canteen. In his right hand he held his lance. He was, in full array, nothing short of an answer to an artist's prayer!

The martial music of the Plains files consisted of the drum beat of horses' hoofs, the rattle of tinklets on the shields, and the war-whoop that rings through all the annals of Southwestern history.

But there was more to this magnificent spectacle than met the eye — if we may believe the settlers' tales. There was an aroma, as powerful and as penetrating to the nose as the war-whoop to the ear. The smell of a single Indian, penetrating a pasture, say the pioneers, was sufficient to cause a stampede! One witness describes it as a cross between a skunk and an old beef hide.

Considering the eccentricities of his diet, as outlined in THE KEEPER OF THE HEARTH, the absence of finger bowls, the fact that his clothing could not be laundered, and that he had a predilection for covering himself with grease and earth, one may well believe the taint of the Indian to have been offensive to a delicate nostril.

Nevertheless, considering the fact that surprise was the main element of Plains attack, it is hard to believe such a tell-tale pungency enveloped the warriors as some of the early narrators would set forth. Besides, it is well-known that the American Indians, like all other mongoloids, were revolted by the odor of the white man. They say he smells "like a dead thing."

Hence, lest we involve ourselves in racial controversy, let us leave the warriors to gallop in the Sun and turn to consideration of the councilors.

FOOTNOTES

[1] The words "mustang" and "hackamore" — now common parlance in Texas — are derivatives from the Spanish-Arabic words *mesteña* (a horse running wild on the *mesta* or pasture) and *jacquima* (a halter made by noosing a rope over the nose).

XXVI
The Robe of State

Parker, speaking of the Plains Tribes:

"Their respective governments are patriarchial, sanctioned by the masses, and guided by the counsels of the elders.

"The Comanches have one head chief and many subordinate ones. They hold regular councils quarterly and a grand council of the whole tribe once a year."

Holley.

MAJESTY OF THE LAW ON THE BUFFALO RANGE

Ranking with the warrior in picturesque appearance, and exceeding him in dignity and prominence, was the councilor whose authority was indicated by the Sun-rayed buffalo robe dropping regally from shoulders constituting "the majesty of the law" in the *Comancheria* and in other Plains sovereignties.

This "toga" of the Buffalo Range, say Anglo-American ambassadors sent forth to parley with the Councils, was never abandoned during state proceedings, no matter how hot the day, no matter though but a breech-clout clad the form beneath it.

Crowning the splendor of the sweeping robe was the feather "bonnet," its plumed train cascading to the foot of the shimmering Sunrays — provided the military achievements of the Plains solon entitled him to such a headdress; otherwise from fourteen to fifty silver buckles adorning the queue might be substituted for Eagle plumes — distinction in the military arts not forming a necessary qualification for distinction in statecraft.

"Absolutism, oligarchy, and democracy," Dodge declares, were the outstanding, though paradoxical features of Plains government. He then goes on to say that each great Tribe was divided into a number of locally independent Bands.

A few further quotations serve to define the several positions of chieftain and to outline the executive system:

> "The hereditary chieftain was always recognized, reverenced and obeyed as sovereign ruler" over the tribe, "even though his age or temperament unfitted him for duties in the field."

> There were "no graduations of rank among the sub-chiefs" who had charge of Bands — all were equal as chiefs and the greater or less power of each came from his own personal standing in the Tribe.

> The sons of chiefs and sub-chiefs had "a certain subordinate rank" and were regarded as chiefs even though they had no following.

> The War Chief, unless he happened to be also the hereditary, or Civil Chief — seemingly an unusual combination — was "elected" by the Council — his function "only to lead in war." In time of war, however, his authority was absolute, and even the hereditary tribal chief subject to it.

The various orders of Medicine Chiefs have already been discussed in THE MEDICINE BAG.

Next to chieftains in rank were councilors, men of an age to be exempt from military duty, serving, like the councilors of the gardening Nations, as executive cabinet and as local judiciary. Legislation can scarcely be said to have existed among Indians, since, as we explained in THE LAW OF THE LAND, any confirmed statute took its authority from a crystallization of custom rather than from legal procedure.

As executive bodies, the Plains Councils passed on such

matters as the selection of a general camp site; the time and place of the Summer Hunt; the time and manner of initiating youth into manhood; the time and form of community religious services; and all matters of diplomatic aspect such as trade or peace treaties, and declaration of war.

As judicial bodies, the Councils interpreted tribal law, acting as arbiters in personal disputes; passed on marriage announcements, assessing the values of properties concerned thereby; and affixed punishments for misdemeanors.

Below councilors in rank were warriors forming the organized military, or Plains police. These, Dodge says, were the adult men who had received warrior's rating, but were not yet of an age to be exempt from military duty. Their official head, selected from among themselves, but elected by the Council, was the War Chief. His power in the military organization was absolute, but his voice in the Council was small — except, of course, when there was intertribal conflict.

The functions of the military, aside from war, which was not, until the encroaching white man made it so, the major item, were the patrolling of the tribal territory, graphically described by Cremony with regard to the *Apacheria;* the enforcement of councilor decrees; and the maintenance of the public commissariat through general supervision of the game supply and control of the Summer Hunt.

CHECKS AND BALANCES

Looking closely into Dodge's analysis, a surprisingly adequate system of checks and balances to prevent the growth of despotism becomes apparent on the Plains. This includes:

Absence of the rule of primogeniture in the descent of the hereditary chieftainship.

The power of the military.

The practice of desertion.

Equality under the economic system.

INDIANS OF THE SOUTHWEST

The absence of a tax system.

Consistent application of the Blood Right.

The authority of the Council.

SELECTION OF THE TRIBAL CHIEF

The position of Tribal Chief descended to the nearest male relative who seemed best equipped to follow in the old chief's footsteps — a qualification usually indicated by confidence and favoritism on the part of the existing ruler. Thus the succeeding civil chieftain might be a son, grandson, or nephew. His succession, however, required the sanction of the Council, which was influenced in its decision not only by the expressed desires of the deceased, but by the voice of public opinion, including that of the womenfolk.

POWER OF THE MILITARY

The "third estate," as Dodge terms the military, though voiceless in the government, prevented, by the latent power of revolution always present in organized humanity, the tipping of the scales towards undue executive authority.

FRENCH LEAVE

The practice of individual desertion as a check on despotism was intimately related to the revolutionary power of the organized military; and was, so Dodge tells us, the customary method of "appeal" from enforced authority in all cases, ranging from unsatisfactory marital ties to judgments of the Council.

A woman might leave her husband; under conditions to be described in THE KEEPER OF THE HEARTH; a warrior or a family leave the Band; or a citizen of one tribe renounce his tribal ties, and become, by adoption, the citizen of another. Thus an *Apache* might become an adopted *Comanche*, or vice versa — a procedure described by Herman

280

Lehmann, who actually underwent the experience. "A change of allegiance . . ." Dodge warns, however, "was always attended with great danger"; but if the discontented person actually succeeded in putting himself under new authority, he was thereafter, by tribal custom, absolved from blame and free from punishment — unless pursued by the personal vengeance of the Blood Right.

THE INDIAN A COMMUNIST

Concerning land and the distribution of raw materials, the Plains Indian, like the gardening Indian, was a communist. Nomadic life, in fact, exaggerated the aspects of common ownership and equality under the economic system.

In the southwest, the entire tribal domain was public property. Neither any one man within the Band, nor any given Band within the Tribe, had a shred of individual right to a single square inch of soil not covered by the tepees — and even that right existed only until the lodge poles came down.

Neither did any man, not even the hereditary chieftain of the Tribe, have a vested interest in the buffalo or mustang herds, other than to the extent of fulfilling his own needs. He might, however, breed mustangs for himself. The game, equal, in this instance, to almost the total supply of raw materials belonged to the people as a whole, and was, as has just been said, under the protection of the military police.

The leveling effects of equality under the Plains economic system, concerned primarily with the common ownership of land and raw materials, was extended to private property, which, being untaxed, allowed for no compilation of public or imperial wealth — and consequently no material recompense for the rendition of official services.

CURRENCY

Ponies and women constituted the ordinary currency of any Plains realm. A man, whether chieftain or commoner, might have as many ponies as he could steal — outside the tribe, of course — and as many wives as he could muster ponies to trade for, suffering no limitation other than his own ability to provide food for them and their offspring. Neither wealth nor wantonness was the privilege of position.

Last Will and Testament — The Give Away Party

Property inheritance was vested in family ties. What a man had left, after his funeral orgy was complete, went to his widows. His estate included the girl children. The sons, being potential warriors and family heads, belonged to themselves alone — or, perhaps, to the Tribe.

What a man wished anyone other than his widows to have, or wished them to withhold from the funeral destruction, he gave away when or before he felt the approach of death. This, in practical analysis, was his "last will and testament," allowing no usurpation of private property by any form of official inheritance tax.

A woman might also dispose of her property this way. The "give away party" is still an event with the aged Indians in Oklahoma and New Mexico.

The Blood Right

The Blood Right, as defined in THE LAW OF THE LAND, was consistently applied throughout Plains society. Though a chieftain might beat a subordinate, or confiscate his personal property, says Dodge, as a father might beat or deprive a son, the privilege of shedding blood was not his. To commit murder was to lay upon the family of the dead the necessity of avenging blood just as surely as though the act had been committed by a less august hand.

The Law and the Statutes

Tribal law as it existed on the Plains and was administered by the Council may be briefly tabulated:

If a man stole another's goods, the Council would investigate his guilt and determine punishment.

If a man took another's wife, the Council would assess her value and he must pay.

If a man made himself obnoxious to the Tribe, particularly as a disturber of the peace by quarreling, the Council would deal with the situation.

If a man made good his desertion of local or tribal authority, no civil judgment followed him — but he could not thus escape the Blood Right.

THEFT

Theft, so far as the Council was concerned, was a much more serious matter than murder, since murder was automatically taken care of by the universal application of the Blood Right. And theft could readily amount to murder for it might set a man afoot on the Plains and leave him at the mercy of wild beasts, or, if it were winter, of the blizzards, as he crossed the *mesas*. It could beggar and make public charges of entire families. There being no locks and no keys, nothing but public sentiment and the fear of punishment to hold such abuses in check, the Council reserved its direst penalties for the convicted thief. Usually lashings were ordered, a form of reproof entailing not so much physical pain as humilation — which was of much more consequence in dealing with the Plains temperament. Habitual offenders, however, were treated with extreme harshness. One instance is cited of a man with whom light-fingeredness was a mania. By edict of the local Council, his eyes were put out for protection of the commonwealth. Although a burden on the community thereafter, he stole no more. The Council was nothing if not effective.

MARRIAGE

All marriages on the Plains, as in the gardening area, were reported to the Council, but the aspects of divorce differed in the two regions due to the differing status of womanhood. Divorce and remarriage on the Buffalo Range were akin to theft because of the property right involved. A *Comanche,* for instance, on taking another man's wife, must pay the assessment of her value as set by the Council. The idea, as Dodge explains, was not that of a "fine" for wrong-doing, but of restitution for stolen goods, the money going, not to the commonwealth, but to the ex-husband. A rich man who took a woman from a poor man, however, was much more likely to have to pay heavily than a poor man who absconded with the wife of an individual of means. So much the Council allowed to the principle of anticapital-ism. If the two men concerned agreed of themselves on a price, the Council customarily took no note of the matter.

DISTURBERS OF THE PEACE

As to the import of quarreling among Indians, there is a story of two *Comanche* warriors who quarreled incessantly. The Council arbitrated again and again. The tribe grew weary of the feud. One day the Civil Chief spoke his mind. An arena was formed. The left arms of the two enemies were bound together with stout straps of buffalo hide. Each was given a knife in his right hand. In that fashion they fought to the death. They fell to the ground, their life streams commingling. There was peace at last!

Lawson tells us Indians in general said of the white men: "They quarrel so. There will be no peace for them until they are dead. Why do they not commit suicide?"

As has been twice pointed out, there was no escaping the edicts of the Council as they were evolved for each indi-vidual case, except to leave the Band, or, in some instances, the Tribe itself. And a fugitive, if caught before he was actually within the limits of the community where he sought sanctuary, was subject to a forced return and increased pun-ishment.

DIPLOMATIC RELATIONS

The Council, acting as an executive cabinet, had all the international affairs of the Tribe on its hands. In the case of the *Comancheria,* to the northwest, in what is now New Mexico, lay the territory of the *Kiowa,* they of the turbaned heads and foxtailed *coup*-sticks. Between them and the *Comanches,* following many years of warfare, was a firm peace, based on a vow of everlasting brotherhood.

To the northeast and east of the *Comancheria* were the areas occupied by the "fighting fringe" of the Mound Dwellers — the *Wichita, Wacos, Tewakana,* and others.

To the direct south, straight in the path of the everspreading *Comanche* hunting ground, was the *Tonkawa,* a planter of beans, a dog of a man by his own tradition, a foul eater of human flesh. The Comanche, though he did an occasional bit of ceremonial nibbling, loathed an habitual cannibal.

Between the outskirts of the *Apacheria* and the woods of the *Tonkawa,* lay that city of wonders, San Antonio, where men lived who made the silver buckles, who traded red cloth, who would give flashing bits of mirror glass for bales of pelts. Magic substances — those mirrors! They reflected a man's face, showing him how to fix his paint symbols and pull his whiskers out. They could be set in the centers of shields to catch the sacred Sun's rays and blind the enemy aim. They could be used for heliographs to direct the activities of the military. A *Comanche* would pay any price, says Hobbs, for a slip of looking glass.

The Council had to consider intertribal relations with all these foreign folk. It had to decide when to dance with the *Kiowa,* when to raid the *Apache* dens, and when to strike lances with the *Pawnee Picts.* It was for the Council to decide when to send bales of tanned wildcat hides, 'coon skins, and deerskins into the 'dobe-walled markets of San Antonio.

ORATORICAL ABILITY

Perhaps the most brilliant displays of Plains eloquence burst forth in the diplomatic proceedings to the Councils, for white man after white man testifes to the genius of the Red Face in the art of oratory. To choose but one of these, Dodge says: "Knowing that he is obliged to speak in public, every Indian man speaks well, spending no little time, not only in the preparation and elaboration of his speech, but, by frequent rehearsing, satisfies himself in the manner."

Thus do we see that to wear the "robe of state" on the Plains amounted to much more than a vain display of rank and title — it was the sign and symbol of tribal sponsorship; the *Comanches,* we are told, coming nearer to true nationhood than any of the other brilliantly flashing, picturesque barbarizations of the wide southwest.

Kiowa Drawing

SINTI AND THE PRAIRIE DOGS

XXVII

The Keeper of the Hearth

"The Comanche women have ever been noted for their chastity."

Gregg.

PRETTY IS AS PRETTY DOES

Superficially speaking, the *Comanche* women, according to many chroniclers, were a lousy lot. Nevertheless, they are admitted to have been industrious, learned in their arts, and accredited, even by fastidious white men, with a large amount of family affection and family pride.

It is usually emphatically stated by persons familiar with the North American peoples that among Indian helpmates, those of the *Comancheria* were outstanding for their virtue, their co-operativeness, and their cheerful dispositions. They were universally kind to children, the several different wives of any given household living and working together, and tending one another's offspring in peace and harmony.

There are those among soldiers and frontiersmen who credit the *Apache* and *Kiowa* matrons with every whit as much superiority as the historians of the *Comanches* credit the latter. However, the women of the *Comancheria* seem to have had three definite advantages over their neighbors.

First, says Noah Smithwick, each had her own **private**

lodge for herself and children, while the man of the family had a central lodge of his own. Each group of harem tents was pitched somewhat separately from all others — this perhaps, being the reason the towns appeared to be laid off in "city blocks" with thoroughfares between. The privacy and individualism engendered by such an arrangement put family life on a much higher plane than in other polygamous areas where a single large tent sheltered the man, all his wives, and their assembled children.

Second, says Gregg *Comanche* women were allowed slaves from among the captives as compensation for the loss of their men in war. This reduced their labors considerably, particularly with regard to the care of stock, and thereby improved their social status.

Third, says Herman Lehmann, *Comanche* women were never taken on the warpath, and were always kept in protected villages when pregnant, denied even the adventure of the chase, at which they were expert, both with the bow and the lasso. *Apache* women, on the other hand, are reputed by some to have gone to war with their men, taken part in battle, and even borne and abandoned babes in the midst of conflict.

MADONNA ON HORSEBACK

Nor are these statements concerning the superior position of *Comanche* women confuted by the picture of the Plains madonna gleaned from the journal of an astonished traveling priest, gazing for the first time at frontier scenes presented on the streets of San Antonio.

He wrote somewhat after this fashion: "These mothers ride along on jolting ponies, their infants swinging at their backs in blanket bags. When the child desires to nurse, it is hauled over the shoulder and permitted to take sustenance, head downwards and heels in the air!"

The good *abbe* further expresses himself as full of pity for these roughly handled babes, and shows no great ad-

miration for their frowzy mamas; but it must be remembered
that he was fresh from the crocheted tidies and flower-
sprigged china wash bowls of the east. Men who lived long
on the frontier sang the praises of the *Comanche* women
for such simple decencies as disrobing under blankets when
bathing in the creeks and rivers, and bringing themselves up
straight in the right stirrup before throwing the left leg over
the saddletree. Indians, not having been subject to court
etiquette, mounted from the right instead of from the left
and never once dreamed of the abnormality of a sidesaddle
for their hardy madonnas on horseback.

THE SADDLE

Though the man of the Plains usually rode bareback,
especially if in vigorous action, his women employed a
crude saddle made of two pairs of crotched boughs held together on each side by slats and padded with hides. This
chicken-coopish conveyance, though not particularly comfortable, either for rider or for horse, made an excellent
rack from which to suspend children, bundles, weapons, and
all manner of household contrivances.

Marcy describes a saddle blanket "used for years" by
American army officers on the frontier which one must
suppose originated with the Indian women. Woven of moss
fibres — *La Barba Español* — it was said to be cool, non-
sweat-absorbing, and in every way superior to blankets
woven of cloth.

THE PLAINS HOUSE

The actual house kept by the Plains woman is described
in considerable detail by Dr. Roemer. The tepees "are round,
twelve to fourteen feet high, and made of tanned buffalo
hides sewed together and spread over a framework made of
poles sixteen to eighteen feet long, crossing each other on
the top. Near the ground is an opening which serves as a
door, but which is usually closed by a bearskin. On the top

is a small slit which can be protected against pressure from the wind by two flaps, ingeniously arranged, and which serve as a vent for the Smoke. The door and the vent of the tents always faced the east. . . .

"A leather rope fastened to a stake driven into the ground and reaching up to a point where the poles cross each other was . . . placed there to give the tent more stability and to keep it from being blown down during a strong wind."

In the original edition of THE TEXAS INDIANS, a tepee is shown with a flap opening like a white man's tent. Chief William Red Fox, of the Sioux, who looked over the illustrations, said emphatically that regardless of the many drawings showing the openings thus made, no Plains Indian ever made such an opening.

Roemer, it will be noticed, says the opening was "near" the ground — not on the ground. Davis, in illustrating his article ON THE BUFFALO RANGE, draws round openings — and Catlin, who did not draw them round, does say that the tents of the *Comanches* were exactly like those of the Sioux. Thus we may feel certain that despite the artistic influence of the American army, whose tents have flaps, the Indian tepee should show a round hole for an entrance — a hole about two feet in diameter and about eighteen inches above the ground.

In the top of the tepees, above the Fire, according to Chief Red Fox, the skins were hung for smoking and drying.[1]

The Fire burned in a circular pit sunk into the Earth that floored the lodge.

THE FIRE DRILL

As keeper of the hearth, it was the oft-repeated task of the Plains woman to make fire by twirling a perpendicular hard stick in a hole in a horizontal soft one until sparks resulted from the friction, and she was able to coax the infinitesimal embers into Flames fed with buffalo chips or wood of her own gathering. She was the backbone of the nation, this custodian of the Fires; for if the buffalo gave the Plains man practically everything he had in the form of raw materials, it was the woman who shaped those materials into food, comforts, and conveniences.

It was she who tanned the hides and stitched them together with sinews and a thorn or a bone to make the sheltering tents. It was she who dressed the deerskins and made them into garments for herself, her husband, and her children.

It was she who piled the surplus hides into stacks for beds, though bedmaking was hardly one of her major problems since members of the family simply crawled beneath the number of skins needed for cover, leaving the rest on the earthen floor as a mattress. Not only was the family thus accommodated, but also the dogs — and innumerable vermin.

Beside her other tasks, the Plains woman acted as personal valet to and hostler for her husband, unless she could substitute captive menials; it being beneath the dignity of the warrior and hunter to catch his own horse when off the trail.

If the camp were picked up bodily and moved to the other side of the river, it was she who moved it, as witness this description of the *Lepan-Apaches* (similar to the *Comanches*) given by Roemer: "The (women) packed all the movable articles . . . in large bundles of untanned buffalo skins. These they carried to the river, set upon each one a pair of black-eyed papooses and propelled the bundles over the swift, swollen stream to the opposite shore with the greatest dexterity. Two (women) always swam near a bundle. Upon arriving there, they carried the bundles up the high bank with great exertion, but always in the best spirits."

INDIANS OF THE SOUTHWEST

PROGRESS

But the lady had her innings. Her husband preferred
meat roasted in the coals or cleanly singed in Flame, but
when the hardware merchants in San Antonio acquired
iron pots to trade, the Plains housewives ceased to turn
the spit.

The lords and masters now had to content themselves
with fishing hunks of meat out of sloppy stew where they
reached in alongside the dirty little digits of the children
and the scarcely cleaner noses of the dogs.

The iron pot released the Plains woman from a lot of
labor, but it added nothing to the flavor, sanitation, or
dignity of Plains meals.

PLAINS CONVENIENCES

While on the subject of household conveniences, it may
be well to mention that throughout the *Apache* country in
West Texas, and on the western edges of the *Comancheria*,
especially about Llano and San Saba, appear innumerable
"pot-holes," round or boat-shaped holes worn in the solid
stone of creek banks or ledges above springs — places where
either the *Apache* women or their predecessors, the ancient
Basket Makers, ground mesquite beans or other bread material in mills of living rock. Each hole was used till the
pestle would no longer reach bottom, then another was
started.

All over West Texas *metates* and *manos*, or "hand"
stones, are found — the *metate* being a flat slab on which
corn or beans were placed, and the *mano* a rounded or semi-
cubic stone operated on the flat stone for crushing purposes,
while grasped in the hand of the breadmaker.

Roughly circular structures of stone, not very high, are
also found in the Big Bend; and ascribed to the *Mescalero-
Apaches* for use as Fire pits in the preparation of *mescal* —
an intoxicating beverage, made from the *agave*, and necessary to the religious ritual of that people.

292

The Carnivorian

Buffalo meat and venison, with honey for a side dish, were the staples of Plains diet. After the Spanish colonials populated the Southwest with livestock, mule meat, horse meat, and beef were added to the list.

When on the trail, and short of rations, Plains Indians, making a "kill," would fling themselves on the ground and drink the warm blood flowing from the carcass of deer or buffalo, thereby evidencing a decided difference between their religious views and those of the gardening Indians who adhered to the strictest taboo of blood, as explained in THE MAGIC ART. On the other hand, while the agricultural Indians partook of many kinds of flesh, the Plains Indian tabooed fish and fowls, and particularly hogs, though according to Lehmann and other captives, they looked on roasted turtle as unobjectionable, perhaps because of the resemblance between the shell and the Sun shield.

The same chroniclers tell us that liver, eaten raw and sauced with gall, was considered inestimable as an *hors d'oeuvre;* while curdled milk taken from the stomachs of young fawns; or the foetus of a mare, cooked in its own liquids; was a supreme delicacy on the Plains menu.

Noah Smithwick describes for us the original "wienie" roast, saying that the tripe or "marrow-guts" were always stripped out by hunters, dragged across the grass, draped on sticks, and broiled over the campfire.

He also says the first morsel of any meal was cut off and buried in the ground; while the heart, when the skeleton of an animal was picked clean, was left hanging intact. The first of these arts was a sacrifice to the gods; the second, in all probability, a ceremonial gesture, intended either to perpetuate or to propitiate the spirit of the slain.

Family meals, he tells us, consisted of meat alone — the different branches of the harem all being served together on the flesh side of a dried skin. Drinking vessels were made of buffalo paunches or "cased" deerskins, the legs and necks of the latter tightly tied with sinews instead of being cemented like those in PRODUCTS OF THE CHASE.

IN THE HOME

"The utmost harmony," records this aged pioneer, "prevailed among the various divisions of the polygamous families. The oldest wife seemed to be the mistress of the harem.

"During the whole period of my sojourn among the tribe — three months — I did not hear a single wrangle among the adult members. The youngsters had an occasional scrimmage, which they were allowed to fight out to the amusement of the onlookers."

The old people of both sexes were treated with deference. He continues:

"I never saw a woman or a child abused. The women . . . were abject slaves, but their inferiority was their protection from the chastisement which 'civilized' husbands sometimes visit upon their wives. An Indian brave would have felt it a burning disgrace to strike a woman.

"Taking them all around they were the most peaceable community I ever lived in."

STYLES ON THE RANGE

Since it was not permitted to the matron of the *Comancheria* to wear her hair long, she wound it over a stick of wood and whacked it off with a knife, presenting the residue to her husband, says Sibley, to braid into his already artificially lengthened "tails" — long or flowing tresses being the privilege of strutting masculinity.

Woman's dress, on the Plains, consisted of ankle-length buckskin tunics, sashed at the waist; moccasins; and leggins that stopped below the knee. Men, on the other hand, were given to all manner of frivolities in dress. Among them were bright shirts of pink, crimson, or purple; fancy breast plates patterned of long, slender beads, presumably "core" beads, or money; queues or pairs of braids wrapped with beaver-

skin which was strong "Medicine"; decorated leather jackets
or jerkins; the various insignia described under THE AEGIS
BEARER and THE ROBE OF STATE; heavy silver bracelets, sometimes beaten out by the wearers themselves from veins of
pure metal found in their native mountains; and, according
to Gregg, long heel tassels of fringed leather or the ermined
brush of the skunk. The proud *Comanche* brave, says this
writer, delighted in the regality of trailing appendages, and
seemed to spurn the very Earth he trod on.

DRY CLEANING IN INDIAN LAND

Of the care of buckskin garments, Roemer tells us the
women "cleaned skins which had become dirty by rubbing
them with white clay until they were white."

Oldtimers in East Texas tell us the Indians laid vermin-
infested bedding on the anthills, and that the ants did a
thorough job, particularly on *chinches,* or bedbugs. "Weren't
the ants just as bad?" someone asked, and was told: "The
ants go home, at night." "Well," the questioner persisted,
"what did the ants want of the bedbugs?" "Oh," was the
offhand answer, "they hang them up in their houses for
hams."

CONFLICTING CUSTOMS

The culture pattern of the Plains, based on nomadism
and polygamy, with its attendant contrast between the social
position of men and women, so opposite to his own familiar
practices, amazed and scandalized the white man. As a consequence, much unnecessary sympathy was poured out in
print on the subject of downtrodden femininity. The Indian, forced into contact with a new and unfamiliar social
pattern, likewise had ideas on the subject.

A "savage" once asked a pioneer neighbor: "Why you
work so hard? Why you have only one wife? Why you no
marry two — three — six women — have somebody do your
work?" And then voiced his opinion of the domestic set-up
in the white world: "White man, he heap big fool!"

Nor was this a masculine bias, for an Indian woman, watching a pioneer woman engaged in the multitudinous duties concerning her household and populous brood of children, inquired succinctly: "Why you work so hard? Why you not make your husband marry some more wives so you not have so much to do?" Though she reserved the statement, very probably she thought: "White *woman, she* heap big fool!"

Difference Between a Woman and a Horse

The supreme degradation of woman's position in the *Comancheria,* in Anglo-American eyes, lay in the fact that she was property, like a horse — but with one outstanding difference. If life became too oppressive she could change masters; the horse could not.

Since marriage was not a sacred rite, to profane it was not a sacrilege. A woman's husband might loan her to a guest for a night, make her a pawn at the gaming board, or put her up for sale. A woman, on the other hand, if sufficiently at outs with the head of the house, might negotiate, through an older woman, with another man, for her own purchase.

Thus, as it is neatly put by Colonel Dodge, any man might be making approaches to any woman, or any woman to any man, at any time and anywhere within the entire tribal domain, regardless of the already existing marital status of either or both.

Furthermore, it was none of the business of either husbands or wives how much love was made to their mates, though the overtures took place directly beneath their flouted noses.

Absence of Decency

This total absence of what he looked on as common decency was the third feature of home life on the Plains that revolted the white man. Though the *Comanche* or *Apache* woman might show a commendable amount of modesty, her husband was totally lacking in respect for her womanhood. His gestures and speech, and the privileges allowed other men in the presence and with the persons of his wives and girl children, reached the extreme of what is known in common English parlance as "vulgarity."

To the Indian this was mere custom. Never having been trained to inhibit his feelings in such regard, he expressed his natural impulses in purely natural fashion — as does the "drugstore cowboy" of today who stands shadowgraphing and passing idle, racy comment on the female figure at every Main Street corner. The Indian, in fair analysis. was neither a "painted red devil" nor "an untutored child of the wilderness" — he was an ordinary human being, living life according to a system adapted to his habitat and using manners handed down from generation to generation.

THE MARK OF INFIDELITY

Despite the general absence of reserve in matters of sex, there was, nevertheless, a definite restriction on sex indulgences in the *Comancheria* and the *Apacheria* that saved society from total promiscuity and fixed the family relationship on a firm basis. This was the barter feature of Plains marriage.

A woman's price was in ponies. It had to be paid before she could legally become the mate of any man — except when gambled off or loaned out, neither of which affected her standing in the community. The whole matter of virtue and chastity hinged on the husband's consent, for a woman who carried on an amour clandestinely, if caught, was turned out of his lodge and branded as a harlot by having her nose either split or chopped off — the local equivalent of the Sacrlet Letter. One so marked was common camp property — a most degrading status, amounting among other disagreeable conditions, to beggary.

WIDOW'S RIGHT

A widow was the only really independent woman in camp, says Dodge. If a widow by death, she became possessed of her husband's property, including the girl children. Provided she disposed of these wisely, she might become a financial power. The other kind of widow was a woman grown old and unwanted whose husband turned her out of his lodge. Under such circumstances, however, she was given her independence, and it was not the privilege of men to accost her; though she might contract another regular marriage if opportunity offered and she chose to take advantage of it.

THE MARRIAGE BROKER

These foot-loose, elderly women were usually the go-betweens for discontented wives and men they thought might make better husbands than the ones they had; the old crones ascertaining whether or not the new inamorato would be willing to add another woman to his household, and if he had a sufficient margin of ponies to bargain for one. Three wives is said to have been the average number in the Plains harem, except for wealthier men and chiefs, with whom nine was not considered excessive.

When an understanding was arrived at, the discontented wife had nothing to do except march over to the headquarters of the man on whom she had set her fancy and begin bringing in the wood and water. The first notice her original husband might have of her disaffection was as likely as not to find her staking out his successor's horse — after which the matter was all over except the bickering about the ponies, which might, or might not be settled out of Council.

CHILDREN OF DIVORCE

The children of such misalliances remained with their father, although it was the privilege of the mother to visit

298

them whenever she chose. In case the father died, the normal course of action was for her to remove them to her new abode.

Summing matters up, it would seem that free love, or a variant thereof, was in vogue on the Plains long before the idea struck the American *literati*. What the system actually amounted to was horizontal polygamy for men and vertical polygamy for women.

CHILD MARRIAGES

The virtue of unmarried girls was in the keeping of their parents. Wantonness does not seem to have been a characteristic of Plains maidens, though the loss of virginity out of wedlock was not attended with such drastic penalties as husbands visited on errant wives — might not, if the parents saw fit, be punished at all. A girl was often allowed her own choice of husbands, and wide laxity was permitted in the wooing process. On the other hand, the guardian might act the tyrant if he wished. He might make the price of ponies exorbitant, thus preventing a match; or he might sell his daughter out-of-hand at a tender age. Although girls were customarily married in their teens, middle-aged and well-to-do *Comanche* men often purchased as wives girls only ten years old or younger. It is frequently recorded by white witnesses that the husbands of these children were most kindly disposed toward the little ones who held the position of household pets.

THE COMING-OUT PARTY

Arrival at the age of puberty is usually a matter of ceremony among primitive peoples. Cremony gives us the following picture of what may be likened to the to the "coming-party" of *Apache* girlhood: "When an *Apache* girl has reached the second year of her puberty, the fact is widely circulated, and all present are invited to a grand feast and

299

dance. She is then deemed marriageable and open to the solicitation of the young warriors.

"On such occasions the girl is dressed in all her finery. Small bells are hung to the skirt of her buckskin robe and along the sides of her high moccasins, which reach the knee. Bits of tinsel are profusely scattered all over her attire until she is fairly weighted down by the quantity of her ornaments.

"Meat in abundance is cooked after their fashion, and the guests partake of it *ad libitum. Twilt-kay-yee,* (probably *tequila*) an intoxicating drink, is freely distributed.

"A dried oxhide is laid upon the ground, and some of the more noted musicians entertain the company with improvised songs, while others beat time upon the oxhide with long and tough sticks. The noise of this drumming can be heard for two miles on a clear, calm night.

"Old warriors meet and recount their exploits; young ones ogle and court the marriageable girls; old women delight in cooking the supper and furnishing it to their hungry applicants.

"Suddenly a shout is riased, and a number of young men, variously attired in the skins of buffaloes, deer, cougars, bear, and other beasts, each looking as natural as possible, make their appearance, and commence dancing to a regular measure around a huge central Fire. The women pretend to be greatly alarmed at this irruption of beasts; the men seize their weapons and brandish them with menacing gestures, to which the human menagerie pays no sort of attention. Finding their efforts to intimidate futile, they lay aside their arms and join in the dance, which is then made more enjoyable by the intermingling of the young girls.

"In the meantime the one in whose honor all these rejoicings are given remains isolated in a huge lodge, in which are assembled the sagamores and principal warriors of the tribe. She is not allowed to participate in or even see what is going on outside; but listens patiently to the responsibilities of her marriageable condition.

"This feast lasts from three to five days, according to the wealth of the girl's father. After it is finished, she is divested of her eye brows, which is intended to publish the fact that she is in the matrimonial market. A month after, the eyelashes are pulled out until not a hair remains."

BRIDAL RITES — BRIDLE RIGHTS

From a ceremonial standpoint, the first marriage of a Plains woman, like first marriages of women in modern society, received much more notice than any marital alliance she might contract thereafter.

One of the main points of eligibility on the part of the groom in her eyes was to be able to furnish her with a pony of her own; another was the ability to pay a goodly price in the same coin to her father. There was prestige in having been sold for many ponies; and the matter of a father's price on his daughter did not lie within the arbitrative scope of the Council. It is suggested by Cremony that the derogatory phrase "a one-horse affair" arose from this Plains custom.

A formal proposal, Gregg tells with regard to the *Comanches* and Cremony with regard to the *Apaches,* consisted of a man's tying his favorite horse beside the tent flap of the desired maiden. If she condescended to untie the animal and return it to the herd, the answer was "yes"; but if she shooed it away, the answer was "no." Four days was the time allotted her to make up her mind. To untie the horse before the second day was considered indecorous, but to allow it actually to suffer — that is, to wait until the fourth day, was looked on as objectionable coquetry.

Occasionally true love matches occurred where a deep and sincere devotion bound man and wife. In such cases, the husband might take no other wives. Again, the favored woman might become also the favorite of her harem companions, and receive, by acclaim, the position of leader among them. Where a love of any great depth was thwarted,

301

either by a parent or an existing husband, the couple concerned might avail themselves of the custom of French leave and fly to the protection of some other community.

What Price Monogamy?

Let us, for a moment, draw a contrast between the lot of the *Comanche* matron and that of the pioneer woman who, for some three centuries, braved the hardships of the American wilderness. Early records show that most pioneer women married between the ages of twelve and seventeen, and that comparatively few lived to celebrate the maturity of their first-born. Many of these records show pioneer men marrying from two to five times. They show, also, that those white women who were long-lived bore from ten to fourteen children, at least half of whom died in infancy. If we had the recorded birth weights of these babies they would probably run between six and twelve pounds, as such weights run today. All, or most, were born without benefit of the medical profession.

Low Birth Rate

With *Comanche* women, historians repeatedly state that children were few and far between, it being unusual to see a mother with more than three, while many women were barren. Further, it is asserted that the newborn were extremely small, thus alleviating many of the difficulties incident to childbirth.

Very often, of course, as is the rule among primitives, babies were puny and died almost at once. The scant number of children, and their small size at birth, has been imputed by scientists not to an all-wise Providence who took sympathetic heed of the Indians and their meager conveniences, but to hard riding, unremitting heavy labor, and diet deficiencies. Recently, however, a plague of sterility struck cattle on the mid-west ranges, resulting in world-wide research on an herb known to Indians as Desert Tea and to botanists as *Lithospermum*. More generally known to the Southwest as the *puccoon*, this herb is now believed to have been an Indian specific, especially with the *Shoshones*. It certainly was used as a dyestuff.[2]

Now, since there were at least three *Comanche* women to do the chores in any one househld, and the three between them not likely to have as many children either to bear or to care for as one pioneer wife, there is certainly something to be said in the affirmative for the *Comanche's* social system.

Polygamy — an Economic Justice

Polygyny, a plurality of wives, balanced the economic scheme of the Plains, since men of the Plains Tribes met death much more often than women — thus proving that despite the many times lamented "hard lot" of the Plains wives, the men bore the brunt of Plains dangers. In other words, since there were never enough men to go around, and no schools to teach, and no stenographic jobs open, it was practically a necessity to distribute the men otherwise than monogamously.

Contrast the condition on the other side of the frontier where it was a requirement, both of law and of religion, to take but one wife at a time, and to let her die as quickly as she would of too many maternities and too much hard work.

Had the wilderness remained the wilderness for another three hundred years, it is probable that the white man, despite his religious scruples and his ancient laws, would have been obliged to turn to polyandry, a plurality of husbands, in order to secure an equitable distribution of womankind in his portion of the universe.

And so perhaps we may feel that, despite the undeniable fact of a Plains woman's being a piece of personal property, to be bought or sold for one or more horses, her economic status was not without its compensations — and her social

303

status by no means so low as we are given to understand by superfically-minded critics gazing upon her seemingly herculean labors, her soiled clothing, and her uneven haircut.

FOOTNOTES

[1] The words "wigwam" and "tepee" (or *tipi*) should not be confused. They are not synonymous. "A "wigwam" is a domed straw house or, more commonly, a rectangular, peak-roofed lodge built by timber Indians such as the *Cherokee* and the *Kickapoo*. It is not, however, a log house. The pioneer log cabin was introduced, we are told, from Scandinavia. Indian walls were of palisading; that is, structured of close-set stick or pole uprights, interwoven with mats or thatching.

The correct term for the Plains house is "tepee." Also spelled "typee" and and "tipi."

[2] See THE SCIENTIFIC AMERICAN, August 1953, p. 48.

XXVIII
The Big Parade

Parker, speaking of the Comanches:

"They eat nothing but meat, and are called, among other Tribes, the Buffalo Eaters."

HARVEST HOME ON THE GREAT PLAINS

All the Plains Tribes had their great annual hunts in preparation for winter. In the *Comancheria*, as elsewhere, the initiatory step in this event was the detailing of scouts by the Council to ascertain a large buffalo herd.

The buffalo moved from south to north, and back again, in seasonal migrations numbering hundreds of thousands. The masses, however, spread out in little groups, many of them often widely separated from the central aggregation. Their general movement, spoken of as "the drift" in old histories, was not unlike the movement of the Plains Tribes, since they, too, split into small segments seeking sustenance, and drifted back and forth with the turn of the seasons.

When the scouts reported to the Council, there was a tremendous stir in the air. Big Medicine was made, and as soon as the marching order was given, the whole citizenship, called in from every quarter, got underway, directed by the military.

MOVING DAY

A woman of the Plains could strike a tent in three minutes and set one up in five. It was a matter of rivalry, says Dodge, to see who got on the road first, for that one, barring accident, would arrive first at the new camp site, having choice of location with regard to water, fuel, and shade.

Moving day processions headed for the Summer Hunt, Catlin says, strung out for miles, the warriors acting as outriders in the wings.

In the old days before the coming of the *mesteña,* the women had only dog-power for aid in transportation; consequently they stooped early from the weight of burdens on their own sturdy backs.

During that weary period they hitched a pair of lodge poles to the trustiest canines, letting these poles trail on the ground, the drag-ends fastened together with thongs to make a primitive rack, or sled. The French gave this conveyance its modern name: the *travois.*

The horse was a vast improvement over the dog and consequently inherited the burden of the pole-drag. It was now possible to pile all the tepee furnishings, consisting for the most part of hides and skins, on the framework and then top off the accumulation with babies and the aged. For the sick, ambulances were fashioned by swinging buffalo hide hammocks between the poles.

Once arrived at the site appointed by the Council, the tepees, each one facing the East, sprouted like fungi.

THE SLAUGHTER

The whole procedure of the Hunt was under absolute command of the War Chief, and any individual found stalking or frightening game on his own account, at this period, was liable to severe punishment.

Hunting methods, according to all reports, were fitted to the occasion. If a *mesa* edge were handy, a stampede might be manipulated, sending the buffalo flying with heads down and tails up to tumble over the bluff in hundreds. But this practice, very popular with some tribes, was contrary in general principle to the *Comanche* temperament. Besides, it engendered waste.

The favorite Comanche maneuver consisted of riding quietly into a grazing herd, each warrior selecting animal after animal of quality and dispatching it with his lance.

Ponies were specially trained for the work, taught to approach from the left, to parry the attacks of wounded animals, and to be guided by knee pressure instead of the hackamore.

This method of hunting, based on the outstanding characteristics of the buffalo, attracted the attention of many frontier historians who give us the following points of description. Neither the sight nor the hearing of the buffalo was acute. He took small notice of sounds, and failed to see clearly through the mat of wool protecting his eyes from prairie gnats. His sharp sense of smell made up in large part for the poorness of his sight and hearing, and it was the custom of stampeded herds to run against the wind in order to scent danger. Practiced hunters made no attempt to approach save from counter-windward — a consideration carefully watched by directors of the summer slaughter.

The brain of the buffalo, due to the weight of the skull bones and the protecting thickness of hair, says Gregg, was well-nigh impregnable, and the heart of the animal hung low. Consequently it was necessary to aim low, either with the lance or the arrow, in order to effect a mortal injury.

The *Comanche* method of killing, leaving the herds unstartled, enabled the hunters with a little judicious effort, to keep the main mass of animals within the vicinity of camp till all the household larders were well filled with dried meat and *pemmican,* and all the women thoroughly supplied with raw materials for their winter's labors.

Each man, though under military supervision, killed for himself and family but the warriors, as a group, killed for the aged and the widowed, definitely designating certain carcasses for the "community chest" — this being the sole existing form of tribal taxation.

The Woman's Part

During the Summer Hunt, Dodge tells us, the women worked from dawn till dark, and sometimes on till dawn again, flaying the huge carcasses, cutting the flesh into strips, twisting the lean strips with fat ones, and suspending them all from drying racks over slow fires.

Hunks of flesh were roasted in the embers, pounded to powder for *pemmican,* and packed in paunches, in *parfleches* — boxes of hide — and in skin bags. The pioneers called *pemmican,* when thoroughly dried out, sliced and dipped in honey, "Indian bread."

Besides curing the meat as fast as it was killed, the women had to work up the hides before they could harden. Ordinarily, says Gregg, these were removed in two pieces, splitting down the back being the first operation. The "hump" was shorn off so as to provide a flat surface when the hide was seamed together again.

For dressing, the hides were staked out on the ground, or laced into upright sapling frames, or thrown over tree limbs. Here they were fleshed, either with flint scrapers or with curved rib "knives." The rack method of stretching is said to have been the better, since the ground would not give to the fleshing motion.

After fleshing, the hides, in order to make them pliable, were massaged with brains — the brain of each animal being sufficient for treatment of its own hide. If it were necessary to remove the hair for any purpose, it was taken off with lye leached from wood ashes, or with lime leached from burnt rocks, after which the hair side of the skin was scraped against the grain.

One method of coloring skins with the hair taken off is described by Parker, who says the women tied them into chimney-shape, hung them to limbs, and built smouldering fires under them, so that they soon changed from white to yellowish brown, on the hair side and light yellow on the flesh side. Sometimes they were darkened with Smoke.

While the preparation of the meat and the hides went on, sinews were shredded out and divided into strong and pliable threads; hair was collected for weaving lariats — and even, sometimes, for lengthening gentlemen's tail braids; and hoofs were singed and dried for glue products.

HOME, SWEET HOME

The Summer Hunt was a time of full stomachs and hard work. Now indeed a man might eat twenty pounds of meat in a single day if he so desired. It was impossible to exhaust the larder. But everything comes to its eventual end, and when the piles of provisions stacked up for winter reached a sufficiency, came the end of the Summer Hunt.

It meant moving again, perhaps for more than a hundred miles — a long trek through the pleasant autumn warmth toward the violet haze that wrapped the Texas hills, or toward the Ozarks on the eastern edge of the Buffalo Range.

It meant packing again, packing more than ever, now. Even the children were fatter and heavier. Small wonder that the *Comanche* woman, though she might know the art of moulding pottery, never made any to shatter into bits on the, for her, seemingly everlasting trail.

But the trail did have a temporary end. It ended for a while in the Winter Camp, which was the *Comanche's* only taste of "Home, sweet Home."

XXIX
The Winter Solstice

"The spot selected for the winter encampment one year may be many miles away from that selected the year before or the year after; but the memory of each is affectionately cherished."

Dodge.

THE GET-TOGETHER

The greatest community gathering in the *Comancheria* or elsewhere on the Plains was the Winter Camp where the entire Tribe remained assembled for several months during the season of uncertain weather.

The site for this tremendous encampment was chosen by the Council after profound consideration of scout reports made at the close of the Summer Hunt, a special detail of men having been sent out to look over favorable situations while the Hunt was in progress. The major requirements were three — access to wood, access to water, and windbreaks; the latter preferably in the form of sheltering rock walls to blunt the keen edges of "whizarrowing" wet northers that were prone to descend, without warning, from a suddenly blue-black sky.[1]

The *Comanche* knew those winds. They came down on him every so often like hosts of howling wolves, sprung from nowhere, as he basked, naked and unsuspecting, in the semitropic Sun. Verily the norther was a prime invention of the Bad God.

Nevertheless, except when an ordinarily brief blizzard whistled through the ice-laden tips of the lodge poles, the great Winter Camp was a place of hilarity. Its semitransparent tents glowed golden and mellow like so many oiled paper lanterns by night, and its hundreds of hearth Fires adorned it with crests of purple-tinged Smoke plumes by day.

The enormous lodge of the Civil Chief, serving as the Council House, and said to have been often as much as forty feet in diameter, was the capitol. Round this Big Top clustered the dwellings of the Chief's wives. Surrounding the leading household were the harem residences of the councilors. Beyond them, were those of the warriors; and so on, according to rank and influence, till the town, with its "blocks" and "thoroughfares," spread out over a vast acreage.

Winter in the leading metropolises of the Buffalo Range, as in London or Paris, was the "social season." The huge, tented town, far removed from enemy eyes and ears, rang with gaiety, the nights passing to the monotonous beat of the *tom-tom,* the shrill squeak of the flute, and the shuffle of moccasined feet. Buckskin-clad men and women "formed figures" and "cut the pigeon wing" so expertly round the Fires blazing on the hard-packed earthen floors that watching soldiers declare them to have been the donors of "the square dance" to white civilization on the frontier. However, the *Comanches* are reputed to have danced less than other Plains Tribes.

Winter was the time for love-making, since there was propinquity as well as leisure for courting; and Dodge tells us the interchange of wives, together with the customary and legitimizing exchange of ponies, went on all winter long.

Meanwhile, the women sewed the year's harvest of skins into new tents and new garments, and even into dolls for the little girls; and the little girls set up miniature towns

of dry cottonwood leaf tepees, pinned together with thorns,
for the dolls to live in; and the little boys shot miniature
arrows at sticks and stones and beaded balls.

Sinti and the Prairie Dogs

Of nights these youngsters watched the dancing till
drowsiness curtained their eyes, or listened to visitors tell
tales — such tales as SINTI AND THE PRAIRIE DOGS, perhaps,
which was a story old among the *Kiowa*. It goes like this:
Sinti was a giant. Sinti was a clown. He liked to make people
laugh. He was a great practical joker. In fact he was one of
the greatest practical jokers in the world.

One day Sinti went into the Prairie Dog Town. He said
to the Chief of the Prairie Dogs: "Nephew" — Sinti called
everybody "Nephew" by the way of being polite; and they
called him "Uncle" — "Nephew," said he, "how would you
like to learn a new game?"

All the Prairie Dogs immediately sat up and cried that
they would like very much to learn a new game — but they
let the Chief answer first, as was fitting and proper.

"Then," said Sinti, "you must all gather round me in a
circle."

The Prairie Dogs were somewhat alarmed because they
were so little and Sinti was so big, and besides he had his
war club in his hand; but he reassured them, and at last they
all sat round in a big circle, while Sinti stood in the middle,
leaning on his war club.

"Now," said Sinti, "you must all do exactly as I say.
First, you must shut your eyes. Then I am going to sing you
a song. It goes like this. 'Little Doggies, thump your tails;
thump your tails; thump your tails; little Doggies, thump
your tails, when I tell you to.'" — and Sinti brought his
war club down with a bang on the "to" — "but you must on
no account open your eyes. Now. Are you ready to play?"

All the little Doggies said they were ready, and they all
squinched their eyes tight; and Sinti began to sing.

Every time he shouted "to!" the little Doggies brought

their tails down with a grand thump, and Sinti brought his war club down with a bang, only he brought it down each time right on top of a little Dog's head.

Far around the circle was a little Dog who suddenly began to think the play was going on a long time. She opened her eyes just as Sinti was about to bring his club down on the last "to." Seeing all the other little Dogs in the circle lying dead, this one leaped straight into her hole without waiting for the end of the song — and that is why we still have Prairie Dogs even though Sinti ate all the rest in one afternoon.

O. O. Howard, who, like Dodge, was an American army officer stationed on the frontier, collected this story from the Buffalo Range and published it in OUR HOSTILE INDIANS. It must have been popular on *Ke-che-ah-qui-ho-no* or Prairie Dog Town Fork of the Red River!

WINTER SPORTS ON THE BUFFALO RANGE

All day long on sunny days, during the winter encampment, men squatted on their heels outside the lodge doors, playing hull-gull and betting on the results, or gambling with colored pebbles or little painted sticks of bone, using dressed deerskins, ivory white and smooth, for gaming boards, staking their possessions to the last item on the "bid."

Through gamblers' luck, though it was usually captive women who were put to such extreme indignities, a woman might change hands — and therefore husbands — a dozen times in a single day.

The native women, if too severely pestered, were like to turn Amazon when the bidding became fast and furious, resorting to physical onset to break up the game. Yet she who hauled hardest on her husband's queue at noon might prove the most docile helpmeet in the *Comancheria* while fetching up his firewood at night; for, themselves incessant gamblers, they resumed their wonted placidity as soon as the threat to their household goods and family ties was withdrawn. Undue excess at the gaming board on the part of their husbands, it is said, was the sole exasperation that changed them into termagants and squalling scolds. However, it seems the rule that such outbursts were taken goodnaturedly by the erring lords and masters — who, perhaps, were thankful for an interruption of their losses.

Clear chill days were for horse racing or for ball play, men and women both betting on results. Visiting rivals with fast horses were always welcomed for the diversion they brought, even though the home tribe might be practically cleaned out when the visit came to an end.

Trick horses, seemingly broken-down old nags, but trustworthy for short quick runs were great favorites. From descriptions furnished by army officers, these Indian races seem to have been the originals of today's quarter-horse races.[2]

Hunting, like horse racing, was a major winter sport. The form varied from lassoing wild turkeys, pony-back, to pursuit of buffalo with the bow and arrow.

Although it was never permissible to destroy game animals wantonly, Noah Smithwick tells us old buffalo bulls were sometimes culled from the shaggy herds and baited in imitation of bullfights seen in San Antonio, until the young bloods of the *Comancheria,* wearying of the sport, dispatched the enraged animal, preserving the tough neck hide for shields.

The capture of wild mustangs offered still another incentive for excursions from camp and for displays of Plains technique. Sometimes these captures were easily effected, like the capture of elephants in India, by building a compound, usually around a water hole, driving the startled animals into it, and closing the opening. Again, mustangs were taken singly with the lasso, choked into exhaustion, subjected to the breath of the captor blown into their nostrils, and let forth from this experience by a "hackamore" — a loop of rope about the nostrils or the underjaw.

A third, not too practical method of capture, dependent on the use of firearms, is described by many early writers. Gregg says: "The mustang is sometimes taken by . . . shooting him through the upper 'crease' of the neck, above the cervical vertebrae; when, the ball cutting a principal nerve, he falls as suddenly as if shot in the brain, and remains senseless for a few minutes, during which he is secured with a rope. He soon recovers from the shock, however, and springs to his feet, but finds himself deprived of his liberty. He is easily tamed after this, and the wound heals without leaving physical injury. But 'creasing' is so nice an operation that many are killed in the attempt. If the ball passes a little too low, it fractures a vertebra and kills the poor brute instantly."

Still another form of diversion in the *Comancheria* was "coursing" the bee — any hunter, either Indian or frontiersman, being only too eager, according to old accounts, to turn aside from his original enterprise for the sake of looting liquid gold. The method of determining the whereabouts of the hive was to sight the course of a bee as it left a water hole, having marked it with a dust of meal or other substance, then time its return, thus calculating distance and direction. Having determined the general position of the honey, whether in hollow tree trunk or cave, the bee hunter could accommodate himself by following the easiest route to the suspected locality.

Stolen sweets were bagged in skin containers exactly as the gardening Indians bagged bear oil in PRODUCTS OF THE CHASE.

So high in favor was honey in the *Comancheria* that one *Comanche* Band received the name of *Panatekas,* or the Honey Eaters.

MUNITIONS MAKERS

The men of the Plains, along with constant gambling and occasional hunting, worked on their weapons throughout the winter, fashioning arrow shafts and lances of ash, arrowpoints of flint — or, if available, of iron — and bows of *Osage* orange, now commonly called *bois d'arc* because of its popularity for bow wood.

War clubs were made of heavy, polished, double-pointed stones, bound on a handle with wet buckskin. Lariats were braided from buckskin strips or buffalo hair; shields were shaped, "tempered" and decorated; war bonnets constructed; and buffalo robes and tents painted with heraldry and Sun symbols.

"The usual length of the bow," says Gregg, speaking of the Plains Tribes in general, "is about three feet, though it is sometimes as much as four. It is generally made of elastic wood, yet elk's horn is occasionally used. Those of the latter are made of two of the longest and straightest shafts, which, being shaved down to the necessary proportions, are united by lapping their ends together and binding them firmly with sinew. Bows have also been made, in the same manner, of a pair of buffalo ribs . . . Even the backs of the wooden bows are often lined the whole length with a broad strip of sinew, and the whole wrapped with shreds of the same. The arrows are generally about thirty inches long."

Catlin, in LAST RAMBLES AMONG THE INDIANS, speaking of arrow-making among the *Apaches,* before iron came into use, says: "Every tribe has its *factory* in which these arrow-heads are made, and in those only certain adepts are able or allowed to make them for the use of the tribe. Erratic bowlders of flint are collected (and sometimes brought an immense distance) and broken with a sort of sledge-hammer, made of a rounded pebble of hornstone set in a twisted withe holding the stone and forming a handle. The flint, at the indiscriminate blows of the sledge, is broken into a hundred pieces, and such flakes selected as from the angles of their fracture and thickness will answer as the basis of an arrowhead.

"The master workman, seated on the ground, lays one of these flakes on the palm of his left hand, holding it firmly with his right hand, between the thumb and two forefingers, places his chisel (or punch) on the point that is to be broken off; and a co-operator (a striker) sitting in front of him, with a mallet of very hard wood, strikes the chisel (or punch) on

316

the upper end, flaking the flint off the under side, below each projecting point that is struck. The flint is then turned and chipped until the required shape and dimensions are obtained — all the fractures being made on the palm of the hand.

"In selecting a flake for the arrowhead ,a nice judgment must be used, or the attempt will fail; a flake with two opposite parallel, or nearly parallel planes, is found, and of the thickness required for the centre of the arrowpoint. The first chipping reaches near to the centre of these planes, but without quite breaking it away, and each chipping is shorter and shorter until the shape and the edge of the arrowhead are formed.

"The yielding elasticity of the palm of the hand enables the chip to come off without breaking the body of the flint, which would be the case if they were broken on a hard substance. These people have no metallic instruments to work with, and the instrument (punch) which they use, I was told, was a piece of bone; but on examining it, I found it to be a substance much harder, made of the tooth (incisor) of the spermwhale, which cetaceans are often stranded on the coast of the Pacific. This punch is about six or seven inches in length, and one inch in diameter, with one rounded side, and two plane sides, therefore presenting one acute and two obtuse angles to suit the points to be broken. This operation is very curious, both the holder and the striker singing, and the strokes of the mallet given exactly in time with the music and with a sharp and *rebounding* blow, in which, the Indians tell us, in the great *medicine* (or mystery) of the operation."

Commenting upon this description, Mr. Stephens, quoted by C. C. Jones, observes "What Catlin has said with reference to a *rebounding* blow, is perfectly true; it is impossible to flake flint with a dull, heavy, smashing blow; it is the measured and rebounding blow — a shock rather than a blow — which, given with judgment, enables the material to take its own line of cleavage, and produces what is so well known as the conchoidal fracture. It is the presence of this conchoidal fracture, resulting from human skill, that distinguishes the mere splinter of flint from the flint-flake."[3]

We are told by other writers, that it was necessary for every man to know how to fashion arrowpoints, whether he made a practice of the art or not, since any man might be caught out alone with all his ammunition expended; thus the expert old men held regular "classes" in which they taught the art of stone flaking to the young boys.

"Their bows," says Marcy, "are made of the tough and elastic wood of the *bois d'arc* or Osage orange, strenghtened and reinforced with the sinews of the deer wrapped firmly around them, and strung with a cord of the same material. They are not more than one half the length of the old English longbow which was said to have been sixteen hands' breadth in length. The arrows are twenty inches long, of flexible wood, with a triangular point of iron at one end, and two feathers, intersecting each other at right angles, at the opposite extremity. At short distances the bow, in the hands of the Indian, is effective, and frequently throws the arrow entirely through the huge carcass of the buffalo."

SHIELD MAKING

Of all the warrior's equipment, his shield was perhaps the most picturesque. It typified the Sun in shape and function. It was, in fact, "Big Medicine," absorbing the Sun's rays and using the magic power thus acquired to turn enemy arrows into hissing nothings. There is many a statement put on record by Minute Men and Texas Rangers to the effect that bullets left no marks on these Sun targets save harmless smudges of lead.

Besides being the protector of his person, the Indian's shield was his compass, says Herman Lehmann. By holding it horizontally he could read the position of the Sun or the stars, according to the position of the devices painted on its surface.

318

Though there were individual differences in the structure of shields, the basis was always the same — a round cut from the toughest possible portion of buffalo hide, the neck of an ancient bull. Accounts appear of single-, double-, and triple-tiered shields, some of them packed with buffalo hair between the tiers of hide. There was nothing, indeed, that added to a warrior's pride and confidence like a properly made and decorated shield.

Once the right section of hide was secured, it was bound to a wooden hoop, says Lehmann, and alternately toasted and scraped until completely fleshed, by which time it was convex on the one side and concave on the other, and almost as hard as iron. The hoop could now be removed. Over the flint-like surface was fitted a buckskin cover, much like a tire cover, drawn in on the under side by means of eyelet slashes and a buckskin thong.

Through the hide itself were bored two pairs of holes, and through these passed two loops of quarter-inch thick thong for hand holds.

On the buckskin cover were arranged the warrior's heraldic devices, and a feather ruffle — the latter made of a narrow strip of cloth with a row of sinew stitches run down the center. Each feather was looped round a stitch, the loop forming a socket. The loose attachment of this cloth strip, which was caught to the shield only occasionally, at the outer edges, and the socket arrangement of each feather, made it possible for the ruffle to be kept in constant motion when the shield was shaken, thus serving to bewilder the eye and disturb the aim of the enemy.

A second cover, made exactly like the first, except that it was much less decorative, was used to protect the feathers and the paintings when the shield was idle.

Human hair might be substituted for the feather fringe, and scalps and horse-tails were frequently pendant from the underside. These were dropped from a light network of buckskin strings attached to the handholds.

INDIANS OF THE SOUTHWEST

When he shield was complete, it was set up and tested, says Lehmann. If the strongest man in camp could nick it with an arrow, it was cast on the rubbish heap at once, regardless of the labor involved in the making.

The Betrayal

Mrs. Alexis Casparis of Austin, Texas, was given such a shield the patina showing the spreading stain where the life blood of its bearer ebbed upon its traitorous surface. Although skillfully made and stamped with the symbol of the Sun, this shield caught a Ranger's bullet on the inner edge, and the steel ball, ricocheting, struck the trustful Indian in his heart. Something must have gone very wrong with his Medicine on the day he fought the battle of Packsaddle Mountain!

Yet, even as this shield betrayed its bearer, so did their perfectly adapted civilization betray the Plains people at the close of their independent history.

Before that betrayal took place, many a winter passed in dance and song, the warriors rising each morning to move in rhythmic circles, chanting a greeting to the appearing Sun, while the women laid down their work each night to mourn its vanishing in the West.

FOOTNOTES

[1] Whiz-ar-rów-ing — a Texanism descriptive of the "norther" (El Norte) which comes on with the swiftness and sharpness of a whizzing arrow.

[2] "Quarter-horses" are a stock bred to run a quarter mile at great speed. Eagle Pass, Texas is the fiesta home of the Quarter Horse Races. Betting follows ancient Indian lines such as "three to one on daylight" — a bet that in the finish daylight will show between the tailtip of the favorite and the nose of the runner-up.

[3] For working flint, see Mewhinney: A MANUAL FOR NEANDERTHALS.

XXX
Closing the Buffalo Holes

"It is not at this late day in our power to atone for all the injustice inflicted upon the red man."

Marcy

THE WEIGHT OF IRON

Soon after the Texas Revolution in 1836, the manufacture of firearms in the United States took an inventive spurt that was to turn the tide of civilization in America. The pioneer, reduced to a pale-faced primitive in cultural status after several generations in the wilderness, stood on the Timberline in Texas impatiently "champing the bit" because of the restraint imposed on his wanderings by the sovereignty of the *Comancheria*.

He promptly dubbed the revolver, which arrived in Texas about 1840 to replace the old single-fire pistols, the "six-shooter" or "six-gun"; and it is said by those having experience that this was the first effective weapon opposed to the Indians' bow and arrows — meaning, in Texas, the *Comanche* Indian; for, by 1840, the *Comanche* and the settler had come to grips. Yet the revolver was only effective as a weapon of defense. It saved the settler's life, but did not daunt the feather-tipped banner, now so far down in the hills that its crimson shadow swept the Texas capitol.

Nearly three more decades were to elapse before the actual crux of the situation, the invention of the high power rifle. In peculiar metaphor, this invention was to "hamstring" the Indian.

A Breathing Space

To go back a bit in recounting history: between the invention of the revolver and the invention of the high power rifle, the Civil War was fought, allowing the North American Indian a breathing space in time while the white usurpers of the continent cut each other's throats instead of his. In four years the flower of southern chivalry, transplanted to Texas from the older southern states, withered and died in the hot blasts of interecine strife, and only the war-orphaned child of the paleface primitive was left to carry on the struggle for control of the southern Buffalo Range.

The Broom-Scratch

Now, indeed, were the Texas woods that once were filled with naked little brown children, full of little white children in their shirttails, their busy mothers having neither the time nor the wherewithal to fashion unnecessary nether garments for their active nether limbs. Instead of the *mitotes* learned to the measures of the rhythm stick and *tom-tom,* these children learned the "Heel! Toe! Poke-'er" or the Broom Scratch to the rhythm of a broomstick vibrated against the puncheon floor boards, accompanied by the drubbing of a rawhide bottom chair. They grew up, as had the Indian children preceding them, with little other knowledge than how to fill their stomachs and save their scalps. Boys were excellent rifle shots long before they were nine, even with the old style guns, said Albert Mills, a "Minute Man"; and they regarded no Indian as a good Indian save a dead Indian — the litany and the creed of their generation being, according to one of Annie Doom Pickrell's anecdotes: "Oh, Lord, put this bullet right between his god-damn eyes!"

322

CLOSING THE BUFFALO HOLES

It was a fight to the death for the survival of the fittest, and the *Comanche* believed he was the child of the Sun!

HAMSTRINGING THE INDIAN

Then came the cataclysm. A market opened in the cold countries for buffalo robes. Enterprising men who set small store by their scalps and large store by adventure, stretched a few stray tents on the Staked Plains, stacked them with ammunition, and set forth with high power rifles to mow down the buffalo, taking only hides and tongues and leaving the Range strewn with rotting carcasses. Said J. N. Atkinson, in recounting A RIDE FOR LIFE ON THE OGLELALLAH TRAIL: "The country round Fort Griffin was covered with buffalo skeletons in 1870 till it was dangerous to ride out of a trot; and in town there was a stack of buffalo hides as long as a city block, as high as a man could reach, throwing hides out of a wagon, and so wide that it must have been made by driving wagons down both sides of the pile to stack from."

Just here we return to Colonel Dodge who offers an explanation of the Buffalo Myth in which he says that since the buffalo migrated to the south for the winter, they, in all probability, returned to the north in spring by an old trail leading through two rock-bound passes. The Indians, grazing from afar, watching the herds teem through these narrow gorges, formulated the theory of the "buffalo holes." Whether this surmise concerning the origin of the myth be correct or not, it is an established fact that Texas was the winter grazing ground of the buffalo — therefore to control the Texas Buffalo Range was practically to control the commissary of the Great Plains.

When the wholesale killing of the American bison for his hides became generally known, a howl went up from some quarters concerning the extermination of that superb game animal and the destruction of an apparently unfailing meat supply. It was silenced by the voice of public opinion

323

expressing this drastic sentiment: "We shall never be able to drive those old Rattlesnakes, the *Comanches*, out of their dens on the Brazos and the Colorado so long as they can depend on the buffalo — let the slaughter go on!" And the slaughter went on till the last bull and cow lay dead on the Texas Plains.

SON OF TWO RACES

Thus did Texas hamstring the Indian, and Quanah Parker, the last *Comanche* chieftain — son of Nocona who lay dead beside the buffalo, and of Cynthia Ann, the blue-eyed captive maid who died in her father's house by an alien hearth — for she was never reconciled to her forced return to civilization — Quanah Parker, the last chieftain to tread on Texas soil, understanding both the white man and the Indian, advised his red brothers to leave the "red man's road for the white man's road"; otherwise they must starve.

And the *Comanche*, looking on the Plains that offered sustenance only to the surfeited *zopilote*, the turkey vulture, devourer of carrion, bowed to the judgment of the last chieftain and departed from Texas forever to take up life on the reservation, thus arriving abruptly, in the fourth century of his might and power, at

THE END OF THE TRAIL

PLAINS MEDICINE MAN

Bibliography

Adair, James Esquire; *History of the American Indians,* Printed for Edward and Charles Dilly in the Poultry, 1775.

Adair's History of the American Indians, edited by Samuel Cole Williams, The Watauga Press, Johnson City, Tennessee, 1930.

American Indians — Taxed and Untaxed; Federal Census, 1890.

Arnold, L. V.; *A True Story of Southwest Texas Fifty Years Ago,* Fort Worth.

Atkinson, Mary Jourdan; *Abstract Element Common to All Cultures,* (chart) Oklahoma Agricultural & Mechanical College, Sitllwater, Oklahoma, 1950; "A Ride for Life on the Oglelallah Trail," *Dallas News,* December 8, 1929.

   Bamboo Cultures of the Southwest, mss. Oklahoma Agricultural & Mechanical College, Stillwater, Oklahoma, 1951.

   Ghost Smoke or *The Trail of the Indian through Texas History,* an Extension Lecture with Sixty Slides, Bureau of Visual Instruction, The University of Texas.

   La Bahia — the Ghostplace, W. M. Morrison, publisher, Houston, 1955. "Texas Indian Flags," *Epic-Century,* April, 1935, Naylor Company, San Antonio, Texas.

Babb, T. A.; *In The Bosom of the Comanches,* Hargreaves Printing Company, Dallas, Texas.

Bancroft, Hubert Howe; *Essay and Miscellany,* Bancroft and Company, N. Y. (This is included for the discussion of Morgan's essay: "Montezuma's Dinner.")

   History of the North American States and Texas, A. L. Bancroft and Company, San Francisco, 1884 and 1889.

Banta, S. E.; *Buckelew — The Indian Captive,* The Mason Herald, Mason, Texas, 1911.

Barde, Frederick S., *Life and Adventures of Billy Dixon,* Guthrie, Oklahoma, 1914.

Bartlett, John Russel; *Personal Narrative of Explorations and Incidents of Texas, New Mexico, California, Sonora and Chihuahua,* D. Appleton and Company, New York, 1845.

Bartram, William; *Travels through North and South Carolina, Georgia, and East and West Florida,* James and Johnson, Philadelphia, 1791.

Bean, Ellis P.; "Memoirs of Ellis P. Bean," Henderson K. Yoakum, *History of Texas,* Vol. 1, Appendix.

Bolton, Herbert Eugene; *Spanish Explorations in the Southwest,* 1542-1706, Charles Scribner's Sons, N. Y. 1930.

INDIANS OF THE SOUTHWEST

Boulding, Kenneth; *The Image,* University of Michigan Press, 1956. (Philosophy.)

Bourke, John G.; *On the Border with Crook,* Sampson, Low, Marston, Searle, and Rivington, St. Dunstan's House, Felter Lane, Fleet Street E. C., London, 1892.

Brown, John Henry; *History of Texas,* 1685-1892, L. E. Daniell, St. Louis, 1893.

Buffalo Range, The — see Davis.

Bushnell, David I. Jr.; "Burials of the Algonquian, Siouan and Caddoan Tribes West of the Mississippi," *Bureau of American Ethnology,* Bulletin 83, 1927.

Campbell, Charles A. R.; *Bats, Mosquitos and Dollars,* Standford, Boston, 1925.

Castañeda, Carlos; "Myths and Customs of the Tejas Indians," *Texas Folklore Society Publication IX,* 1931.

"The Six Flags of Texas," *Texas Catholic Historical Society,* Vol. II, No. 4, January, 1933.

Our Catholic Heritage, Vol. I, Van Boeckmann-Jones, Austin, 1936.

Carter, Captain Robert G.; *The Old Sergeant's Story,* F. H. Hitchcock, New York, 1926.

Catlin, George; *Illustrations of the Manners and Customs of the North American Indian,* Chatto and Windus, London, 1876.

Notes of Eight Years Travel and Residence in Europe with his North American Indian Collection, The Author, 1848.

Celiz, Fray Francisco; *Diary of the Alarcon Expedition into Texas,* 1718-1719, tr. Fritz Leo Hoffman, The Quivira Society, Los Angeles, 1930.

Charlevoix, Pierre Francois Xavier de; *Letters to the Duchess of Lesguierres; an account of a Voyage to Canada and travels through . . . Louisiana to the Gulf of Mexico, London,* 1763.

Christian, Asa Kyrus; *Mirabeau Buonaparte Lamar,* Thesis, University of Pennsylvania, 1919; *Southwestern Historical Quarterly,* Jan. 1920, April 1921; Von Boeckmann-Jones Company, Austin, Texas, 1922.

Colman, Harold S., *Hopi Kachina Dolls,* University of New Mexico, Albuquerque, 1949.

Covarrubias, Miguel; *The Eagle, the Jaguar, and the Serpent,* Alfred Knopf, New York, 1954.

Cremony, John C.; *Life Among the Apaches,* A. Roman and Company, San Francisco, 1868.

Cushman, Horatio Bardwell: *History of the Choctaw, Chickasaw and Natchez Indians,* Headlight Printing House, Greenville, Texas, 1899.

Daniell, L. E.; *Texas: The Country and its Men,* Austin, 1924.

Davenport, "Expedition of Pamfilio Narvaez," *Southwestern Historical Quarterly,* Vol. XXVII, 1923-24.

Davis, Theodore R.; "The Buffalo Range," *Harper's New Monthly Magazine,* Vol. XXXVIII, No. 224.

De la Vega, Garcilaso; *Historia de la Florida,* N. Rodriguez Franco, Madrid, 1723.

De Mézières, Athanasio; *Report on the Texas Indians,* Mss. The University of Texas Archives.

De Mézières and the Lousiana-Texas Border, edited by Herbert Eugene Bolton, Arthur H. Clark Company, Cleveland, Ohio, 1914.

DeShields, James T.; *Border Wars of Texas,* The Herald Company, Tioga, Texas, 1912.

De Solis, *Diary of a Visit of Inspection of the Texas Missions Made by Fray*

BIBLIOGRAPHY

Gaspar José de Solis in the Year 1767-1768; tr. by Margaret K. Kress with Introductory by Mattie Austin Hatcher, *Southwestern Historical Quarterly*, Vol. 35, No. 1, July, 1931.

De Soto, *Narratives of de Soto*, tr. Buckingham Smith, Allerton Book Company, New York, 1922.

Diaz, Bernal del Castillo; *The True History of the Conquest of Mexico*, written in 1568, tr. Maurice Keatinge, Esquire, Robert M. McBride & Co., N. Y. 1938.

Dixon, Olive K.; *Life of "Billy Dixon,"* P. L. Turner Company, Dallas, Texas, 1927.

Dixon, Sam Houston;*Romance and Tragedy of Texas History*, Texas Historical Publishing Company, Houston, Texas, 1924.

Dobie, J. Frank; *The Vaquero of the Brush Country*, Southwest Press, Dallas, Texas, 1919.

Dockstader, Frederick J.; *The Kachina and the White Man*, Cranbrock Institute of Science, Bloomfield Hills, Michigan.

Dodge, Colonel Richard Irving; *Our Wild Indians*, A. D. Worthington, and Company, Hartford, Connecticut, 1883.

Domenech, Abbe; Missionary Adventures in Texas and Mexico, tr. from the French, Longman, Bowman, Green, Longmans and Roberts, London, 1856.

Seven Years Residence in the Great Deserts of North America, Vols. 1 and 11, Longman, Green, Longman and Roberts, London, 1800.

Duel, Thorne; "Basic Cultures of the Mississippi Valley," *American Anthropologist*, Vol. 37, No. 3, Part 1, July — September, 1935.

Du Pratz, Le Page; *L'histoire Louisianne, Paris*, 1758.

Du Pratz; *The History of Louisiana*, tr. Roberta Ely Kendall 1935 in manuscript, Austin, Texas.

Duval, John C.; *The Adventures of Big-Foot Wallace*, The W. Burke Company, Macon, Georgia, 1870.

Duval, J. C.; *Early Times in Texas*, J. W. Burke and Company, Macon, Georgia, 1885.

Eastman, Edwin; *Seven and Nine Years Among the Comanches and Apaches*, C. Johnson, Jersey City, N. J., 1873.

Emmet, Chris; "Texas — As It Was Then; Cabeza de Vaca meets the Caranqua Indians," *Naylor's Epic-Century*, Fall, 1934.

Espinosa, Frary Isidro Felis de; *Chronica Apostolica y Seraphica*, Mexico, Viuda de Bernardo de Hogal, Impressora del Real y Apostolico; Tribunal de la Santa Cruzada en todo este Reyno, 1746.

Espinosas' Chronicle, tr. Roberta Ely Kendall, 1935, in manuscript, Austin, Texas.

Foik, Rev. Paul J.; "Fray Juan de Padilla," *Texas Catholic Historical Society*, Vol. 1, No. 5, 1930; *Mid-America*, Vol. XIII, No. 2, October, 1930.

"Captain Don Domingo Ramón's Diary of his Expedition into Texas in 1716," *Preliminary Studies of the Catholic Historical Society of Texas*, Vol. II, No. 5, April, 1933.

Forrestal, Rev. Peter P.; "The Solis Diary of 1767," *Texas Catholic Historical Society*, Vol. I, No. VI, March 1931. "The Venerable Padre Fray Antonio Margil de Jesus," *Texas Catholic Historical Society*, Vol. II, No. 2, April, Reprint from *Mid-America*, Vol. III, No. 4, April, 1932.

French, B. F.; *Historical Collection of Louisiana*, Wiley and Purnam, New York, 1846, 1853.

French, B. F.; *Historical Collections of Louisiana and Florida*, A. Mason, New York, 1875.

329

INDIANS OF THE SOUTHWEST

Gamio, Manuel; *The Population of the Valley of San Juan Teotihuacan,* Talleres Graficos de la Nacion, Mexico, 1922.

Gatschet, Albert S.; *The Karankawa Indians,* Papers of the Peabody Museum, Volume I, 1888-1904.

Geronimo — *Apache Chief,* Taken down and edited by S. M. Barrett, Duffield and Company, New York, 1906.

Glover, William B.: *A History of the Caddo Indians,* Thesis, University of Texas, 1932.

Goldschmidt, Walter R.; *Some Archaeological Sites in Titus County and Their Relation to East Texas Pre-History.* Thesis, University of Texas, 1935.

Goodnight, Charles and others; *Pioneer Days in the Southwest from 1850 to 1879,* The State Capitol Company, Guthrie, Oklahoma, 1909.

Gregg, Josiah; *Commerce of the Prairies* or *The Journal of a Santa Fe Trader,* J. W. Moore, 193 Chestnut Street, Philadelphia, 1855.

Hamilton, Henry W.; *The Spiro Mound,* The Missouri Archaeological Society (The Missouri Archaeologist, Vol. 14) Columbia, 1952.

Harriot's Narrative, *The First Plantation of Virginia in* 1585, B. Quaritch, London, 1893.

Hatcher, Mattie Austin; "Descriptions of the Tejas or Asinai Indians," *Southern Historical Quarterly,* Vol. 31, No. 1, July 1927 — October, 1927. *Diary of a Journey from Bexar to Santa Fe,* 1808, Mss. Translation, University of Texas Archives.

"The Expedition of Don Domingo de los Rios," *Texas Catholic Historical Society,* Vol. 2, No. 1, January, 1931.

Letters of An Early American Traveler, The Southwest Press, Dallas, Texas, 1933.

"Myths of the Texas Indians," *Texas and Southwestern Lore,* Edited by J. Frank Dobie, Publication of the Texas Folk-lore Society, No. VI.

"Texas in 1820," *Southwestern Historical Quarterly,* Vol. 23, No. 1, July, 1919.

Helm, Mary S.; *Scraps of Early Texas History,* The Author, Austin, Texas, 1884.

Hennepin, Louis; *A New Discovery of a Vast Country in America,* 2 vols. reprinted from the second London issue of 1698 by Reuben Gold Thwaites, 1903.

Herzog, George; "Plains Ghost Dance and Great Basin Music," *American Anthropologist,* Vol. 37, No. 3, Part 1, July — September, 1935.

Hewitt, Alexander; *South Carolina and Georgia,* Alexander Donaldson, No. 48 St. Pauls Church-Yard, London, 1779.

Hobbs, Captain James; *Wild Life in the Far West,* Wiley, Waterman, and Eaton, Hartford, 1872.

Hodge, Frederick Webb; *Handbook of the American Indian North of Mexico,* Buereau of American Ethnology, Washington, 1907.

Holden, W. C.; "The Buffalo of the Plains Area," *West Texas Historical Association Year Book,* June, 1926.

Rollie Burns, The Southwest Press, Dallas, Texas, 1932.

Holley, Mary Austin; *Holley's Texas,* J. Clarke and Company, Lexington, Kentucky, 1836.

Howard, O. O.; *My Life and Experience Among Our Hostile Indians,* A. D. Worthington, and Company, Hartford, Connecticut, 1907.

Hunter, John Dunn; *Memoirs of a Captive Among the Indians of North America,* Longman, Hurst, Bees, Orme, Brown, and Green, Paternosterrow, London, 1824.

BIBLIOGRAPHY

Jackson, A. T.; *Picture Writing of the Texas Indians*, Anthropological Papers, Vol. II, No. 25. The University of Texas, Austin, Texas.

James, Marquis; *The Raven*, The Bobbs-Merrill Company, Indianapolis, 1929.

James J. Franklin; editor; *Spanish Explorers in the Southern United States*, 1528-1543;
The Narrative of Alvar Nuñez Cabeza de Vaca.
The Narrative of the Expedition of Hernando de Soto.
The Narrative of the Expedition of Coronado.

Jones, Charles C. Jr.; *Antiquities of the Southern Indians*, D. Appleton and Company, New York, 1873.

Jones, Jonathan H.; *A Condensed History of the Apache and Comanche Indian Tribes*, Johnson Brothers Printing Company, San Antonio, Texas, 1899.

Joutel's Journal of La Salle's Voyage, 1684-7; tr. B. F. French, Joseph McDonough, Albany, New York, 1906.

Joyce, Thomas Athol; *Mexican Archaeology*, P. L. Warner, 1914, London.

Kellog, Louise Phelps; tr. *Journal of a Voyage to North America*, The Caxton Club, Chicago, 1923.

Kendall, George Wilkins; *Narrative of the Texan Santa Fe Expedition*, Harper and Brothers, New York, 1856.

Kennedy, Louise Phelps; tr. Journal of a Voyage to North America, The Caxton Club, Chicago. 1923.

Kennedy, William; *Texas — The Rise, Progress, and Prospects of the Republic*, R. Hasings, London, 1841.

Kroeber, Alfred Louis; *Anthropology*, Harcourt, Brace, and Company, New York, 1923.

Lafitau, P.; de la campagnie de Jesus; *Moeurs des Sauvages,,* Paris, 1724.

Laubin, Reginald and Gladys; *The Indian Tipi*, University of Oklahoma Press, Norman, 1957.

Lawson, John; *The History of Carolina*, W. Taylor at the Ship and F. Baker at the Black Boy, London, 1714; Strohler and Marcom, Raleigh, 1860.

Lehmann, Herman; *Nine Years with the Indians*, 1870-1879; Von Boeckman-Jones Company, Printers, Austin, Texas, 1927.

Linton, Ralph; "The Comanche Sun Dance," *American Anthropologist*, Vol. 37, No. 3, Part 1, July-September, 1935.

Loon's Necklace, Encyclopedia Britannica Films (made from Indian folklore and masks at the National Museum of Natural History, Ottawa, Canada).
Note: This 16 mm film, made by Crawley Films Limited, can be rented or bought at the office of Encyclopedia Britannica Films Inc., at 1414 Dragon Street, Dallas.

Maillard, N. Doran; *History of the Republic of Texas from the Discovery of the Country to The Present Time*, London, 1842.

Malone, P. V.; "The Alabama Cooshatte Indians," (thesis in mss.) Texas Southern University, History and Geography Department.

Marcy, Randolph B.; *Exploration of the Red River*, Washington, D. C., 1845.

Marquina, Ignacio; *Monumentos Arquelogicos de Mexico*, Talleres Graficos de la Nacion, Mexico, 1928.

Marriott, Alice; *Maria, the Potter of San Ildefonso*, University of Oklahoma Press, Norman. 1948.

Matthews, Sallie Reynolds; *Interwoven*, Anson Jones Press, Houston, 1936.

INDIANS OF THE SOUTHWEST

Maverick, Mary A.; *Memoirs of Mary A. Maverick*, Mss. University of Texas Archives.
   Memoirs of Mary A. Maverick, 1818-1918, Alamo Printing Company, San Antonio, Texas, 1921.
Means, P. A.; *Ancient Civilizations of the Ande*, Scribner, N. Y., 1931.
McDonough, Joseph; *Joutel's Journal of La Salle's Voyage*, 1684-7, Albany, New York, 1906.
Morfi, Father Juan de; *Memorias for the History of Texas*, tr. Frederick C. Chabot. The Naylor Company, San Antonio, Texas, 1932.
Morgan, L. H.; *League of the Ho-de-no-sau-nee of Iroquois*, Dodd, 1922, New York.
Nuñez Cabeza de Vaca, Alvar; *Schriffbrüche die unglücksfahrt der Narvaez-Expedition nach der südküste Nordamerikes in den jahren 1528 bis 1536*, Stuttgart, Strecker and Schroder, 1925.
Nuttal, Thomas; *Journal of Travels into the Arkansas Territory*, T. H. Palmer, Philadelphia, 1821.
Owens, Elizabeth McAnulty; *The Story of Her Life*, The Naylor Company, San Antonio, Texas, 1936.
Palmer, J. W.; "The Tribes of the Thirty-Fifth Parallel," *Harper's Magazine*, Vol. XVII, p. 448.
Parker, W. B.; *Unexplored Texas*, Hayes and Zell, No. 193 Market Street, Philadelphia, 1821.
Payne, John Howard; "The Green Corn Dance," *The Continental Monthly*, Vol. I, No. 1 p. 17, January, 1862.
Pearce, James Edwin; *The Archaeology of East Texas*, Reprint from *American Anthropologist*, Volume 34, No. 4, October-December, 1932.
   The Tale that Dead Men Tell, Anthropological Papers, Vol. 1, No. 1, The University of Texas, 1931.
Pearce, J. E. and Jackson, A. T.; *A Prehistoric Rock Shelter in Val Verde County*, Anthropological Papers, Vol. 1, No. 3, The University of Texas, Austin, Texas.
Peña's Diary of the Aguayo Expedition, Translated by Rev. Peter Forrestal, *Records and Studies of U. S. Catholic Historical Society*, Reprint from Volume 24, October, 1934; *Texas Historical Association* Vol. 2, No. 7, January, 1933.
Pichardo — Jose Antonio, tr. Charles W. Hackett, The University of Texas Press, Austin, Texas, 1931.
Pickrell, Annie Doom; *Pioneer Women in Texas*, Steck, Austin, Texas, 1930.
Popul Vuh, Sacred Book of the Maya, trs. Delia Goetz and Syvanus G. Morley (from the translation from the Indian by Adrián Recinos) University of Oklahoma Press, Norman, 1950.
Posnansky, Arthur; *Tiahuanacu, The Cradle of American Man*, Vols. I and II, tr. James F. Shearer, J. J. Augustin, N. Y. 1945.
Rabb, Mrs. John;*Reminiscences of Mrs. John Rabb*, Photostat of Mss. University of Texas Archives, Original with Miss Lillian Rabb, Smithville, Texas.
Raht, Carlysle Graham; *Romance of the Davis Mountains and the Big Bend Country*, The Rahtbooks Company, El Paso, 1919.
Ramón's Diary — See Foik.
"Report of the Post Surgeon at Fort Phantom Hill, 1852," from Texas State Gazette, Austin, 1857, *West Texas Historical Association Year Book*, June 1926.
Reports of the Secretary of War, Washington, D. C., 1850, Marcy, et. als.

BIBLIOGRAPHY

Report of the Secretary of War, Letter of W. A. Trimble, Washington, D. C. 1822.

Richardson, Rupert Norval; *The Comanche Barrier to South Plains Settlement,* The Arthur H. Clark Company, Glendale, California, 1933.
   "Documents Relating to West Texas and Her Indian Troubles," *West Texas Historical Association Year Book,* June, 1925.

Roberts, Mrs. D. W.; *A Woman's Reminiscences of Six Years in Camp with the Texas Rangers,* Press of Von Boeckmann-Jones Co., Austin, Texas, 1928.

Roberts, Emmett; "Frontier Experiences of Emmett Roberts of Nugent, Texas," *West Texas Historical Association Year Book,* June 1927.

Roemer, Dr. Ferdinand von; *Texas.* tr. from the German by Oswald Mueller, Standard Printing Company, San Antonio, Texas, 1935.

Sayles, E. B.; *An Archaeological Survey of Texas,* Gila-Pueblo Press, Globe, Arizona, 1935.

Schoolcraft, Henry Rouel; *History of the Indian Tribes of the United States,* U. S. Indian Bureau, 1852-57.

Shea, Dawson Gilmary; *Discovery and Exploration of the Mississippi; With the original narratives of Marquette, Allouez, Membré, Hennepin, and Anatase Doudy,* New York, 1852.

Shetrone, Henry Clyde; *The Mound-Builders,* D. Appleton and Co., New York, London, 1930.

Shipman, Daniel; *Frontier Life in Texas* . . . (n. p.) 1879.

Sibley, Dr. John; *A Report from Natchitoches in* 1807, Edited by Annie Heloise Abel, Heye Foundation, 1922.

Simonds, F. W.; *Geography of Texas,* Ginn and Co., Boston, 1914.

Sinks, Julia Lee; "Religious Beliefs and Customs of Texas Indians,' *Southwestern Historical Quarterly,* 1897-99, Vol. I, p. 127.

Smith, Clinton L. and Smith, Jeff D.; *The Boy Captives,* Frontier Times, Bandera, Texas, 1927.

Smithwick, Noah; *The Evolution of a State,* Gammel Book Company, Ausin, Texas, 1900.

Sowell, A. J.; *Early Settlers and Indian Fighters of Southwest Texas,* B. C. Jones and Company, Austin, Texas, 1900.

Spence, Lewis; *Myths of Mexico and Peru,* Farrar and Rinehart, New York, 1931.

Spinden, Herbert Joseph; *Ancient Civilizations of Mexico and Central America,* American Museum of Natural History, Handbook Series, No. 3, New York, 1917.

Steck, Rev. Francis Borgia; "Forerunners of Captain de Leon's Expedition to Texas, 1670-1675. *"Texas Catholic Historical Society* Vol. 3, No. 3, September; *Southwestern Historical Quarterly,* Vol. XXXVI, No. 1, July, 1932. Neglected Aspects of the De Soto Expedition," *Texas Catholic Historical Society,* Vol. 25, No. 1, July, 1932, Reprint from *Mid-America.*

Stephenson, A. B.; *Album of Texas Indians,* Forty photographs collected by A. B. Stephenson, University of Texas Archives.

Swanton, John R.; "Notes on the Cultural Provinces of the Southwest," *American Anthropologist,* Vol. 37, No. 3, Part 1, July-September, 1935.

Sweet, Alex and Knox, J. Armory; *On a Mexican Mustang through Texas,* and, McNally and Company, Chicago, 1892.

Texas Almanac
   1859   The Indian Reserves of Texas, p. 130.
   1860-1861   Indian Wars in Texas.

INDIANS OF THE SOUTHWEST

1867 Constitution of the State of Texas — Ordinance concerning Indians.
1869-1870 Texas Indians, p. 157.
1872 Frontier Legends, p. 162.
    Historical Reminiscences, p. 164.
    The Carancaway (Karankawa) Indians, p. 171.
    The Last of the Alabamas, p. 174.
    Waco — A Leaf from its History, p. 175.
    Aboriginal Antiquities of Texas, p. 175.
Thomas, Sidney Johnson; *The Archaeological Investigation of Fate Bell Shelter, Seminole Canyon, Val Verde County, Texas,* Thesis, University of Texas,1933.
Thrall, Homer S.; *A Pictorial History of Texas,* N. D. Thompson, and Company, St. Louis, Missouri, 1879.
Timberlake, Lt. Henry; *Memoirs, 1756-65,* Edited by Samuel Cole Williams, The Watauga Press, Johnson City, Tennessee, 1927.
Torquemada, Fray Juan de; *La Monarquia Indiana,* Madrid, 1723.
Tribes of the Thirty-Fifth Parallel — see Palmer.
Underhill, Ruth M.; *The Navajos,* University of Oklahoma Press, 1956.
Wallis, Johnnie Lockhart, and Hill, Lawrence L.; *Sixty Years on the Brazos,* Press of Dunn Brothers, Los Angeles, 1930.
Washburn, Rev. Cephas, *Reminiscences of the Indians,* Presbyterian Committee of Publications, Richmond, Virginia.
Webb, Walter Prescott; *The Great Plains,* Ginn and Company, Boston, 1931.
Wilbarger, J. W.; *Indian Depredations in Texas,* Hutchings Printing House, Austin, Texas, 1889.
Wissler, Clark; *The American Indian,* Oxford University Press, New York, 1922.
Woodman, David, Jr.; *Guide to Texas Immigrants,* M. Hawes, Boston 1835.
Yarrow, Dr. H. C.; *Study of Mortuary Customs,* Washington, D. C., 1880.

ADDENDA

Books of philosophy applicable to the authors interpretation of Indian philosophy:
Allier, Raoul; Doyen of the Faculty of Protestant Theology, Paris; *The Mind of the Savage,* tr. from the French, 1927, Harcourt, Brace & Co., New York.
Atkinson, M. Jourdan; *Fourteen Steps in Cultural Anthropology for the Primary Child,* doctoral thesis, Oklahoma State University, Stillwater, Oklahoma (Oklahoma Agricultural and Mechanical College) 1955.
Briffault, Robert; *The Making of Humanity,* George Allen and Union, Ltd., Ruskin House, 40 Museum Street, London, W.C. 1, 1919.
Heard, Gerald; *The Source of Civilization,* Harper and Brothers, New York, 1937.
Huntington, Ellsworth: *The Mainsprings of Civilization,* John Wiley and Sons, New York, 1945.
Spencer, Lilian White; *Arrowheads,* (poetry) The Parade Publishing Company, New York, 1929.
Tylor, Edward B.; *Primitive Cultures,* Chapter I, "The Science of Culture — Definite Laws," 1873, Brentano Reprint, 1905.

Index

Wolf, 205
Yaupon Boughs, 83

Death Song, 147, 193, 229
deer decoy, 103-104
diseases and remedies:
  epidemics, 71, 244
  exorcism, 68, 70
  healing art (witch doctors), 69, 70,
    186, 199
  malaria, 71, 244
  smallpox and measles, 174, 244
  sweat lodge, 238, 243

dogs, 45, 107, 145, 178, 184, 204, 236,
  237, 250, 291, 292, 306
dragonfly, 244
dreams, 236
duck hunt (gourds), 105
dug-out:
  canoes — see *pirogues*
  desert shelter, 205
  Tonkawa sleeping area, 207
dyes and paints, 112, 117, 118, 119,
  132
  cochineal, 59
  mineral, 60
  vermilion, 39, 59, 119, 131, 232
  warpaint, 200

eagle:
  dance, 55
  tail feathers, 49, 50, 64, 152, 269,
    278
  wooden, 38

Earth Mother, 156, 227, 228, 233
eclipse, 44, 48
estufas, 42
  wall painting, 50

ethnic groups:
  Adeaseños, 4
  Alibama-Cooshatte, 193
  Anadarko, 165
  Apache, 2, 55, 59, 60, 61, 102, 105,
    171, 198, 241, 279
  Asinai, 1, 4, 15, 17, 54, 59, 97,
    123, 128, 136, 163, 165, 245
  Athapascan (Apache), 195, 220
  Attakapa, 1, 175, 178
  Azteca, 47, 87, 141
  Basket Makers, 197
  Bidai, 69, 178
  Buffalo Eaters, 305

Buffalo Hunters — see Cibolero
Caddo, 1, 4, 14, 15, 54, 121, 128,
  136, 157, 165, 171, 191, 245
  household, 10
Cajun, 134
Cherokee, 4, 82, 168, 194, 219, 304
Cheyenne, 267
Choctaw, 4, 20, 25, 130
Cibolero (Buffalo Hunters), 141,
  142, 195
Coahuilteca, 2, 175, 178, 196, 202,
  204, 210
Coenis (Asinai), 17, 32
Comanche, 2, 21, 59, 60, 61, 67,
  102, 132, 166, 167, 170, 199, 201,
  204, 211, 212, 213, 220-324
Conquistadores, 22, 207, 223
Coupane, 179
Coxane, 179
Creek, 25, 90, 122, 158, 193, 194
Creole, 4, 53, 129
Crusaders, 49
Dog Lovers (Karankawa), 178
Guapites, 179
Honey Eaters (Panatekas)
Inca, 164
Ionie, 165
Jicarillo, 196, 197
Jumana, 135, 166
Karankawa, 1, 54, 118, 175, 177-191
Keechie, 178
Kickapoo, 4, 194, 304
  migration to Nacimiento, 195
Kiowa, 59, 195. 198, 220, 224,
  225, 252, 272, 285, 287
Ku Klux Klan, 191, 215, 219
Lipan-Apache, 165, 178, 179, 182,
  196, 220, 291
Lumbee, 215, 219
Mandan, 156, 158
Man Eaters — see Attakapa
Maya, 38
Mescalero, 196, 197, 220, 292
Mound Builder Nations, 1, 4-8, 52,
  59, 136, 137, 140
  frontier, 19, 61, 165, 167, 285, 309
  league members, 60
  league pledges, 55
Muscoghe, 193, 195
Natchez, 11, 18, 19, 28, 37, 48,
  164
Navajo, 198, 219
Orejone (Big Ears), 210
Paneteka, 315
Pani-Pique, 166

PERSONS AND REFERENCES NOT OTHERWISE LISTED

CHART OF OLD IN

COLORADO

KIOWA

SANTA FÉ

HOPI

ZUNI   ACOMA

NAVAJO

A   P   A   C   H   E   R

GILA

MESCALLERO APACHES

EL PASO
DEL NORTE

JICARILLO APACHES

TOBOSA
OR
CONCHOS

JUMANA

RIO   YAGUI

☀ SUN WORSHIP — ALL TRIBES AND NATIONS
+ NEW FIRES — ch. 5   ⊙ ALABAMA-COOSHATTE
Y PERPETUAL FIRES — ch. 5   ⊡ NACIMIENTO
⚰ PEACE PIPE — chs. 7, 11, 23   ≢ TIMBER LINE
△△ NOMAD TRIBES ——————— COMANCHE
⛩ HORSE INDIANS ——————— KIOWA
⌂⌂ MOUND BUILDERS —————— APACHE
💀 CANNIBALS - - -   WACO
                              WICHITA
🚣 INDIAN NAVIES ————   JUMANA
🏠 PRAIRIE & DESERT ————   CADDO
🛶 COASTAL TRIBES ————   ASINAI
🦅 GREEN CORN DANCE ———   NATCHEZ
                              TONKAWA
PUEBLOS ➤ ADVANCE   COAHUILTECA
   OF HORSE INDIANS   KARANKAWA
      OVER OTHERS   ATTACAPA
                            PUEBLOS

BOLSON
DE
MARIMI

J. T. JONES